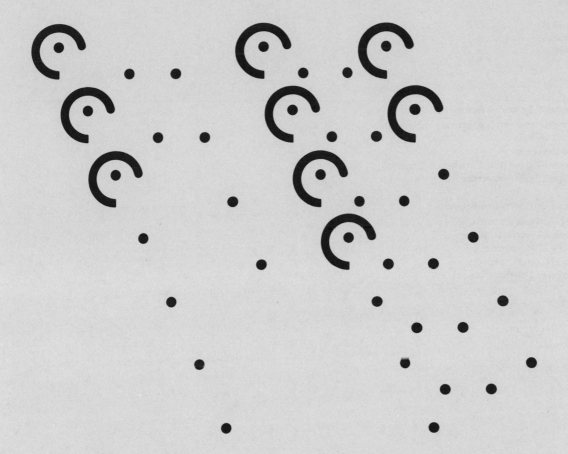

**Hermeneia
—A Critical
and Historical
Commentary
on the Bible**

Micah

A Commentary on the
Book of the Prophet Micah

by Delbert R. Hillers

Edited by
Paul D. Hanson
with
Loren Fisher

**Fortress
Press**   Philadelphia

Library of Congress Catalog Card Number 83–48002
ISBN 0–8006–6012–9

Printed in the United States of America
Design by Kenneth Hiebert
Type set on an Ibycus System at Polebridge Press
K358A84   20–6012

TO MY CHILDREN
  EVE ELIZABETH HILLERS
  AND
  SAMUEL THOMAS HILLERS

Contents
Micah

The name *Hermeneia,* Greek ἑρμηνεία, has been chosen as the title of the commentary series to which this volume belongs. The word *Hermeneia* has a rich background in the history of biblical interpretation as a term used in the ancient Greek-speaking world for the detailed, systematic exposition of a scriptural work. It is hoped that the series, like its name, will carry forward this old and venerable tradition. A second entirely practical reason for selecting the name lies in the desire to avoid a long descriptive title and its inevitable acronym, or worse, an unpronounceable abbreviation.

The series is designed to be a critical and historical commentary to the Bible without arbitrary limits in size or scope. It will utilize the full range of philological and historical tools, including textual criticism (often slighted in modern commentaries), the methods of the history of tradition (including genre and prosodic analysis), and the history of religion.

Hermeneia is designed for the serious student of the Bible. It will make full use of ancient Semitic and classical languages; at the same time, English translations of all comparative materials—Greek, Latin, Canaanite, or Akkadian—will be supplied alongside the citation of the source in its original language. Insofar as possible, the aim is to provide the student or scholar with full critical discussion of each problem of interpretation and with the primary data upon which the discussion is based.

Hermeneia is designed to be international and interconfessional in the selection of authors; its editorial boards were formed with this end in view. Occasionally the series will offer translations of distinguished commentaries which originally appeared in languages other than English. Published volumes of the series will be revised continually, and eventually, new commentaries will replace older works in order to preserve the currency of the series. Commentaries are also being assigned for important literary works in the categories of apocryphal and pseudepigraphical works relating to the Old and New Testaments, including some of Essene or Gnostic authorship.

The editors of *Hermeneia* impose no systematic-theological perspective upon the series (directly, or indirectly by selection of authors). It is expected that authors will struggle to lay bare the ancient meaning of a biblical work or pericope. In this way the text's human relevance should become transparent, as is always the case in competent historical discourse. However, the series eschews for itself homiletical translation of the Bible.

The editors are heavily indebted to Fortress Press for its energy and courage in taking up an expensive, long-term project, the rewards of which will accrue chiefly to the field of biblical scholarship.

Dr. Loren R. Fisher provided valuable assistance in copy editing this volume. The editor responsible for this volume is Paul D. Hanson of Harvard University.

January, 1984

Frank Moore Cross
For the Old Testament
Editorial Board

Helmut Koester
For the New Testament
Editorial Board

Author's Foreword

Many people have contributed skilled labor to bringing out this volume; the following seem to me to deserve special mention and thanks. Prof. Frank Cross invited me to contribute to this series, years ago; in more recent times, Prof. Paul Hanson and Dr. Loren Fisher have seen to revising and fitting the work for publication. Mrs. Florence Felter and Miss Adelaide Eisenhart of the Milton S. Eisenhower Library at Johns Hopkins were most efficient and helpful with interlibrary loan transactions. Mr. Ebenezer Afful, my student, verified references for me, and the map is the work of Miss Ann Kort, also my student. Colleagues here at Johns Hopkins, and in the Biblical Colloquium, discussed the whole, and parts, with me, sympathetically and critically. To all, thanks, and absolution of any responsibility for remaining errors, which are solely mine.

The Johns
Hopkins University

Delbert R. Hillers

1. Sources and Abbreviations

The abbreviations used for biblical books are in common use.

α'	Aquila
AASOR	Annual, American Schools of Oriental Research
Ach	Achmimic Coptic version
AJSL	*American Journal of Semitic Languages*
*ANET*³	*Ancient Near Eastern Texts Relating to the Old Testament* (Princeton: Princeton University, ³1969)
ATD	Das Alte Testament Deutsch
ATR	*Anglican Theological Review*
Aug	*Augustinianum*
AUSS	*Andrews University Seminary Studies*
AV	Authorized Version
BA	*Biblical Archeologist*
BASOR	*Bulletin of the American Schools of Oriental Research*
Bd.	Band
*BH*³	*Biblia hebraica*, ed. Kittel, 3rd ed.
BHS	*Biblia hebraica stuttgartensia*
BJPES	*Bulletin of the Jewish Palestine Exploration Society*
BK	Biblischer Kommentar
BO	*Bibliotheca Orientalis*
BZ	*Biblische Zeitschrift*
BZAW	Beiheft, Zeitschrift für die alttestamentliche Wissenschaft
CBQ	*Catholic Biblical Quarterly*
cf.	compare
chap(s).	chapter(s)
col(s).	column(s)
CTA	*Corpus des tablettes en cunéiformes alphabétiques*, by Andrée Herdner
DBS	*Dictionnaire de la Bible Supplément* (Paris: Letouzey et Ané, 1938)
de Rossi	G. de Rossi, *Variae lectiones Veteris Testamenti*
DJD	Discoveries in the Judaean Desert
DJDJ	Discoveries in the Judaean Desert of Jordan
EAEHL	*Encyclopedia of Archaeological Excavations in the Holy Land*, edd. Michael Avi-Yonah and Ephraim Stern. Vol. III (Englewood Cliffs, M. J.: Prentice-Hall, 1977).
EB	*Études Bibliques*
ed., edd.	editor(s), edition(s), edited by
EM	*Entsiklopediyah Mikra'it* (Jerusalem: Bialik, 1955–).
FRLANT	Forschungen zur Religion und Literatur des Alten und Neuen Testaments.

Gesenius'	*Gesenius' Hebrew Grammar*, ed and rev. E. Kautzsch, tr. and rev. A. E. Cowley (Oxford: at the Clarendon Press, ²1910).
HAT	Handbuch zum Alten Testament
HK	Handkommentar zum Alten Testament
HS	*Die Heilige Schrift des Alten Testaments* (Feldmann and Herkenne)
HTR	*Harvard Theological Review*
HUCA	Hebrew Union College Annual
IB	*Interpreter's Bible*
Ibn Ezra	Abraham ben Meir (–1167)
ICC	International Critical Commentary
IDB	*Interpreter's Dictionary of the Bible*
IDBS	*Interpreter's Dictionary of the Bible, Supplementary Volume*
IEJ	*Israel Exploration Journal*
JAOS	*Journal of the American Oriental Society*
JBL	*Journal of Biblical Literature*
JJS	*Journal of Jewish Studies*
JNES	*Journal of Near Eastern Studies*
JPOS	*Journal of the Palestine Oriental Society*
JQR	*Jewish Quarterly Review*
JRAS	*Journal of the Royal Asiatic Society*
JSS	*Journal of Semitic Studies*
JTS	*Journal of Theological Studies*
K	Ketib
KAI	*Kanaanäische und aramäische Inschriften*, H. Donner and W. Röllig
KAT	Kommentar zum Alten Testament
KeH	Kurzgefasstes exegetisches Handbuch zum Alten Testament
Kenn.	B. Kennicott, *Vetus Testamentum Hebraicum cum variis Lectionibus*
KHC	Kurzer Hand-Commentar über das Alte Testament
l, ll	line(s)
LXX	Septuagint (often – the text of Ziegler)
MT	Masoretic Text
ms(s)	manuscript(s)
Mur 88	a scroll from Murabba'at (see Bibliography under F. Benoit)
NJPS	New Jewish Publication Society Translation
NT	New Testament
NTT	*Norsk Teologisk Tidsskrift*
OrAnt	*Oriens Antiquus*
OT	Old Testament
p, pp	page(s)
para.	paragraph
PEFQSt	*Palestine Exploration Fund Quarterly Statement*
PEQ	*Palestine Exploration Quarterly*
PJB	*Palästinajahrbuch*

Pl.	Plate(s)
Q	Qere
R	A Greek text of the Minor Prophets published by D. Barthélemey, *Les devanciers d'Aquila.*
Rashi	Solomon ben Isaac, 1040–1105
RB	*Revue biblique*
Redaq	David ben Qimchi, ca. 1160–ca. 1235
RGG	*Die Religion in Geschichte und Gegenwart*
RHR	*Revue de l'histoire des religions*
RQ	*Revue de Qumrân*
RSV	Revised Standard Version
S	Syriac version (Peshitto)
σ'	Symmachus
Sa	Sahidic version
SAT	Die Schriften des Alten Testaments (Gunkel and Gressmann)
SEÅ	*Svensk Exegetisk Årsbok*
Sf	Sefire
Syh	Syrohexaplar
SZ	*Kurzgefasster Kommentar,* edd. Strack and Zöckler
T	Targum
θ'	Theodotion
Teilbd.	Teilband
THAT	*Theologisches Handwörterbuch zum Alten Testament,* edd. Ernst Jenni and Claus Westermann. 2 vols. (Munich: Chr. Kaiser, 1971, 1976).
TrTZ	*Trierer Theologische Zeitschrift*
ThR	*Theologische Rundschau*
TWAT	*Theologisches Wörterbuch zum Alten Testament,* edd. Botterweck and Ringgren (Stuttgart: Kohlhammer, 1970–)
UF	*Ugarit-Forschungen*
V	Vulgate
VT	*Vetus Testamentum*
VTS	Vetus Testamentum, Supplements
v, vv	verse(s)
WMANT	Wissenschaftliche Monographien zum Alten und Neuen Testament
ZA	*Zeitschrift für Assyriologie*
ZAW	*Zeitschrift für die alttestamentliche Wissenschaft*
ZDMG	*Zeitschrift der Deutschen Morgenländischen Gesellschaft*
ZDPV	*Zeitschrift des Deutschen Palästina-Vereins*
ZS	*Zeitschrift für Semitistik*

2. Short titles of Commentaries, Studies, and Articles Often Cited

Allen
  Leslie C. Allen, *The Books of Joel, Obadiah, Jonah, and Micah,* The New International Commentary on the Old Testament (Grand Rapids: Mich.: Eerdmans, 1976).
Alt, "Micha 2,1–5"
  Albrecht Alt, "Micha 2,1–5 Γης αναδασμος in Juda," *NTT* 56 (1955): 13–23.
Bewer
  Julius A Bewer, *The Book of the Twelve Prophets: Vol. I Amos, Hosea and Micah,* Harper's Annotated Bible (New York: Harper, 1949).
Brown-Driver-Briggs, *Lexicon*
  Brown, Francis, S. R. Driver, and Charles A. Briggs, *A Hebrew and English Lexicon of the Old Testament* (Oxford: Clarendon, 1907).
Budde, "Das Rätsel"
  Karl Budde, "Das Rätsel von Micha I," *ZAW* 37 (1917/18): 77–108.
Budde, "Micha 2 und 3"
  Karl Budde, "Micha 2 und 3," *ZAW* 38 (1919/20): 2–22.
Cathcart, *Micah 5, 4–5*
  Kevin J. Cathcart, "Micah 5, 4–5 and Semitic Incantations," *Biblica* 59 (1978): 38–48.
Cross, *Canaanite Myth*
  Frank Moore Cross, *Canaanite Myth and Hebrew Epic* (Cambridge, Mass.: Harvard, 1973).
Duhm, "Anmerkungen"
  B. Duhm, "Anmerkungen zu den Zwölf Propheten," *ZAW* 31 (1911): 81–110.
Ehrlich, *Randglossen*
  Arnold B. Ehrlich, *Randglossen zur hebräischen Bibel V* (Leipzig: Hinrichs, 1912).
Elliger, "Die Heimat"
  Karl Elliger, "Die Heimat des Propheten Micha," *ZDPV* 57 (1934): 81–152.
George
  Augustin George, *Michée Sophonie Nahum. La Sainte Bible,* Vol. 27 (Paris: Cerf, 1952).
Gesenius'
  Gesenius' Hebrew Grammar, ed. and rev. E. Kautzsch, tr. and rev. A. E. Cowley (Oxford: at the Clarendon Press, ²1910).
Graetz, *Emendationes*
  H. Graetz, *Emendationes in plerosque Sacrae Scripturae Veteris Testamenti libros,* ed. W. Bacher (Breslau: Schlesische Buchdruckerei, ²1895).
Hillers, *Treaty-Curses*
  Delbert R. Hillers, *Treaty-Curses and the Old Testament Prophets,* Biblica et Orientalia 16 (Rome: Pontifical Biblical Institute, 1964).
Hitzig
  Ferdinand Hitzig, *Die zwölf kleinen Propheten,* ed. Heinrich Steiner, Kurzgefasstes exegetisches Handbuch (Leipzig: S. Hirzel, ⁴1881).

Horgan, *Pesharim*
  Maurya P. Horgon, *Pesharim: Qumran Interpretations of Biblical Books,* Catholic Biblical Quarterly Monograph Series, 8 (Washington, D. C.: Catholic Biblical Association, 1979).
Jeremias, *Theophanie*
  Jörg Jeremias, *Theophanie: Die Geschichte einer alttestamentlichen Gattung.* WMANT, Vol. 10 (Neukirchen-Vluyn: Neukirchener, 1965).
Lindblom, *Micha*
  Johannes Lindblom, *Micha literarisch untersucht,* Acta Academiae Aboensis, Humaniora VI. 2 (Helsingfors: Åbo Akademi, 1929).
Margolis
  Max L. Margolis, *Micah* (Philadelphia: Jewish Publication Society, 1908).
Marti
  Karl Marti, *Das Dodekapropheton,* KHC 13 (Tübingen: J. C. B. Mohr, 1904).
Mays
  James Luther Mays, *Micah: A Commentary* (Philadelphia: Westminster, 1976).
McKeating
  Henry McKeating, *The Books of Amos, Hosea and Micah,* Cambridge Bible Commentary (Cambridge: University Press, 1971).
Milik, *Midrash*
  J. T. Milik, "Fragments d'un Midrash de Michée dans les manuscrits de Qumran," *RB* 59 (1952): 412–18.
Nowack
  W. Nowack, *Die kleinen Propheten,* HK III, Abteilung 4 (Göttingen: Vandenhoeck & Ruprecht, ³1922).
von Orelli
  Conrad von Orelli, *Die zwölf kleinen Propheten,* Kurzgefasster Kommentar zu den Heiligen Schriften Alten und Neuen Testamentes, A., 5 Abteilung, 2 Hälfte (Munich: Becksche, ³1908).
Proksch
  Otto Proksch, *Die kleinen prophetischen Schriften vor dem Exil,* Erläuterungen zum Alten Testament, 3 Teil (Calw & Stuttgart: Vereinsbuchhandlung, 1910).
Renaud, *La formation*
  B. Renaud, *La formation du livre de Michée,* Études Bibliques (Paris: Gabalda, 1977).
Robinson
  Theodore H. Robinson, *Die zwölf kleinen Propheten,* HAT 14 (Tübingen: Mohr, 1938).
Rudolph
  Wilhelm Rudolph, *Micha–Nahum–Habakuk–Zephanja,* KAT 13/3 (Gütersloh: Gütersloher Verlagshaus Gerd Mohn, 1975).
Ryssel, *Textgestalt*
  Viktor Ryssel, *Untersuchungen über die Textgestalt und die Echtheit des Buches Micha* (Leipzig: S. Hirzel, 1887).

Schmidt

Hans Schmidt, *Micha*, SAT, Abteilung 2, Band 2, *Die grossen Propheten* (Göttingen: Vandenhoeck & Ruprecht, [2]1923).

Sebök, *Syrische*

Mark Sebök, *Die syrische Uebersetzung der zwölf kleinen Propheten* (Breslau: Preuss und Jünger, 1887).

Sellin

Ernst Sellin, *Das Zwölfprophetenbuch*, KAT 12/1 (Leipzig: Deichertsche, [2]1929, [3]1930).

G. A. Smith

George Adam Smith, *The Book of the Twelve Prophets*. I. Expositor's Bible (New York: A. C. Armstrong, 1896).

Smith

J. M. P. Smith, William Hayes Ward, and Julius A. Bewer, *A Critical and Exegetical Commentary on Micah, Zephaniah, Nahum, Hababbuk, Obadiah and Joel*, ICC (Edinburgh: T. & T. Clark, 1911).

Weiser

Artur Weiser, *Das Buch der zwölf Kleinen Propheten I: Die Propheten Josea, Joel, Amos, Ojadja, Jona, Micha*, ATD Teilbd. 24 (Göttingen: Vandenhoeck & Ruprecht, 1956).

Wellhausen

J. Wellhausen, *Skizzen und Vorarbeiten*, Fünftes Heft: *Die kleinen Propheten übersetzt, mit Noten* (Berlin: Reimer, 1892).

Wildberger, *Jesaja*

Hans Wildberger, *Jesaja*, BK 10/1 (Neukirchen-Vluyn: Neukirchener Verlag, 1972).

Willi-Plein, *Vorformen*

Ina Willi-Plein, *Vorformen der Schriftexegese innerhalb des Alten Testaments*, BZAW 123 (1971).

Wolff

Hans Walter Wolff, *Micah the Prophet*, tr. Ralph D. Gehrke (Philadelphia: Fortress, 1981).

Wolff, *Hosea*

Hans Walter Wolff, *Hosea: A Commentary on the Book of the Prophet Hosea*, tr. Gary Stansell; Hermeneia (Philadelphia: Fortress, 1974).

van der Woude

A. S. van der Woude, *Micah* (Nijkerk: Callenback, 1976).

Ziegler, *Duodecim Prophetae*

Septuaginta: Vetus Testamentum Auctoritate Litterarum Göttingensis editum. XIII. *Duodecim Prophetae*, J. Ziegler (Göttingen: Vandenhoeck and Ruprecht, 1943, [2]1967).

Ziegler, "Beiträge"

Joseph Ziegler, "Beiträge zum griechischen Dodekapropheton," *Nachrichten von der Akademie der Wissenschaften in Göttingen*, Philolog.-Hist. Klasse (Göttingen: Vandenhoeck & Ruprecht, 1943), pp 345–412 equal *Sylloge*, 71–138.

Ziegler, *Sylloge*

Joseph Ziegler, *Sylloge: Gesammelte Aufsätze zur Septuaginta*. Mitteilungen des Septuaginta—Unternehmens der Akademie der Wissenschaften in Göttingen, X (Göttingen: Vandenhoeck & Ruprecht, 1971).

The translation of the Book of Micah presented by
Professor Hillers in this volume is new, and is based on
a thorough study of the ancient texts.

Pictured on the endpapers are the two halves of a
column from a scroll of the Minor Prophets found in
the *Wâdī Murabba'ât* dating to the late first century
C. E. It is inscribed in an elegant Late Herodian
Formal script, ancestral to the medieval bookhand, and
witnesses to the text of Micah 1:5–3:4. It is presumed
that the scroll was deposited by partisans of Bar
Kokhba in ca. 135 C. E. The photographic prints were
provided through the courtesy of the Israel Depart-
ment of Antiquities and Museum through the agency
of Pierre Benoit, O. P., of the *Ecole biblique et archéo-
logique française* in Jerusalem; they are reproduced with
the permission of the Oxford University Press,
publisher of the *editio princeps* of Mur XII(88): P.
Benoit, O. P., J. T. Milik, and R. de Vaux, O. P., *Les
grottes de Murabba'ât,* 2 vols. ("*Texte*" and "*Planches*"),
DJD 2 (Oxford: At the Clarendon Press, 1961).

1. Micah: Some Preliminaries.

The book of Micah stands sixth among the Minor Prophets as they are ordered in the Hebrew canon (and in "R"; see below on the *Text*). In the Greek ordering it is third, after Hosea and Amos. In either case the principle of arrangement seems to have been chronological, so that Micah is placed with books believed to be approximately contemporary.[1]

Little is known of the man Micah. He is called "of Moresheth," in all likelihood a reference to the Moresheth-Gath of 1:14, a town in southwest Judah. Jeremiah 26:18 confirms a part of the superscription to Micah with the information: "Micah of Moresheth prophesied in the days of Hezekiah." According to Micah 1:1 the prophet's ministry may have been even longer, going back to Jotham and Ahaz, but the correctness of this information is disputed, especially the mention of Jotham, for nothing in the book seems to require so early a date. Beyond this bare positioning of Micah in place and time we can only conjecture concerning the life and experiences of the prophet, since the information added in Jeremiah 26 is problematic.[2]

The chronological problems of this period are as great as any in Israel's history. The following table may be of some use for ready reference in connection with the commentary, but some of the dates and synchronisms are not to be accepted uncritically.

Kings of Judah		Outside Judah	
Uzziah	783–742		
Jotham	742–735		
Ahaz	735–715	Fall of Samaria	722
Hezekiah	715–687	Sargon II comes	
		against Ashdod	713/712
		Sennacherib's invasion	701

This table is very meagre, but adequate to place chronologically the events and persons actually mentioned in Micah. As passionately involved as the prophet was in the situation of his people, he was either unconcerned or vague about happenings in national and world politics.

If it is impossible to speak at any length of the life and times of Micah, it might be thought possible to offer a sketch of his thought and message, as an introduction to the commentary. Regrettably, this is made very difficult by two sorts of problems. Micah abounds in textual problems; the discussion of *Text* below, and the notes within the commentary will give the details. Not all portions are equally affected, some being very lucid and well-preserved, but others, such as the last poem in chap 1 (10–16), are well-nigh hopeless.

Textual difficulties, however, tend to affect our grasp of Micah's thought only in detail. A much more serious problem is an apparent incoherence of thought which must impress the reader who approaches the book for the first time, and which is not necessarily alleviated by prolonged study. It is difficult to understand how Micah hangs together in a logical, systematic, or historical way. The following sketch of the *Course of Micah Studies* is meant to show how various critical difficulties have emerged over a century of Micah study, and some of the solutions proposed. It is intended to qualify and set in perspective the point of view advanced in this commentary. This commentary argues that Micah consists largely of materials connected with a movement of protest and revitalization, but it is important that the reader realize the degree to which that view is also hypothetical and provisional.

2. The Course of Micah Studies.

It is not surprising, given the general trend and interests of early biblical interpretation, that critical problems in Micah seem to have passed unnoticed from earliest times down to the nineteenth century. Though Mic 4:1–4 recurs almost verbatim in Isa 2:2–4, early Jewish and Christian interpreters apparently did not think the fact worth a comment.

Critical views become effective in the works of Ewald. In the first edition of his *Propheten des Alten Bundes*[3] he called Micah "complete in itself and lacking nothing," only the superscription being by a later hand. In the second edition (1867) a different view is presented (pp 501, 525–27), for though chapters 1–5 are described as before, 6–7 "belong to a different prophet." They are from completely different times, being from the days of Manasseh, are cast in completely different language, and

1   For further details, see Karl Marti, *Das Dodeka-propheton*, KHC 13 (Tübingen: J.C.B. Mohr, 1904), XII–XV.

2   See *Jeremiah 26 and Micah*, below.

3   Heinrich Ewald, *Die Propheten des Alten Bundes*, Volume I (Göttingen: Vandenhoeck & Ruprecht,

show a different "art of representation." No detailed demonstration of the last two points is offered.[4]

A critical observation made already in 1800 by Hartmann was repeated by Wellhausen in 1878 (in his edition of Bleek's *Einleitung*)[5] :Mic 7:7–20 presupposes a completely different historical situation than 7:1–6, and strongly resembles Isaiah 40–66. Thus it is at least a century later than 7:1–6.

It was Bernhard Stade, however, who most decisively affected criticism of the book of Micah and gave it a shape still recognizable today. In the first issue of the *Zeitschrift für die alttestamentliche Wissenschaft* (1881), which he edited, he took up and went beyond the observations of Ewald, attempting to show that Micah received its present form only after the exile, and that to Micah we can ascribe only chaps 1–3, minus 2:12–13. According to Stade, 2:12–13 interrupts the clear plan of chaps 1–3, and does not fit well with Isaiah as the other chapters do. The hopeful material of chaps 4–5 states the direct opposite of 1–3, which is a most implausible situation in itself, still more implausible when Jeremiah 26 is taken into account, for in Jeremiah the prophet Micah is remembered for the judgment speech of 3:12. So chaps 4–5 were added to secure Micah a place in the canon.[6] In brief notes in 1883,[7] 1884,[8] and 1903,[9] Stade answered his critics and added details.

Further literary criticism of Micah has tended to move within the bounds marked out by Stade and Ewald. Thus the remaining authentic material in Micah is, in the opinion of many twentieth-century scholars, chaps 1–3 minus 2:12–13. Further dissection of this part of the book has been carried out, but has often concerned only details, and has not been as convincing. As far as the rest of Micah is concerned the burden of proof has come to rest with anyone who would wish to claim large or small parts of chaps 4–7 for the eighth-century prophet. Of course, there have been those, such as Sellin[10] and Rudolph,[11] who have taken up the challenge.[12]

It is worth noting that the chief criteria in carrying out this reduction of Micah have been historical and religious or psychological, rather than linguistic or stylistic. Thus given Micah's firm place in the time of Hezekiah, reference to deliverance from Babylon (4:10) is a historical difficulty of an obvious sort; similar though less obvious are references to rebuilding walls (7:11), scattering of the nation (2:12), and the like. If the book refers to the streaming of all nations to Zion this has seemed to some to be at odds with the history of Israel's religious thought. Still other elements, while not anachronistic, have seemed out of harmony with Micah's character or religious convictions as expressed in chaps 1–3, where he is the one sent to "declare to Jacob his transgression (3:8)." From this point of view much of chaps 4–5 has fallen as too hopeful. Vocabulary study and stylistic comparison have played only a limited role, due mostly to the brevity of the book and of the units under consideration.

Hermann Gunkel in 1924 contributed notably to Micah criticism by his identification of 7:7–20 as a "prophetic liturgy,"[13] a viewpoint anticipated by Stade in 1903.[14] Aside from its exegetical significance this essay had the effect of turning attention away from the

1840), 327.

4   Heinrich Ewald, *Die Propheten des Alten Bundes* (Göttingen: Vandenhoeck & Ruprecht, [2]1867), 1:501, 525–27.

5   J. Wellhausen in Friedrich Bleek, *Einleitung in das Alte Testament*, ed. J. Wellhausen (Berlin: Reimer, [4]1878), 425–26.

6   Bernhard Stade, "Bemerkungen über das Buch Micha," *ZAW* 1 (1881): 161–72.

7   Bernhard Stade, "Weitere Bemerkungen zu Micha 4.5," *ZAW* 3 (1883): 1–16.

8   Bernhard Stade, "Bemerkungen zu vorstehendem Aufsatze," *ZAW* 4 (1884): 291–97.

9   Bernhard Stade, "Streiflichter auf die Entstehung der jetzigen Gestalt der alttestamentlichen Prophetenschriften," *ZAW* 23 (1903): 153–71.

10   Ernst Sellin, *Das Zwölfprophetenbuch*, KAT 12/1 (Leipzig: Deichertsche, [2]1929, [3]1930).

11   Wilhelm Rudolph, *Micha-Nahum-Habakuk-Zephanja*, KAT 13/3 (Gütersloh: Gütersloher Verlagshaus Gerd Mohn, 1975).

12   The earlier period of Micah criticism is reviewed in detail in a valuable survey by J.M.P. Smith in J.M.P. Smith, W.H. Ward, and Julius Bewer, *A Critical and Exegetical Commentary on Micah, Zephaniah, Nahum, Habakkuk, Obadiah and Joel*, ICC (Edinburgh: T. & T. Clark, 1911), 8–16.

13   H. Gunkel, "Der Micha-Schluss," *ZS* 2 (1924): 145–78.

14   See note 9 above.

individual prophetic figure and toward the studying and worshipping community which shaped and preserved the prophet's words.

Recent fresh contributions to Micah studies have taken the form of attempts to show the growth of the Micah collection from an original core through various stages of editing, each with its own intention. This sort of transmission or redaction-history was attempted very early in the course of Micah studies, but in recent decades has been pursued with far greater keenness. Lescow, Jeremias, Mays, Willi-Plein, van der Woude, and Renaud,[15] all writing in the 1960's or 1970's, have tried approaches at many points strikingly different, but united in the desire to remedy the incoherence of Micah by exposing the process of redaction which produced the present book. But the judgment of Childs, in a survey of this period of intense activity, is apt: "Although these scholars all agree on a complex history of redaction which passed through many stages, the analyses are so strikingly different that no common conclusions have emerged."[16]

A summary of one recent attempt at a redaction-history of Micah is given here to illustrate the promise and achievements of this line of approach (though scarcely the variety of results), and also the difficulties it encounters in the case of Micah. Hans Walter Wolff's scheme has been chosen as recent (thus not included in Childs's survey, quoted above) and to some degree representative, for his views, though individual, are not eccentric. Wolff's commentary,[17] of course, states, defends, and amplifies this scheme much more fully. The present brief summary is intended to provide the occasion and framework for my assessment of the shortcomings of this widely-used interpretive method, and by contrast to characterize my own approach.

Wolff[18] regards the book of Micah as the result of centuries of accretion to a core coming from Micah, consisting of 1:6, 7b–13a; 14–16; 2:1–4, 6–11; and 3:1–12. The earliest additions came in the form of "deutero-nomic commentary" (1:5, 7a, 13b, and the "introit" to the liturgical use of the Micah collection, 1:3–4).[19]

The hopeful oracles of chaps 4–5 come from prophets of weal in post-exilic times (6th century B.C.). At the end of the process, 1:2, "Listen, all you peoples," was prefixed. This form of the book reflects a post-exilic movement where in ceremonies of lament over Jerusalem, Micah's words of doom (now fulfilled) were recited with the addition of new words of salvation and materials pertaining to foreign nations.

At the same time, within these circles, men under the influence of Micah's judgment oracles added oracles of social criticism (6:2–7:7). Finally a liturgical ending was added (7:8–20), to fit the whole for use in worship.

If convincing, such an interpretive approach would go far to resolve a central dilemma in Micah: the presence of widely disparate, almost clashing elements. It does so by adopting a diachronic approach. The disparate sayings come from separate groups in different ages, employing and amplifying the words of the eighth-century prophet for their own purposes, mostly for worship.

Redaction-criticism of Micah fails to carry a satisfying degree of conviction, however. In the first place, it is evident that there is a great lack of fixed points in the scheme of Wolff. We have only one form of the book, and nothing like direct evidence for the variety of text-forms the theory calls for. Moreover, we have no evidence for the existence of the groups of tradents supposed to be involved, or the worship situations in which they are supposed to have functioned. Jeffrey Tigay has been able to discuss the development of the Gilgamesh Epic on the basis of a variety of extant forms of the legend and epic, related to a number of known groups who transmitted and transformed it. Since we lack everything except the final form of Micah, for even the initial "core" of Micah material is not a given, it would seem that a redaction-criticism is hypothetical at too many points to be interesting.

---

15 See Bibliography.

16 Brevard S. Childs, *Introduction to the Old Testament as Scripture* (Philadelphia: Fortress, 1979), 430.

17 Hans Walter Wolff, *Micah*, BK 14/12 (Neukirchen-Vluyn: Neukirchener, 1980).

18 Ibid. XXXVI–XXXVII.

19 Throughout this summary some details have been disregarded.

It is not only the hypothetical character of redaction-criticism which reduces its usefulness, but a certain inattention to two factors which I would summarily label "loss" and "chance." By loss I mean the accidental or deliberate omission of materials in the process of transmission. The history of Micah is treated by Wolff and others under a metaphor of constant growth: to a small original nucleus time steadily brings additions. But another common editorial tool is the blue pencil. Redactors may change objectionable texts by leaving things out, by simply dropping them or by substituting other material. This is a truism, but if so, it renders even more uncertain any attempt to write a redaction-history, since a potentially important part of the process is and will remain out of our control. "Chance" also seems somewhat overlooked. Wolff's redaction-critical scheme, like others, seems to depict an ultimately rational, comprehensible process, for the smallest verse in the book can be assigned a date and a life-situation. Indeed this kind of perspicuity seems to be presupposed in this critical approach. But it seems to me that this underestimates the place that chance, the irrational, the unpredictable, may have in the forming of a text.

Here and there in this commentary I have speculated that the present text shows signs of editing or alteration with the needs of a later, exilic community in mind (thus at 5:2[EV 3]), but in general have looked away from redaction-criticism. This is not only out of despair over the insufficient evidence, but out of preference for the promise that may lie in a synchronic approach, to reading the book as arising for the most part out of one situation. I do not, of course, revert to biographical explanation or historical explanation, relating oracles to (unknown) events in the prophet's life and times. Instead a unifying explanatory approach is sought in a type of social situation which has recurred over and over in human history, a movement of "revitalization", a "millennial" movement. (The terms are discussed in the following section of the introduction.) Micah, it is proposed, was associated with such a movement in his time, and the oracles in the book, from him or others associated with it, reflect typical themes of such movements. Such a movement in eighth-century Judah is as

hypothetical as anything in redaction-criticism, of course; the difference is that what is posited, or deduced from the Micah text, is a recurring and typical state of affairs.

3.   Micah as Prophet of a New Age.

From time immemorial, all over the world, groups of those who believe themselves oppressed have voiced their complaints and banded together to seek changes in their condition. In most cases the changes sought have been of a practical sort: more land, lighter taxes, a more equitable deal in the market, or some other realizable gain. Now and then, however, a movement takes another turn, and those involved look for an imminent, radical reordering of life on earth, conceived in ways that are imaginative and even fantastic rather than practical.

Scholars in history or the social sciences who encounter such movements in their studies have not adopted a uniform terminology in discussing them. Perhaps most commonly they have used the term "millennium" and the adjectives "millennial" and "millennarian." The narrower sense of millennium is of course derived from Rev 20:4–6 with its prophecy of a thousand-year reign of Christ, but the term has been extended to apply to any movement of the oppressed which looks for a radical alteration in the conditions of earthly life, in the not too-distant future, ushering in a reign of plenty and peace. It may, however, invite misunderstanding to import into study of an Old Testament book a term more at home in New Testament studies and with a technical sense in dogmatics, so although the term "millenium" might be particularly valuable as calling attention to comparable phenomena outside the biblical field, it will be used only sparingly in this commentary, and will usually be enclosed in quotation marks ("millennial") as a reminder that the technical theological sense is not intended. By preference protest movements with hopes of a radically new age will be called movements of "revitalization," using an alternate term in use by historians in the sense "a deliberate, organized, conscious effort by members of a society to construct a more satisfying culture."[20]

An entry into the study of movements of revitalization throughout the world may be made through the works of Cohn, Thrupp, Mühlmann, Guariglia, Adas, Lanternari,

---

20   Or the term "navitistic" will be used, a word which stresses the characteristic rejection of foreign elements of a culture.

and Bloch,[21] and the works they cite. Since one of the main characteristics of such movements is their variety, it is not surprising that no rigid laws emerge which might describe the necessary origin and course of development of "millennial" protest at any time and place. Some rather commonly found themes may be stated, however, and the procedure in the following will be to sum up some aspect of movements of revitalization, and then to compare relevant materials in Micah, also very briefly. Since the intent is to seek possible connections between the seemingly disparate materials in Micah, the common critical division after chap 3 has been disregarded for the most part. Those features which belong to the phase of protest are taken up first, then those belonging to the vision of the new age, but of course the whole point is that protest at oppression and dreams of a new age often occur together.

One commonly identified causal factor in such movements is deprivation. This may be absolute, where a group is being cut off from the means of supporting life, or more often relative deprivation, that is where a group finds itself worse off than it was before, or badly off in comparison to a new group it has come to be associated with. A second major factor is thus described by Norman Cohn: "The supposed defection of authority traditionally responsible for regulating relations between society and the powers governing the cosmos."[22]

Turning to Micah, it is not difficult to identify either the economic or the spiritual factor. The prophet complains—beyond doubt voicing the feelings of many in his region—"Ah you who think up evil and deeds of wrong on your beds, then perform it when day breaks because it lies within your power; you who covet fields, and steal them, houses, and take them; who oppress a man and his household, an owner and his property!" (2:1–2) Elsewhere this is echoed in the brief, obscure saying: "You drive the women of my people out of her pleasant dwelling" (2:9). The grisly passage about the cannibalism of the heads and rulers no doubt refers to this same economic oppression for which "deprivation" is almost a euphemism. (cf. also 6:9–11, 16).

Looking outside Micah for confirmation of this bleak picture, one finds comparable complaints in Isaiah, and some historical and archaeological evidence that may be relevant. The father of Jotham, the great Uzziah (783–742) carried on an aggressive program of armament and fortification (2 Chron 26:9, 11–15) and enlarged Judaean borders by warlike means. According to the same source, Hezekiah also fortified and armed Judah (2 Chronicles 32), which seems to be confirmed by archaeological data.[23] A further financial burden must have been added when Judah had to make up the tribute repeatedly exacted by the Assyrians from the kings beginning with Ahaz. If the powerful in the time of Isaiah and Micah placed onerous financial burdens on the poor, they may have only been passing their costs on.

The fall of the Northern Kingdom in 722 would have had an economic and social effect in the south as well. In the late eighth century, Jerusalem grew to three or four times its previous size, according to archaeological data. Broshi accounts for this growth as follows: ". . . the main reasons behind the expansion was (sic) the immigration of Israelites who came to Judah from the Northern Kingdom after the fall of Samaria in 721 B.C. and the influx of dispossessed refugees from the territories that Sennacherib took from Judah and gave to the Philistine cities."[24] As far as Micah is concerned, the importance of the latter point is doubtful, for chronological reasons. Even so, during his time there must have been a substantial increase in the population, and this in a region where resources were not abundant. It is likely that this jump in population overtaxed the resources of Judah, gave extra incentive to owning land and reduced wages.[25] Micah's comment on the process seems to have been: "You who build Zion at the price of bloodshed" (3:10).

Consonant with the above is the evidence of the stamped jar-handles. The jar-handles found by exca-

---

21   See Bibliography.
22   Norman Cohn, "Medieval Millenarism: Its Bearing on the Comparative Study of Millenarian Movements," *Millennial Dreams in Action*, Comparative Studies in Society and History, Sup. II, ed. Sylvia L. Thrupp (The Hague: Mouton, 1962), 40.
23   Jonathan Rosenbaum, "Hezekiah's Reform and the Deuteronomistic Tradition," *HTR* 72 (1979): 32–33.

24   Magen Broshi, "The Expansion of Jerusalem in the Reigns of Hezekiah and Manasseh," *IEJ* 24 (1974): 21.
25   Hans Bardtke, "Die Latifundien in Juda während der zweiten Hälfte des achten Jahrhunderts v. Chr." in Hommages à André Dupont-Sommer (Paris: Adrien-Maisonneuve, 1971), 235–54.

vators which bear the stamp *lmlk* "of the king" seem to have had a kind of administrative function. In some way they symbolize an assertion of greater royal control of affairs in Judah.[26] Though the date has been disputed, it now seems likely that they were used first under Hezekiah, in the time before Sennacherib's invasion.[27] One of the main areas in which finds of handles are concentrated is the Shephelah, Micah's home territory.

Reference has been made to the "defection of authority" which Cohn identifies as a factor associated with "millennialism."[28] The relevant passage in Micah is 3:9–12, culminating in the charge: "Her heads judge for bribes and her priests give instruction for pay and her prophets give oracles for money. All the while they rely on Yahweh, and say, 'Surely Yahweh is in our midst.'" Prophets, priests, and judges (who are also sacred figures here), have in the most literal sense sold out.

The effect on the populace of the destruction of their lives' social and economic fabric is portrayed in 7:1–6. The phrase "Put no trust in a neighbor" and what follows is to some extent conventional, but not to be dismissed on that account. Conditions which have produced this kind of disintegration have thereby prepared the ground for protest leading to visions of a reordered society.

Five elements in Micah, best attested in the latter part of the book, have parallels in movements of revitalization, as they look to the future. First is the removal of foreign elements. Micah 5:10–15 predicts a "cutting-off" of horses and chariots, cities and strongholds, sorceries and soothsayers, images and pillars, Asherim and idols.[29] This is followed by the assertion, "And in anger and wrath I will execute vengeance upon the nations that did not obey." In *Chiliasmus und Nativismus*, Mühlmann discusses this phenomenon. In numerous less developed societies, after a period of contact with a technically superior civilization in which the natives freely accept the goods and customs of the foreign society, there is a sudden reversal and utter rejection of foreign cultural elements. This is an element of preparation for the coming righteous kingdom, a necessary preliminary stage.[30] The Micah passage may be viewed from this nativistic perspective. The things proscribed "in that day" are foreign to Israel, either historically and demonstrably, such as horses and chariots, images and Asherim, or in the prophet's ideology, thus cities and strongholds. Note the congruence in detail with a passage from early on in Micah (1:13), where Lachish is taunted for her horses and chariots, which are "the beginning of sin." Note too that this purging culminates in a promise that God will punish the nations; the removal of foreign elements is preparation for the new age.

A second common "millennial" theme is that of the time of troubles. Before the onset of the golden Messianic age, must be a time of distress, the birth-pangs of the Messiah. This receives classic expression in Micah 5. The coming of the ruler from Bethlehem having been announced, the oracle goes on: "Therefore he will give them over until the time when the mother has given birth." After this will come the age of peace. Reference to a parturient mother is probably not a prediction of the *birth* of the Messiah. She who is in labor is rather a figure doubly symbolic, of the severity of the distress during the time when he (God) has given them up, and of the brevity of that time. In its allusive, enigmatic way this is a classic statement of the Messianic woes that precede the end. Another reference to this time may be the problematic 4:9–10. If one eliminates as an anachronistic contemporizing gloss the reference to Babylon, the idea of exile from the city, a time of suffering and then of redemption is congruent with this second "millennial" theme.

A third feature of movements of revitalization is the reversal of social classes, with expectation of the dominance of the pariah class. In general the poor play a prominent role in these movements, and the expectation is that these underdogs will come out on top. "In that day, says the Lord, I will gather the one who limps and collect the one who has strayed, and the one I did harm. Then I will make the one who limps a remnant, and the

---

26 See now, A. F. Rainey, "Wine from the Royal Vineyards," *BASOR* No. 245 (1982): 57–62, for a review of the subject consonant with the view expressed here.

27 N. Na'aman, "Sennacherib's Campaign to Judah and the Date of the LMLK Stamps," *VT* 29 (1979): 61–86.

28 See note 22.

29 Or cities, see the notes to the text.

30 Wilhelm E. Mühlmann, *Chiliasmus und Nativismus* (Berlin: Dietrich Reimer, 1961), 291–96.

far off one a populous nation."[31] It is difficult to be sure what group in Israel is meant, for the language is figurative; perhaps the prophet is deliberately vague.

A characteristic, and important, shift is illustrated in this passage. The old theme remains: the rule of God over his people from Mount Zion, but the promise is appropriated by a smaller group. It has not perhaps been noticed sufficiently that this point of view is prepared for already in passages everyone agrees are by Micah. In 2:5, after a blistering attack on the land-hungry, Micah says: "Therefore you (the rich) will have no one to cast the cord over your allotted land in the assembly of Yahweh." We do not know of any actual redistribution of land in Judaean society, though no evidence completely rules out the existence of such an institution.[32] Thus most likely this is a reference to the age to come, when in a sacred assembly land will be divided among the righteous. Several times "my people" is used in a way that if pressed, would exclude the leaders, lay and spiritual, from the people of God. Thus "who eat the flesh of my people" (3:3); "who mislead my people" (3:5); "you drive the women of my people out" (2:9). Note also 6:16 where the leaders of the city will have to bear "the scorn of my people." Thus at least an approach is made in Micah to identifying a portion of the historic people as the whole people. The tension between the "judgment" and "grace" in Micah is somewhat eased if we recognize the motif of the exaltation of the pariahs, for to some extent doom and hope are not addressed to the same group.

The idea of a righteous, peaceable ruler is a common feature of the movements under discussion, and is of course present in Micah. The relation of Micah 5 to other Messianic dreams would be easier to trace if the passage were less ambiguous, especially as to whether this ruler is David come again. If that view, adopted in this Commentary, is true, one may compare the widespread myth of a king who belongs to the glorious past and yet is somehow still alive and will return—a Constantine, Charlemagne, Barbarossa, or Arthur.[33]

Finally, the new age itself is depicted abundantly in Micah. As in many "millennialist" schemes,[34] triumph over enemies is a prominent feature. The remnant will be like a lion, or, in a more bizarre figure, Zion will be a great cow with iron horns and brazen hoofs to thresh out the nations. Part of the conception of the coming golden age is the belief in the glorificiation of the city of God. Since the principal passage on this theme recurs almost verbatim in Isaiah, it has long been denied to Micah. But if not by the man of Moresheth, it may be more in harmony with his thought than is usually recognized (see *Commentary*). Micah's protest against cities, and against Jerusalem, never strikes at the notion of a *holy* city. Many "millennialists" have conceived of the great age of peace as having a center of symbolic and spiritual value.

A final touch in 4:4 returns this picture to its village roots: each will live under his own vine and his own fig tree. In the future each will hold his land secure, undisturbed, and with some measure of prosperity—an agrarian millennium. Though the imagery is conventional, it is noteworthy that this passage is absent from the Isaiah version, and fits well in its position in Micah.

To sum up, disparate elements in the book of Micah appear more closely connected on the assumption that the prophet was somehow associated with a movement of revitalization, a hypothesis which also promises to deepen our understanding of individual passages. A phrase such as "somehow associated with a movement of revitalization" is, of course, vague. It is chosen deliberately because we lack any biographical or historical information which might permit greater definiteness. Comparative evidence fails us here, though it provides a warning: in medieval European "millennial" movements the leaders were most often not of the lower classes they led, frequently being of the lower clergy or even nobility. Note that in describing Micah as a prophet of a new age there is no intention of limiting his thought to this sphere; passages such as the great controversy in 6:1–8 have nothing much to do with visions of the future.

---

31 Mic 4:6, 7a.

32 Contra Alt. See Albrecht Alt, "Micha 2, 1–5 Γης αναδασμος in Juda, "*NTT* 56 (1955): 13–23.

33 See Hans Schmidt, *Der Mythos vom wiederkehrenden König im Alten Testament, Schriften der Hessischen Hochschulen*, Universität Giessen, Jahrgang 25, Heft 1 (Giessen: Töpelmann, 1925).

34 Wilhelm E. Mühlmann, *ad loc.* 281–82.

One objection may be anticipated here. At least since Wellhausen, some of the elements identified here as "millennial" have been assigned to the exilic or post-exilic period, on the basis of comparison with Second Isaiah or other late materials. To rephrase this line of argument, there was a phase in Israel's religion which might be called "millennialistic" in a broad sense, but it was later than Micah. Some reply to this is made in comments on individual passages, but one general point is perhaps best made here. Revitalization is a recurring phenomenon in human history and the history of given societies. Over and over again in the centuries of medieval history men's minds turned in this direction, again and again in the centuries of czarist rule in Russia movements of rebellion were characterized by "millennialist" features. We must leave open the possibility for the same sort of recurrence in Israel.

4. The Form of the Book of Micah.

It is relatively easy to distinguish the smaller units of composition which make up the book of Micah. There are problematic cases (e.g., 4:14 [EV 5:1]), but in general the divisions made in this commentary are those long and widely accepted. It is not as easy to discover any larger units—groups of oracles or the like—which are of significance for understanding the book. (If chaps 6–7 were a "Northern" collection, this conclusion would require modification, but in my opinion there is no good evidence for such a theory; see the *Commentary*.) Rather frequently, units are joined on a catchword principle; thus the אַתָּה ("you") and עַתָּה ("now") of chaps 4 and 5 seem to have been decisive in the placing together of materials in those chapters. Often, too, there are thematic links between adjacent oracles. Yet nothing like an overall plan or structure is discernible. Lindblom put it this way: "We must stick to the viewpoint that the prophetic books of the Old Testament are *collections* and in principle abandon any claims to topical or chronological order or disposition among various units. The

individual pieces are for the most part joined on the basis of very superficial and purely accidental resemblances"[35]

Larger divisions and groupings have been proposed by commentators, and may claim some limited validity or at least convenience for the student. A tripartite plan has often been proposed, approximately as follows: chap 1–3 "doom"; 4–5 "grace"; 6–7 "further admonitions and comfort." Others, such as Rudolph, have objected to a detail of this division, pointing to the "hopeful" passage 2:12–13 and the possible structural clue in the thrice-repeated "Hear ye" (1:2; 3:1; 6:1), and have divided at 3:1, yielding a kind of progression in all three divisions from judgment to grace.[36] Still other permutations have been proposed. Renaud[37] and Willis[38] have described rather more intricate structures within the book, but neither attempt has persuaded very many. When Mays[39] refers to a "discernible pattern in the material which is the result of an accumulative and sustained intention to say something which incorporates all the smaller parts into a larger message," he is unduly pressing the significance of structure in Micah, in the interests of his own redaction-critical scheme.

5. Jeremiah 26 and Micah.

Jer 26:1–19 is part of the biographical material concerning Jeremiah, presumably from Baruch.[40] At the beginning of the reign of Jehoiakim, Jeremiah preached a sermon at the Jerusalem temple in which he warned the worshippers that if they did not obey the law and prophets God would "make this house like Shiloh," and also destroy the city. It is worth noting that in Jeremiah's formulation (vv 4–6) the threat is conditional, though those who arrest him cite it as an absolute prediction (v 9). Arrested by priests and prophets, who pressed for a death sentence, Jeremiah in his defense urged reform, calling on his hearers in this way to avoid disaster. Then the princes and "all the people" took up the defense, and certain elders declared (vv 18–19): "Micah of Moresheth used to prophesy in the time of Hezekiah, king of Judah,

35 Johannes Lindblom, *Micha literarisch Untersucht*, Acta Academiae Aboensis, Humaniora, VI, 2 (Helsingfors: Åbo Akademi, 1929), 9. This is my translation.

36 Rudolph, p. 24.

37 B. Renaud, *Structure et attaches littéraires de Michée IV–V*, Cahiers de la Revue Biblique, 2 (Paris: Gabalda, 1964).

38 J.T. Willis, "The Structure of the Book of Micah,"

Svensk Exegetisk Årsbok 34 (1969): 5–42.

39 James Luther Mays, *Micah: A Commentary* (Philadelphia: Westminster, 1976), p 3.

40 This is Mowinckel's source B. For a summary see Aage Bentzen, *Introduction to the Old Testament, volume 2* (Copenhagen: G.E.C. Gad Publisher, ³1957) 120–21.

and he said to all the people of Judah: 'Thus says Yahweh of Hosts: "Zion shall be plowed as a field, and Jerusalem shall become heaps of rubble, and the temple mount will belong to the wild beasts."' Do you think Hezekiah king of Judah, and all Judah, put him to death? Did he not fear Yahweh and seek to appease him, so that Yahweh changed his mind about the calamity he had predicted for them? But we are doing ourselves great harm." Jeremiah was finally rescued by Ahikam son of Shaphan.

A number of conclusions for Micah can legitimately be drawn from this, but not exactly the ones usually drawn. First, Micah's words were remembered in a different context from that in the book of Micah. It is not the case that the oracle of Micah (3:9–12) is shortened in Jeremiah by dropping off the basis for the threat, or altered by the insertion of "thus says Yahweh of Hosts." Rather the words are remembered as part of a prophetic narrative. Micah's harsh words about city and temple are laid specifically in the time of Hezekiah. They are thought of as having been spoken in the king's hearing or brought to his notice, and were thought to have been followed by the king's repentance. This reconstructed narrative setting recalls in outline and in some details an extant prophetic narrative about Hezekiah, Isa 38:1–8, and brings to mind the notice about Hezekiah's reform, 2 Kgs 18:1–8. Thus, though often described as a direct quotation of Micah, Jeremiah 26 offers something slightly different, namely, evidence for the persistence of prophetic legend concerning Micah, about a century after his time.

In the second place, in this narrative setting the sense of Micah's words is affected. Just as Jeremiah's temple prediction is specifically cast in conditional terms, so the elders rightly take Micah's words as an earlier example of the same sort of prophetic pronouncement, conditional in intention if not in form. In the story of Hezekiah's illness, Isaiah speaks in peremptory fashion: "Thus says Yahweh, 'Set your house in order, you will die and not recover.'", but this is averted by the king's prayer. The concept illustrated was familiar in Israel: Yahweh remains sovereign over his word and sometimes uses a prophetic word of doom not to rule out, but to invite human response, which will evoke his own gracious response in turn.

If these inferences are legitimate, it will be evident that others commonly drawn involve a measure of misreading. Jer 26:18–19, whether a true report or a legend, does not define the scope of Micah's prophecy. It is but a single narrative and may be as unrepresentative of the prophet's whole message as the story of Hezekiah's illness is of Isaiah's. Still less does Jeremiah 26 define the chronological scope of Micah's activity. And as an unconfirmed late report of events in Hezekiah's time it does not really inform us about Micah's relation to the king, or the effect of Micah's message in his own time.

6. The Text of Micah.

To the traditional sources for the text and versions of Micah certain recent additions have been made. Three new sources for the Hebrew text from finds in the Judaean Desert have been published, and are cited in the commentary. They are:

IQpMi (IQ14): A sectarian commentary on Micah, citing 1:2–5, with *pešer* ("commentary") on 1:5–7, 8–9, 6:14–16, plus fragments. There are several material variants and exegetical items of interest.[41]

4QpMi(?) (4Q 168): A sectarian commentary on Micah, or simply a text of Micah, citing 4:8–12. This is very fragmentary; it only has one material variant (see on 4:9).[42]

---

41 Dominique Barthélemy and J.T. Milik, *Qumran Cave I, Discoveries in the Judaean Desert I* (Oxford: Clarendon, 1955), 77–80 and Pl. XV. Also see the preliminary publication by J.T. Milik, "Fragments d'un Midrash de Michée dans les manuscrits de Qumran," *RB* 59 (1952): 412–18. There is a review article by J. Carmignac, "Notes sur les Pešârîm," *RQ* 3 (1962): 505–38, and a discussion by Maurya P. Horgan, *Pesharim: Qumran Interpretations of Biblical Books.* Catholic Biblical Quarterly Monograph Series, 8 (Washington, D.C.: Catholic Biblical Association, 1979).

42 John M. Allegro, *Qumran Cave 4*, Discoveries in the Judaean Desert of Jordan, V (Oxford: Clarendon, 1968), 36 and Pl. XII. Also see Horgan as cited in note 40 above.

Mur 88: A long roll of the Minor Prophets with extant portions covering from Joel 2:20 to Zech 1:4; it was written about the time of the second Jewish revolt. This text is very close to the MT, even to divisions in the text; there are scarcely any variants.[43]

In the commentary an attempt is made to report all the variants of the above three manuscripts, including orthographic variants.

Since Ziegler's edition of the LXX to the Minor Prophets,[44] one important new witness to an early form of the Greek text has been announced by D. Barthélemy, and published with extensive discussion, though not in definitive form, in *Les devanciers d'Aquila*.[45] This is a scroll of the Minor Prophets in Greek of the middle of the first century A. D. In this commentary Barthélemy's siglum R is used. Extant portions contain Jonah 1:4–Zech 9:4, the Hebrew order of the books being observed. Of Micah, 1:1–5:6, with gaps, is preserved. Since readings of this manuscript are not in Ziegler's edition, all variants from the LXX have been reported here except for orthographic variants.

In view of the substantial span between even the later portions of Micah and our extant manscripts and versions, and in view of the evidently corrupt text of some passages, conjectural emendations retain considerable importance. But in the more corrupt passages of the book—and Micah is often placed among the worst books in the canon in this respect—so many conjectures have been proposed that it would be impossible to list them all even if it made any sense to do so. In making a selection of those that deserve consideration, I have in part been guided by the practical consideration that most users of this commentary will have *BHS* or *BH*[3] before them, and I have made it a general rule to comment on those emendations which have won a place in the apparatus of these editions.

Certain types of minor variants are rather common in the LXX, the S, and other versions, and at the same time offer little basis for a choice between readings. These cases involve addition or omission of the conjunction *w*, presence or absence of the definite article, use or omission of a possessive suffix, singular for plural and vice versa. Such cases are not ordinarily reported in this commentary.

7. Poetic Form in Micah.

Except for the heading (1:1), which is clearly non-poetic, the book of Micah is evidently in some sort of verse. There are textually corrupt passages, such as 1:10–16, where verse form (if any) is obscured, and isolated lines which are not especially rhythmic or parallelistic (2:3, 2:5, 2:4a; 3:4; 4:5; 5:14) including formulas of introduction which are not obviously metrical (4:1a; 5:9a (EV 10a); 3:5; 3:1 [?]), but on the whole the book, in all its divisions, is meant to be verse. The characteristic mark of this is the pervasive parallelism. Units parallel to each other in sense are of roughly the same length, whether one reckons by number of words, accents, or syllables. But there is no rigidity in this regard. Until some theory of Hebrew meter more adequate than present ones is available, metric considerations must be used with great caution in judging textual matters. Having studied the poetic style of the eighth-century prophets, Freedman and Andersen find in them, including Micah, a style that is a mixture of prose sentences and poetic elements.[46] "It is not a matter of an obvious mixture of prose sentences and poetic verses, but rather a distinctive oratorical style which blends features of both".[47] If this is true, it suggests still more caution in restoring a supposed original verse form in Micah.

The arrangement of the translation will permit users of this commentary to see which lines are regarded as parallel to one another, the second member of a bicolon being indented.

43 F. Benoit, J.T. Milik, and R. de Vaux, *Les Grottes de Murabba'ât, Discoveries in the Judaean Desert*, II (Oxford: Clarendon, 1961), 181–205, Pls. LVI–LXXIII.

44 *Septuaginta: Vetus Testamentum Graecum auctoritate Academiae Litterarum Gottingensis editum. XIII. Duodecim Prophetae*, J. Ziegler, 1943 (Göttingen: Vandenhoeck & Ruprecht, ²1967).

45 Dominique Barthélemy, "Redécouverte d'un chaînon manquant de l'histoire de la Septante," *RB* 60 (1953): 18–29, and *Les devanciers d'Aquila, VTS* X (1963).

46 Francis I. Andersen and David Noel Freedman, *Hosea*, The Anchor Bible (Garden City, N.Y.: Doubleday, 1980), 60–66.

47 Ibid., 61.

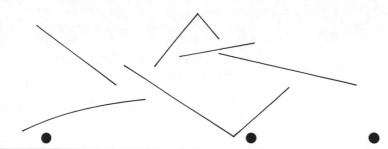

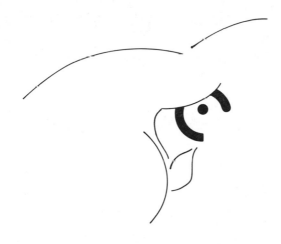

■ **The Heading**

1

1

The word of Yahweh which came^a to Micah of Moresheth^b in the days of Jotham, Ahaz, and Hezekiah, kings^c of Judah, which^d he prophesied^e concerning Samaria and Jerusalem.

a   The LXX, σ′, θ′, read καὶ ἐγένετο λόγος κυρίου which stands for ויהי דבר יהוה. Against Viktor Ryssel (*Untersuchungen über die Textgestalt und die Echtheit des Buches Micha* [Leipzig: S. Hirzel, 1887]) and Smith there is no reason to think this is simply free rendering of the MT. ויהי דבר יהוה occurs at the beginning of the book of Jonah, and of many individual prophetic oracles, e.g., Isa 38:4; Jer 28:12 et passim, and in the Twelve, at Hag 1:3; 2:20; Jonah 3:1; Zech 4:8; 6:9; 7:4, 8; 8:1, and 18. The LXX to the Twelve, the work of one translator, is, outside of the present problematic instance, completely consistent in distinguishing this Hebrew phrase from דבר יהוה אשר היה which occurs at Hos 1:1; Joel 1:1; and Zeph 1:1. In spite of the translator's inconsistencies in other respects, this is not altogether without significance.

b   This is the same as Moresheth-Gath of 1:14. The MT has it here (defective spelling; 33 MSS Kenn. plene) and in Jer 26:18 (plene) and the LXX and V in both passages. Mareshah is a separate place, as 1:14–15 indicates. The S and T (and Syh) have "of Mareshah" (accepted by Rashi and Redak), but this is contrary to the oldest evidence for the vocalization. On the identification of these sites, see the comments on 1:14, 15.

c   The LXX has βασιλέων, but LXX^{ms} and R read –ως. Ziegler (in his *Duodecim Prophetae*) compares the situation at Hos 1:1.

d   The LXX ὑπὲρ ὧν ("concerning the things") is not a different reading, but an attempt to smooth out an apparent difficulty with the relative clause (see below), so Ryssel, *Textgestalt*. R ὅν is a correction according to the MT.

e   Or, we could translate "received" (in his capacity as a prophet). חזה though its basic sense is "see," is from early times (Num 24:4, 16) used of a prophetic figure's reception of a communication mostly or entirely verbal (see Alfred Jepsen, "חזה, ḥāzāh," *TWAT*, s.v. for full discussion and bibliography), so that there is no difficulty involved in joining it with the object דָּבָר ("word") here, as in Isa 2:1 and Amos 1:1. A translation "saw" might be misleading, because it would be overly concrete. חֹזֶה is a prophet, in all his activities as a channel for divine communications. Certain passages closely associate חזה and derivatives with prophetic *speaking*: 2 Sam 7:17 (1 Chr 17:15); Jer 14:3; 23:16; and especially Zech 10:2. Ezek 13:1–16 not only associates חזה with words denoting speech, but asserts (in v 3) that the false prophets (v 3 נְבִיאִים, or v 9 חֹזִים) "have not seen (anything)." In such a context חֲזוּ שָׁוְא (v 6) is well rendered by RSV: "They have spoken falsehood." The T to Mic 1:1 uses ד אתנבי, "which he prophesied" or "who prophesied"; this is the T's preferred rendering of חזה and derivatives when prophetic activity, not ordinary seeing, is in question. NJPS has adopted this at appropriate places: here, Isa 1:1; 2:1, etc. Cf. Rudolph (tentatively) "der Seher war."

In contrast to NJPS at Isa 1:1, the antecedent of the relative clause is perhaps best taken as "word" (cf. NJPS at Isa 2:1) rather than "Micah," if view of the syntax. Even so, the second relative clause is uncoordinated with the first and separated from its antecedent (דְּבָר) in a way that has been felt to be unusual or awkward by many. Yet the construction is unobjectionable, compare Lev 25:45; Num 35:34; Deut 9:26; 21:3; 2 Kgs 11:10; Isa 39:7, etc. If the whole sentence seems overloaded this is perhaps to be excused in a superscription (so Artur Weiser, *Das Buch der zwölf Kleinen Propheten, I: Die Propheten Josea, Joel, Amos, Obadja, Jona, Micha*. ATD Teilbd. 24 [Göttingen: Vandenhoeck & Ruprecht, 1956]). One cannot rule out the possibility or even probability of additions, alterations, etc., in the superscription to Micah over the centuries, but the present working provides no firm basis for a tradition history. B. Renaud's effort along these lines (*La formation du livre de Michée*, Études Bibliques [Paris: Gabalda, 1977]) is strikingly over-elaborate and over-confident.

Commentary

The superscription to Micah is of a type not uncommonly prefixed to prophetic books; rather close parallels are Isa 1:1; 2:1; Jer 1:1–3; Hos 1:1; Joel 1:1; Amos 1:1; and Zeph 1:1. It designates the collection that follows as "the word of Yahweh," names the prophet and gives a bit of further information about him, and specifies the time in which he worked and those he addressed. It is no doubt the work of an editor at some stage in the collection and arrangement of the work, and though we cannot define precisely when just this form of superscription was first prefixed to a Micah collection, it is the only transmitted title for the extant book. As such it deserves—and has received—detailed examination.

The book is "the word of Yahweh," which "came to" (הָיָה אֶל) the prophet. As Grether has shown, "word of Yahweh" is almost always a technical term for revelation of a divine message to a prophet.[1] Though Wolff would associate "the word of Yahweh" (with "came to" [הָיָה אֶל]) specifically with writings from Deuteronomistic circles, this is over-precise.[2] Grether's more neutral formulation is preferable. The expression is found occasionally outside Deuteronomistic writings, e.g., Gen 15:1, 4, and is totally absent from Deuteronomy itself (aside from 5:5, which is textually suspect). Though in other contexts the phrase may express a rather specific conception of how communication from God to a prophet took place, in editorial superscriptions such as this it stands before collections of the most disparate materials, so that it is not to be taken as expressing anything about the means of communication, but only the idea that all that follows is somehow from God. For this editor, scripture is "the word of Yahweh." (See below on "the word of Yahweh" [דְּבַר יהוה] in 4:2).

Micah is said to be "of Moresheth" (see Note). The Old Testament often identifies men by their place of origin; compare, among the prophets, Ahijah of Shiloh (the Shilonite) and "Jeremiah of Anathoth" (Jer 29:27). Whatever the editor's intention in the present case, such

an identification serves to set this Micah apart from others who bore this common name (eight are mentioned in the OT). Even so, Micaiah ben Imlah was confused with our Micah; see note a on Mic 1:2 and 1 Kgs 22:28. "Micah" means "Who is like (Yahweh)?", an oblique way of asserting the incomparability of the deity; whatever interest there may be in this name-type, found far outside the confines of the Bible, the prophet's name is of no significance at all for his book. Though the prophet is identified by his home town and not by his father, no conclusion as to Micah's family, social status, or his "self-effacing character"[3] is in place (cf. "Goliath of Gath"). Moresheth-Gath has not been certainly identified.[4]

Identification of Micah as "of Moresheth" rests on tradition concerning the prophet independent of the rest of the book, for it could not have been deduced from 1:14 or 15. Similarly only the heading to Hosea, not the body of the book, supplies the information that he is the son of Beeri. Also Jer 1:2; Hos 1:1; Joel 1:1; Amos 1:1; Nah 1:1; and Zeph 1:1 give us bits of information about the prophets which must come from traditions independent of the contents of the extant books.

This point is of some importance in considering the list of Judaean kings which follows. This has, since Wellhausen, been commonly dismissed as secondary addition, on various grounds: 1) No word of Micah goes back as early as to Jotham (some would say, to Ahaz); 2) It is an imitation of Hos 1:1 and Isa 1:1; 3) The information is vague and indefinite (in contrast to the precision of "of Moresheth"); 4) Jer 26:18 knows only of Micah's activity under Hezekiah. The last argument is fallacious; see Introduction, 5. *Jeremiah 26 and Micah.* The others are also suspect. What is especially vague or indefinite about the naming of three specific kings, unless one (unreasonably) demands the precision of Haggai and Zechariah? Micah 1:1 is not *identical* in its listing to Hos 1:1 and Isa 1:1, and taking into account chronological notices elsewhere (Jer 1:2; Amos 1:1; Zeph 1:1, etc.), it is surely

1   Oskar Grether, *Name und Wort Gottes im Alten Testament,* BZAW 64 (1934) 67–76.
2   Hans Walter Wolff, *Hosea: A Commentary on the Book of the Prophet Hosea,* tr. Gary Stansell; Hermeneia (Philadelphia: Fortress, 1974). See on Hosea 1:1.
3   So Smith.
4   See on 1:14.

better to hold that editors of prophetic materials generally had some concern for the date of a prophet's activity, and that this accounts for Micah 1:1 better than supposing that they imitated any one model. Finally, if it proves true that nothing in the extant book actually comes from the time of Jotham or even Ahaz, this does not bear on the integrity of the superscription. The editor and his contemporaries may have read portions of the book as being from the early time of Jotham and Ahaz, whether correctly or quite erroneously, as later Jewish and Christian interpretation read Lam 4:20 as referring to Josiah. In my opinion, it is probable that the editor had access to independent traditions, now lost. It is best to keep an open mind as to the accuracy and value of this dating, and at least not to imagine that one has here a firm foothold for redaction-criticism.

Only kings of Judah are named. If one must explain this, it seems most likely that the editor, like most readers of Micah since, thought of the prophet as active chiefly in the southern kingdom.

In describing Micah as prophesying "concerning Samaria and Jerusalem," instead of "Israel and Judah," the editor seems to have been influenced chiefly by the first oracle in the book, 1:2–7, where these two cities are singled out as foci and symbols of the sins of the two kingdoms. In some degree this emphasis on the *city* is maintained throughout the book, that is, in the rest of chap 1, chap 3, the salvation oracles of chap 4, and even in 6:9–16.

The writer of the superscription writes from a perspective later than the time of Micah. In view of the content of the present collection and the interest already during exilic times and shortly thereafter in gathering and interpreting earlier prophetic words of doom and salvation, the present title may have been attached to a Micah collection containing much of what is in the present book as early as the sixth century. Though the title could have been written all at once, in its present form, it is plausible to suppose that the present title replaced an older form, and not very difficult to conjecture what such an earlier form might have been. Such efforts, however, and attempts to fit the superscription into a detailed account of the growth of the collection, do not rise above the level of guesses. It is significant that the painstaking studies of Lescow and Jörg Jeremias reach opposite conclusions as to what is new and old here.[5]

---

5   Theodor Lescow, "Redaktionsgeschichtliche Analyse von Micha 1–5," ZAW 84 (1972): 61–64, and Jörg Jeremias, "Die Deutung der Gerichtsworte Michas in der Exilszeit," ZAW 83 (1971): 330–54. Also see Renaud, *La formation* and Hans F. Fuhs, *Sehen und Schauen. Die Wurzel ḥzh im alten Orient und im alten Testament,* Forschung zur Bibel, 32 (Würzburg: Echter Verlag, 1978), 194–97.

1

■ **The Wrath to Come on Samaria**

The heavenly ruler is coming down in destructive splendor to execute judgment on Samaria and Jerusalem.

2   Listen, all[a] you peoples,
     Give ear, O earth and all that is in you,[b]
   That the Lord Yahweh[c] may testify against you,[d]
     The Lord, from his holy temple.

3   For Yahweh[e] will soon come out of his place,
     Descend and tread[f] on the heights of the world.[g]

4   Then the mountains will melt beneath him
     And the valleys will be split open,[h]
   Like wax[i] before a fire,
     Like water poured down a slope.

5   All[j] this happens for the rebellion of Jacob,
     For the sins[k] of the house of Israel.[l]
   What[m] is the rebellion of Jacob? Samaria!
     What is the high place[n] of Judah?[o] Jerusalem![p]

6   So I will make Samaria a ruin,
     An open field[q] for planting of vineyards.
   I will roll her stones down into the valley[r]
     And uncover her foundations.

7   All her carved statues will be smashed,[s]
     And all her whore's fees[t] will be burned in fire.
   I will make all her idols a ruin,
     For as she got[u] them from whore's fees,[v]
     They will go back[w] to being whore's fees.

---

a   The LXX λόγους ("words") is plausibly explained by Karl Vollers ("Das Dodekapropheten der Alexandriner [Schluss]," *ZAW* 4 [1884]: 2) as a translation of מלים, a slight miswriting of the correct text. If not totally convincing this is more plausible than alternate suggestions, for which one may see Rudolph.

     Syriac "all of you" smoothes out the text by using the second person pronoun following the vocative, and Sellin and T. H. Robinson (*Die zwölf kleinen Propheten*, HAT 14 [Tübingen: Mohr, 1938]) have emended to כֻּלְּכֶם, but the MT displays good Hebrew syntax, where after a vocative, modifying clauses regularly use the third person (as also in classical Arabic). (See C. Brockelmann, *Hebräische Syntax* [Neukirchen Kreis Moers: Buchhandlung des Erziehungsvereins, 1956], para. 10, 153 c; C. Brockelmann, *Grundriss der vergleichenden Grammatik der semitischen Sprachen*, Vol. ii, Syntax [Hildesheim: Olms, 1961] [reprint of Berlin, 1913 ed.], 589, para. 385c; H. Reckendorf, *Arabische Syntax* [Heidelberg: Carl Winter, 1921], 423, 443, and 444). For Hebrew examples see Isa 44:23; 54:1; Ezek 21:30 (EV 21:25) and Isa 22:16b (חֹצְבִי מָרוֹם קִבְרוֹ). To the MT, Redaq and Ibn Ezra compare Job 17:10 וְאוּלָם כֻּלָּם תָּשֻׁבוּ. Smith notes that the Syriac also for Job 17:10 changes to a second person suffix. As Wellhausen noted (J. Wellhausen, *Skizzen und Vorarbeiten. Fünftes Heft: Die kleinen Propheten übersetzt, mit Noten* [Berlin: Reimer, 1892]), the MT at this point is confirmed by the verbatim citation in 1 Kgs 22:28 (again in 2 Chr 18:27). The elaborate attempt of Meir Rottenberg, "שמעו עמים כלם" *Beth Miqra* 78 (1979): 266–68, to deal with the syntax here is unnecessary and unconvincing.

     The words שִׁמְעוּ עַמִּים כֻּלָּם have been inserted in the MT at 1 Kgs 22:28 and 2 Chr 18:27 (not in the original LXX text at either point), as a result of the mistaken identification of Micah of Moresheth with Micaiah ben Imlah.

b   The LXX freely translates, καὶ πάντες οἱ ἐν αὐτῇ which is revised by R to καὶ τὸ π[λήρωμα α]ὐτῆς (like the MT).

c   The MT of this colon seems long metrically, and the verbatim repetition of אֲדֹנָי seems unacceptable, thus many have deleted the first occurrence, citing the LXX where the original text seems to have only κύριος for אדני יהוה. IQpMi(14) has ה[יהו אדני]הוה[י]. Milik, *Midrash*, argues that since אדני יהוה is very common and the reverse order occurs only five times (Hab 3:19; Pss 68:21 [EV 20]; 109:21; 140:8 [EV 7]; and 141:8), the reading of the commentary could be original. A choice is difficult because with the easy confusion of *w* and *y*, either reading could arise out of the other by slight scribal error.

d   Hebrew usage favors "*against* you," cf. 1 Sam 12:5; Jer 42:5 and many other passages. Since this context does not otherwise speak of judgment against the nations, and "you" hardly refers to Israel (contra Conrad von Orelli, *Die zwölf kleinen Propheten,* Kurzgefasster Kommentar zu den Heiligen Schriften Alten und Neuen Testamentes. A., 5. Abteilung, 2. Hälfte [Munich: Becksche, ³1908], and Carl Friedrich Keil, *Biblischer Commentar über die Zwölf Kleinen Propheten.* BC III/4 [Leipzig: Dörffling und Franke, 1866, ²1873, and ³1888]) many have favored a rendering "among you," i.e., Yahweh is witness along with the nations to Israel's transgressions (so B. Duhm, "Anmerkungen zu den Zwölf Propheten," *ZAW* 31 [1911]: 81–110; Weiser; Rudolph; and Wolff). But the latter idea is odd, in the context of Israel's religion, and it seems best to suppose that here, if only briefly, Micah touches on the idea of judgment against the heathen. Compare the strategy of the opening chapters of Amos (cf. Ferdinand Hitzig, *Die zwölf kleinen Propheten,* ed. Heinrich Steiner, Kurzgefasstes exegetisches Handbuch [Leipzig: S. Hirzel, ⁴1881]; Smith; and W. Nowack, *Die kleinen Propheten,* HK III, Abteilung. 4 [Göttingen: Vandenhoeck & Ruprecht, ³1922]; see comments).

e   Meter is an insufficient basis for shortening this colon by reading הִנֵּהוּ "behold, he," (is coming; so Otto Proksch, *Die Kleinen prophetischen Schriften vor dem Exil,* Erläuterungen zum Alten Testament, 3. Teil [Calw & Stuttgart: Vereinsbuchhandlung, 1910], BH³, BHS, Karl Elliger, "Die Heimat des Propheten Micha," ZDPV 57 [1934]: 81–152, and Duhm, "Anmerkungen"). The first colon is appoximately as long as the second no matter how the second is read.

f   The versions (contra Proksch and BH³) reflect both verbs; only a portion of the Lucianic recension lacks the second, probably due to homoioteleuton (βήσεται, so Rudolph and Ina Willi-Plein, *Vorformen der Schriftexegese innerhalb des Alten Testaments,* BZAW 123 (1971). IQpMi(14) seems to lack one of the verbs, judging from the size of a lacuna in the ms. Many commentators have wished to delete one or the other, partly on metrical grounds. דרך, the common verb in referring to moving over the heights of the earth (Hab 3:19; Isa 58:14; Job 9:8; Amos 4:13; and Deut 33:29), is more likely to be secondary, and must have been omitted in IQpMi in the opinion of Milik, *Midrash,* and Horgan, Pesharim, but there are no compelling grounds for omitting either.

g   IQpMi(14) has הארץ for the MT ארץ.

h   For the MT וְנָמַסּוּ . . . יתבקעו the LXX has σαλευθήσεται, ("will be shaken") . . . τακήσονται ("will melt"). Though σαλευθήσεται is difficult to account for as the equivalent of either Hebrew verb, τακήσονται is the appropriate translation of נמסו and suggests that the LXX has trans-

posed the two. Ryssel, *Textgestalt,* conjectures that this was done to put the appropriate verb as close as possible to the comparison that follows from it ("melt like wax"). Joseph Ziegler, (*Sylloge: Gesammelte Aufsätze zur Septuaginta.* Mitteilungen des Septuaginta—Unternehmens der Akademie der Wissenschaften in Göttingen, X [Göttingen: Vandenhoeck & Ruprecht, 1971], 366 [112]) does not think of a transposition, but of free translation. For ונמסו R reads . . . τακή]σον[ται (cf. α' and θ'), and for יתבקעו it reads . . . [. . . ρα]γήσον[τα]ι.

i   Commentators have felt a difficulty in this simile, coming after the line about valleys splitting, and have resolved the supposed problem in various ways, Smith by deleting the simile, Nowack by extensive reordering, Wolfe by a forced translation: (the mountains) "shall flow down (be cleft) into the valleys." But this is a case where the simile attaches to the head word (i.e., the A word) "mountains," ignoring the parallel term (the B. word) "valleys." Cf. 5:6 (EV 7), where the relative clause attaches to the first noun (in the singular), not the second (plural).

There is no serious reason to question מוֹרָד ("slope, cliff") here in spite of G. Köbert, "môrād (Mi 1, 4) Tränke," *Biblica* 39 (1958): 82–83. Cf. O. Garcia de la Fuente, "Notas al texto de Miqueas," *Aug* 7 (1967): 145–54.

j   IQpMi(14) has כול (plene).

k   The LXX and T^mss have the singular. Most commentators prefer singular but the versions are especially unreliable as to number, and either singular or plural is possible.

l   Israel is from ancient times the customary "B word" to the "A word" Jacob. The only reason for substituting "Judah" as the "B word" here is that it appears later in the verse (Sellin, Smith, Henry McKeating, *The Book of Amos, Hosea and Micah,* Cambridge Bible Commentary [Cambridge: University Press, 1971], and BHS), but even if that line is retained as original to the poem—a disputed point—Jacob as a parallel to Israel is tolerable here since it seems to be Micah's name for the whole people. In 3:9 the rulers of Jerusalem are "heads of the house of Jacob and judges of the house of Israel."

m   The Hebrew uses the personal interrogative מִי, normally "who?" with an abstract, impersonal noun as predicate. There is no exact parallel. Closest comparable cases are Gen 33:8; Deut 4:7; Judg 9:28; and 13:17. Note also (unless it is an accident) the spelling of "what" as מי in Isa 52:5 (K; Q מה). Wellhausen's explanation, that sin and sinner are hereby identified, is very much *ad hoc,* as is the similar view of Weiser, that sin has a sort of personal character here. IQpMi(14) has, in the commentary on the second occurrence ומה, a reading we may presume would have been used in the first instance also; this is simply an easing of the difficulty. For the sequence . . . מִי הֲלֹא see Exod 4:11; Isa 42:24; and 45:21.

n   The MT is difficult because of the plural and because of "high places" where one expects a term parallel to פֶּשַׁע "rebellion." The LXX has ἁμαρτία, the S ḥṭîteh ("sin"); and the T also implies "sin." Thus many have emended to חַטָּאת "sin." במות is then taken to be a gloss which was first added to identify the sin, and then replaced the original term. The MT is defended by Roorda (Taco Roorda, *Commentarius in Vaticinium Michae* [Leipzig: Weigel, 1869]), Wellhausen, and Vaughan (Patrick H. Vaughan, *The Meaning of "bāmâ" in the Old Testament.* Society for Old Testament Study, Monograph Series 3 [New York: Cambridge University, 1974], 14, 15) though reading singular בָּמָה instead of the MT plural; the argument being that "sin" of the versions can readily be understood as an easing of the difficult MT, while the reverse is implausible. Wellhausen, however, supposes that the line is a late addition to the poem; others have concurred. In my opinion, the MT is textually preferable, if a singular is read; perhaps the development was from בומת to במות by metathesis, cf. the spelling in IQIs[a] 53:9. If not absolutely original, the line may be the result of an early reworking by Micah of a poem on Samaria. Rudolph's conjecture of בְּמוֹת (beth essentiae: "Wer ist <geradezu der Tod> Judas") is very fanciful.

o   The LXX οἴκου, "house of," is probably an addition.

p   The MT has הלוא before the word "Jerusalem"; at this point, IQpMi(14) has הלא.

q   The MT's "a ruin-heap of the field" is unparalleled and scarcely right, though defended by G. A. Smith: "A ruin in the midst of soil gone out of cultivation, where before there had been a city among vineyards, is a striking figure of desolation" (George Adam Smith, *The Book of the Twelve Prophets.* I. Expositor's Bible [New York: A. C. Armstrong, 1896]). Hos 12:2 is not a close parallel. The LXX ὀπωροφυλάκιον ("watchman's hut") is probably a guess according to context, perhaps influenced by Isa 1:8. The same rendering of עי occurs in Mic 3:12 and Ps 78:1 (Heb 79:1) (Hitzig and Rudolph have alternate explanations of the LXX rendering, but implausible). Wellhausen suggested either "Ackerdorf" cf. 1 Sam 27:5, or לְיַעַר הַשָּׂדֶה ("forest land") cf. Ezek 21:2 (EV 20:46). The translation given here is based on a reading influenced by proposals of Karl Budde ("Das Rätsel von Micha I," *ZAW* 37 [1917/18]: 77–108), Marti, Sellin, and Nowack: לְעִי שָׂדֶה לְמַטָּעִי. Rudolph similarly reads for the MT השדה, שָׂדֶה ("her territory"). Though use of

"vineyard" as figure for destruction seems to be unparalleled, recourse to Akkadian *karmu* ("ruin") does not seem to solve the problem (so Smith and S. J. Schwantes, "Critical Notes on Micah 1:10–16," *VT* 14 (1964): 454–61.

r   The LXX εἰς χάος ("to a chasm") and R εἰς τὴν φάραγγα ("to the ravine") are less free. The S "and I will pile up her stones in a heap" is puzzling; Sebök suggests (Mark Sebök, *Die syrische Uebersetzung der zwölf kleinen Propheten* [Breslau: Preuss und Jünger, 1887]) the Vorlage was והגרתי לגל אבניה, which is not altogether convincing.

s   The LXX κατακόψουσι means "they will smash"; the active form with an indefinite subject does not necessarily reflect anything other than the MT. Similarly ἐμπρήσουσιν, literally, "they will burn," translates יִשָּׂרֵפוּ.

t   Because this is repetitious, some (BH³, BHS) would delete the whole colon, whereas others follow Wellhausen in reading אֲשֵׁרֶיהָ. But already Smith pointed out that this would require a feminine verb. "Whore's fees" is appropriate as a parallel to "statues." The S and T with "her idols" have caught the sense. It is unnecessary to emend or to propose a new etymology to yield the sense "images."

u   The MT lacks an object, and implies a feminine subject (in this context, Samaria). This is defended by Ryssel, *Textgestalt,* and others, but most have preferred to follow the S, T, and V and read a passive plural קֻבְּצוּ ("they were gathered"). So also a few mss, Kenn. and de Rossi read קובצה.

v   The LXX πορνείας, "of fornication," is a free translation.

w   The LXX καὶ ἐκ . . . συνέστρεψεν ("and from . . . she collected") apparently was translated under the influence of the first colon, thus misunderstanding the whole line.

Commentary

This oracle announces a number of themes of the book, including the fundamental idea, the rule of God. This irresistible rule first appears in its destructive force, in conformity with another fundamental idea of the book: rebellion within mankind, especially the people of God, calls forth divine fury. This strikes at the central symbol of authority, the capital city.

The book's heading, with its "concerning Samaria and Jerusalem" was probably framed with this oracle in view. The brief reference to "Judah" and "Jerusalem" (v 5) links an oracle mostly about the Northern Kingdom to the following passages having to do with what is happening to the Southern Kingdom.

This is apt to be an early oracle of Micah, first composed prior to the fall of Samaria. Since the point of view is theocentric, one would not necessarily expect a realistic account of Samaria's destruction even if the poem dated from after the fall of the city to the Assyrians, yet it may deserve mention that nothing in these verses refers necessarily to the actions of a conqueror. The reference to Judah and Jerusalem (v 5) is apparently a later addition, since it is not tightly integrated with the rest of the poem. The possibility remains open that the addition was made already by Micah or an early collector of his sayings. The line about Judah may have *replaced* an earlier line referring to Israel and Samaria. Aside from this line, it seems unnecessary and hyper-critical to make further excisions; a valuable detailed review of critical opinions on this poem and the rest of chap 1 is found in Fohrer, "Micha 1."[1]

The components of the oracle are: v 2: Yahweh in the divine council; 3-4: the theophany; 5: the reason for his wrath; 6–7: the resulting overthrow of Samaria. Especially the first two of these components incorporate fragments of very old traditional material, which gain in point if read in the light of fuller formulations of the same type.

The problems and exegetical possibilities of v 2 are reviewed almost exhaustively by Willis.[2] In my view, this verse and what follows from it is a transformation of the conception of the divine council. In ancient Near Eastern religion one encounters the idea of a chief god surrounded by a heavenly council, where he exercises judicial power over the presiding powers in the cosmos. This originally polytheistic conception is adopted at points in Old Testament religion, and here, to make a point about the nature of Yahweh's rule.[3] The most illuminating Old Testament parallel to Mic 1:2 is perhaps Psalm 82. There God stands up for judgment in the midst of the gods. He condemns them for injustice in the world of men. Implicit in this charge is the notion that the kingdoms of the world are allotted to the "sons of God," the patron deities (Deut 32:8). Because of their unjust rule, the world is threatened again by chaos, and the psalm ends with an appeal for God to judge: "Arise, O God, judge the earth, for to thee belong all the nations!" Thus, though the psalm finishes at this point, it looks forward to the intervention of God. Of passages reflecting a similar conception of the council of Yahweh, one of the richest is 1 Kgs 22:19–28.

Elsewhere in the Old Testament the members of the council may be reduced to "heaven and earth," "mountains," and the like (cf. 6:1–2). Here at the beginning of Micah the process of removing polytheistic traces has gone even farther, and for the original patron deities, i.e., the heavenly order, is substituted the nations, the

earthly order (cf. Ps 29 to Ps 96:7 for a similar development). Yet the old sequence is preserved in condensed form; there is a condemnation of other sources of justice before Yahweh arises to judge the earth. The same transformation and condensation is attested in Isaiah 34. There the "nations" and "peoples" are assembled to learn of Yahweh's wrath against them. "Let the earth listen, and all that fills it; the world, and all that comes from it." Yet there is clearly a cosmic setting in mind, for "all the host of heaven" are likewise condemned. All this is prelude to judgment on a single nation, Edom. "For my sword has drunk its fill in the heavens, behold it descends for judgment upon Edom." Parallels to details are found in Jer 6:18; Ps 49:2 (EV 1); Isa 26:21; Jer 25:30–31. Amos 1 and 2 may be regarded as a transformation of the same schema: the Lord roars from his place (Zion), there is judgment against the nations, then judgment on Israel (and Judah, as an afterthought). Allen[4] compares Isa 3:13–14 and argues for retention of the MT: "The Lord has taken his place to contend, he stands to judge the peoples. The Lord enters into judgment with the elders and princes of his people." (נִצָּב לָרִיב יְהוָה וְעֹמֵד לָדִין עַמִּים [LXX, τὸν λαὸν αὐτοῦ] יְהוָה בְּמִשְׁפָּט יָבוֹא עִם־זִקְנֵי עַמּוֹ וְשָׂרָיו). Most, however, follow the LXX and read "his people" (singular).

If this analysis of the mythological background is correct, it makes clearer the function of an initial testimony *against* the nations. This sets Yahweh's judgment on an individual nation in the context of his universal zeal to establish justice. The fate of God's own people is not the result of caprice, but the carrying out of a broader order. The first verse prepares for the oracles against injustice and persecution of the defenseless that fill the first portion of the book.[5]

In view of the present form of the poem, which includes an indictment of Jerusalem, "his place" and "his holy temple" refer primarily to the heavenly palace of God (cf. Isa 6:2; 2 Sam 22:7 = Ps 18:7). It is a mistake, however, to separate too sharply between a heavenly and

---

1 Georg Fohrer, "Micha 1." *Das Ferne und nahe Wort* (Festschrift Rost), BZAW 105 (1967): 65–80.

2 J.T. Willis, "Some Suggestions on the Interpretation of Micah I[2]," *VT* 18 (1968): 372–79.

3 For a recent treatment see Frank Moore Cross, *Canaanite Myth and Hebrew Epic* (Cambridge, Mass.: Harvard, 1973).

4 Leslie C. Allen, *The Books of Joel, Obadiah, Jonah and Micah.* The New International Commentary on the Old Testament (Grand Rapids, Mich.: Eerdmans, 1976).

5 Franz Hesse, "Wurzelt die prophetische Gerichtsrede im israelischen Kult?" *ZAW* 65 (1953): 48–49, recognizes the pattern followed in the opening verses of Micah, but he wrongly stresses its cultic origin and the psychological motives for prophetic employment.

an earthly temple, and especially in the earlier form of the poem where reference to the temple could have been like Amos 1:2, "Yahweh roars from Zion" (cf. Isa 6:6).

The theophany of vv 3–4 is, as shown by Jeremias, close in form to other ancient specimens of this sort of composition, with a division into two parts: the coming of the deity out of his place, and the destructive effect on nature, cf. Judg 5:4–5 and Ps 68:8–9 (EV 7–9).[6] The third person form of vv 3–4, contrasting with the first person of v 6, is explained by Jeremias as due to the inherited, fixed form. "Go out" (יָצָא) is often used of the deity's setting out in these contexts, thus Judg 5:4; Ps 68:8 (EV 8); Zech 14:3; Isa 26:21; and Assumption of Moses 10:3; "For the Heavenly One will arise from his royal throne, and he will go forth from his holy habitation . . . and the earth shall tremble; to its confines shall it be shaken." "Come down" (יָרַד) is used in Isa 63:19 (EV 64:1); Ps 18:10 = 2 Sam 22:10; Exod 19:18; 34:5; and Isa 31:4. It is misguided to look for a naturalistic explanation of the melting of the mountains, especially for natural events contemporary with Micah; as Jeremias amply demonstrates, this is part of the stock imagery in descriptions of theophany. For specific reference to mountains, note Judg 5:4, "the mountains quaked" (הָרִים נָזֹלּוּ); Isa 63:19, "before you the mountains quaked" (מִפָּנֶיךָ הָרִים נָזֹלּוּ); Ben Sira 43:16; and Ps 97:5, "the mountains melted like wax" (הָרִים כַּדוֹנַג נָמַסּוּ). There are many others. A possible parallel in the Ugaritic epic of Baal may include mention of the mountains tottering and the trembling of the "high places of the earth"; the text is, however, damaged at key points.[7]

All of "this," that is, the destructive appearance of God, is over the sin of Jacob, designated by two terms ultimately related to political life (both meaning approximately "rebel"): פֶּשַׁע and חַטָּאת, though the image is not developed, and in the following context idolatry is stressed. The chief city is named as the main focus of sin, cf. Isa 7:8–9 "For the head of Syria is Damascus, . . . and the head of Ephraim is Samaria . . ." (כִּי רֹאשׁ אֲרָם דַּמֶּשֶׂק וְרֹאשׁ אֶפְרַיִם שֹׁמְרוֹן . . .).

The additional line concerning Judah preserves the same form as that against Samaria, but for the expected "sin(s)" (חַטָּאת) the text reads "high places" (בָּמוֹת). That is, the nature of the sin is designated. Worship at shrines called "high places" is widely but not universally condemned in the Old Testament, for reasons that are not completely clear to us and that probably varied from time to time. Micah, or an editor, boldly uses the term here to designate Jerusalem, no doubt with the temple in mind. In the reform associated with Hezekiah (2 Kgs 18:1–6) the king is said to have "removed the high places." If historically accurate, this would testify to sentiment against the high places in Micah's time, but the historical worth of this passage has been questioned.[8] Amos condemned the high places of Israel, Amos 7:9 "the high places of Isaac shall be desolate" (וְנָשַׁמּוּ בָּמוֹת יִשְׂחָק).

Samaria is to be ruined, an uninhabited land, available for cultivation. The reference to rolling the stones of the city into the valley may be in part traditional imagery, but is happens to fit well with the hilltop location of Samaria. Wellhausen aptly cites the (doubtless exaggerated) account of Hyrcanus' destruction of Samaria, Josephus, *Ant* xiii 281: "He effaced it entirely and left it to be swept away by the mountain-torrents, for he dug beneath it until it fell into the beds of the torrents."

The divine wrath strikes especially the images used in the worship at Samaria and the wealth assembled in the sanctuaries. This is contemptuously referred to as "whore's fees," invoking the common biblical picture of idolatry as illicit sexual behavior. (For a *city* as harlot, cf. Nah 3:4.) This is in part figurative, having to do with the cycle of images connected with Yahweh as the husband of the faithless wife, Israel, made much of by Micah's earlier contemporary, Hosea. At the same time there is a literal component, in that sacred prostitution was practised at the shrines. The last line "they will go back to being whore's fees" is susceptible of rather literal inter-

6   Jörg Jeremias, *Theophanie: Die Geschichte einer alt-testamentlichen Gattung.* WMANT Vol. 10 (Neu-kirchen-Vluyn: Neukirchener, 1965), 11, 12.

7   See Cross, *Canaanite Myth,* 47 with a discussion and translation of CTA 4 VII 32–35; also Jeremias, *Theophanie,* 73–90 gives copious extra-biblical parallels.

8   Jonathan Rosenbaum, "Hezekiah's Reform and the Deuteronomistic Tradition," *HTR* 72 (1979): 23–43.

pretation. The idols and cult-vessels made of gold and silver will be broken up by conquering soldiers and used to hire prostitutes, perhaps at shrines in their own land. This is possible, but it should be remembered that this would then be the only place in the poem where the prophet refers, even obliquely, to conquest by a foreign enemy; elsewhere it is Yahweh himself who is the destroyer. Perhaps it is best, then, to leave the sense vague: as the precious things were gained, so they will be lost, the end will be like the beginning. Keil aptly quotes Gen 3:19 "For dust thou art, and unto dust shalt thou return" (כִּי עָפָר אַתָּה וְאֶל־עָפָר תָּשׁוּב).

Reference to Samaria as a center of idolatrous worship has disturbed finicky commentators who remind us that Bethel and Dan were the great northern cult centers. But surely Samaria had shrines, since they were all over, and Amos (8:14) and Hosea (8:6) assure us of what we would have supposed on general principles. In any case Micah's point of view is that the chief city, which he may never have seen, embodied all the sins of the people.

Why the prominence given to idol worship? Micah, interpreters point out, is otherwise concerned with crimes against the social order. This is poor grounds for denying this passage to Micah,[9] but does call for reflection. In 3:9–12, it is evident that the capital is condemned for a false confidence. Her leaders "lean upon Yahweh" in the absence of those qualities in society which could give that reliance meaning. In referring to the idols of Samaria—and her walls—Micah may be expressing a related idea: Samaria's sources of trust will be destroyed and exposed as delusory. Mic 5:10–15, taken as an integral portion of a prophetic view of cleansing in preparation for the new age (see Introduction), very much in harmony with 1:6–7.

"Smashing" (כתת) and "burning" of idols is enjoined in Deuteronomy (7:15, 25; 9:21; 12:3) and elsewhere; note 2 Kgs 18:4 (of Hezekiah).

---

9   This is done recently by Volkmar Fritz, "Das Wort gegen Samaria Mi 1, 2–7," ZAW 86 (1974): 316–31.

1

■ **Lament as the Disaster Spreads**

The prophet grieves over the
blow to the Northern Kingdom,
for it has reached Jerusalem
also.

8   Over this I[a] will lament and wail.
       I will go[b] barefoot[c] and naked.
     I will make lament as jackals[d] do,
       Mourning as the ostriches.[e]
9   For her wound[f] is deadly,[g]
       For it has come as far as Judah.
     It has touched[h] the gate of my people,
       Has reached Jerusalem.[i]

a   The MT throughout v 8 has first singular verbs; the
    LXX has third singular; the T has third plural; and the S
    has imperative feminine singular. The versions seem, in
    different ways, to have altered the MT to tie these verses
    more closely to the context (Ryssel, *Textgestalt,* and
    Rudolph).

b   The MT has an unusual plene spelling; many mss have
    the more normal אלכה. BH³ identifies the latter as Q,
    but there is no marginal Q here.

c   The MT has שׁילל; Q and many mss have שׁולָל.
    1QpMi(14) has שׁלל (cf. 3 mss Kenn.). This rare adjective
    is probably connected with the verb שׁלל, "pull out,"
    (Ruth 2:16) with a sense "stripped as to walking" (BDB)
    i.e., "barefoot," since it occurs only with הלך, "to walk,"
    (so the LXX and S). Others (Ibn Ezra, Redaq, and Keil)
    connect it with שָׁלָל, "plunder," in a sense "plundered"
    or "naked" (robbed of clothes), or "raving like a mad-
    man," comparing Ps 76:6 (EV 5) and Isa 59:15.

d   The LXX δρακόντων and the V *draconum* arise from
    confusion with תַּנִּין.

e   The S has *dbart yārōrā* ("like the daughter of the jackals")
    which repeats the translation of the first term, perhaps
    from ignorance. The LXX σειρήνων ("sirens") as at Isa
    13:21, is of uncertain origin; Rudolph, following Karl
    Vollers, "Das Dodekapropheten der Alexandriner
    (Schluss)," *ZAW* 4 (1884): 3, thinks ענה "to sing" influ-
    enced the translation.

f   The plural noun of the MT does not agree with the
    singular adjective. This is probably a mistake for מַכָּתָה
    (the LXX has ἡ πληγὴ αὐτῆς ["her wound"]). Budde,
    "Das Rätsel," Duhm, and others prefer מַכַּת יה(וה) "the
    blow of Yah(weh)."

g   The LXX κατεκράτησεν ("prevailed over") is a free
    translation, or else unexplained.

h   If the subject is "wound," a change to the feminine נֶגְעָה
    is required (Wellhausen et al.), cf. the S and T. But
    perhaps the subject is indefinite, a vague "destruction,
    ruin" being in mind, in which case the masculine may
    stand (Hitzig). Rudolph's suggestion of Yahweh as
    subject seems unlikely.

i   Wellhausen deletes on the basis that this has been
    introduced from Obad 11, 13, but the parallel is inexact,
    and even if it were exact, it would be poor ground for
    deletion. Marty (Jacques Marty, *La Sainte Bible,* Bible du
    Centenaire, Tome II: Les Prophètes [Paris: Société
    Biblique de Paris, 1947], 768–783 and xxxiii–xxxiv) and
    Sellin read עָדָיִךְ "to you" (0 Jerusalem), but this is
    unnecessary.

Commentary

This section is a short bridge from the opening theophany, with its announcement of doom for Samaria, to the
following lament over the towns of Judah. As such it
looks both back ("over this") and forward ("my people").
The connection with the preceding theophany has some-

times been denied[1] on various grounds. The lament is supposed to contradict the announcement of doom for sin, v 5, and the difference in mood and the difference in the nature of the destruction (earthquake in 2–7; invasion in 8–16) are noted. This is, however, overly pedantic. If in v 5 the stern voice of God speaks, a shift to the prophet's own person and feelings is quite in the style of Old Testament prophetic books. It is pedestrian to suppose that 2–7 describes an earthquake; these verses depict a theophany, and the succeeding oracles which refer to invasion by an enemy explicate this vision without contradicting it. Moreover, "over this" (עַל זֹאת, i.e., עַל plus a demonstrative pronoun) typically refers back, not forward; note Jer 31:26; Ps 32:6; Isa 57:6; 64:11 (EV 12); Jer 5:9, 29; 9:8; and Amos 8:8 (Jer 4:28; Lam 1:16 are debatable). This is not to say that the elements of chap. 1 were composed at one time, for the oracle on Samaria may well be earlier. But the present arrangement does make for an intelligible sequence.

The "I" who mourns is the prophet, as in Jer 8:23 and Isa 22:4, where after a description of the destruction of Jerusalem the prophet himself speaks: "So I said, Look away from me, that I may weep bitterly. Do not labor to comfort me for the destruction of the daughter of my people" (עַל־כֵּן אָמַרְתִּי שְׁעוּ מִנִּי אֲמָרֵר בַּבֶּכִי אַל־תָּאִיצוּ לְנַחֲמֵנִי עַל־שֹׁד בַּת־עַמִּי). It was part of the prophet's dissociation from what he received as the word of God that he could react to what was in a sense his own message in horror or grief.[2]

The prophet gives outward expression to his feelings by asserting that he will go barefoot and naked. Both are gestures of mourning or consternation; cf. Ezek 24:17–23 and Isa 20:2, where the prophet goes "naked and barefoot" (עָרוֹם וְיָחֵף) to symbolize the coming captivity. In 2 Sam 15:30 David is said to go weeping and "bare-foot" (יָחֵף) at the rebellion of Absalom. The prophet will cry out like a howling jackal or an ostrich: the same pair of beasts is linked in poetic parallelism in Job 30:29. The ostrich does, in fact, have a loud, strident call.[3]

The blow that has struck Samaria has reached Jerusalem also. McKeating fittingly compares Isa 10:11 "Shall I not do to Jerusalem and her idols as I have done to Samaria and her images" (הֲלֹא כַּאֲשֶׁר עָשִׂיתִי לְשֹׁמְרוֹן וְלֶאֱלִילֶיהָ כֵּן אֶעֱשֶׂה לִירוּשָׁלַם וְלַעֲצַבֶּיהָ).

Jerusalem is called the "gate" of the people, apparently as being the center of political and religious life for the people. "Gate" (שַׁעַר) is used as a kind of synonym for "city" in Isa 14:31 "Wail, O gate; cry, O city" (הֵילִילִי שַׁעַר זַעֲקִי־עִיר). The phrase "gate of my people" (שַׁעַר עַמִּי) occurs twice elsewhere; in Obad 13 it is also used of Jerusalem; in Ruth 3:11 the expression is extended to mean "body of citizens" (of Bethlehem). It is unlikely that the reference is to the strategic position of Jerusalem, as "gate" to the conquest of Judah.[4] Attack on Judah could bypass Jerusalem entirely.

Since vv 8–9 prepare for 10–16, it is likely that the same military campaign is in mind here as in the following verses, which fit best with Sennacherib's invasion of 701 (so already Ibn Ezra).

In dealing with passages about the exaltation of Jerusalem in chap. 4, and their relation to the message of Micah, it is well to keep in mind the sympathetic, sorrowing treatment of Jerusalem here.

---

1   Denied by such scholars as: Johannes Lindblom, *Micha literarisch untersucht.* Acta Academiae Aboensis, Humanioria VI. 2 (Helsingfors: Åbo Akademi, 1929), Weiser, and Augustin George, *Michée Sophonie Nahum. La Sainte Bible,* Vol. 27 (Paris: Cerf, 1952).

2   See the examples cited in Delbert R. Hillers, "A Convention in Hebrew Literature: The Reaction to Bad News," *ZAW* 77 (1965): 86–90.

3   Driver, however, rejects unanimous ancient tradition and identifies the bird as the "eagle-owl." See G.R. Driver, "Birds in the Old Testament," *PEQ* 87 (1955): 5–20.

4   Albrecht Alt, "Micha 2, 1–5 in Juda," *NTT* 56 (1955): 13–23 or as reprinted in *Kleine Schriften zur Geschichte des Volkes Israel,* III (Munich: Beck'sche, 1959), 373.

■ **Lament Over the Towns of Judah**

Mourning and taunt are combined
as the prophet takes up the
fate of the towns of Judah and
their chief, Jerusalem.

1

10　Exult not in Gath,[a] but break down and weep![b]
　　In Beth-Leaphra,[c] roll yourselves[d] in the dust.
11　Pass on,[e] O inhabitants of Shaphir, in shameful nakedness.[f]
　　The dwellers in Zaanan have not come forth.[g]
　　Mourn greatly, Beth Ezel;
　　　He takes away your treasures.[h]
12　Surely they waited[i] for sweetness,
　　　The dwellers in Maroth!
　　Yet calamity has come down from Yahweh
　　　To the gates of[j] Jerusalem.
13　Hitch[k] the horses to the chariot,
　　　Dwellers in Lachish!
　　You are the beginning of sin for Zion;
　　　In you the rebellions of Israel were found.
14　Therefore you[l] must give[m] a dowry[n]
　　　To Moresheth-Gath.
　　The houses[p] of Achzib have become a dry watercourse
　　　To the kings[q] of Israel.
15　Again[r] I will bring[s] the conqueror[t] to you,
　　　Dwellers in Maresha.
　　To[u] Adullam will come the glory[v] of Israel.[w]
16　Make yourself bald and cut off your hair[x]
　　　For your delicate children.
　　Make yourself bald[y] as an eagle,
　　　Because they have gone away from you into exile.

Prefatory Note

This is textually the most difficult passage in the book. Most commentators have no doubt felt more than ordinarily diffident about their explanations at this point, which brought from St. Jerome a fervent prayer for divine illumination. Where so many individual details are obscure, and the versions of little help, commentators have sought help from general considerations as to the sense or form of the passage. All concede that it is a series of addresses to places which either expect calamity or have already experienced it. Comparing Isa 10:27–32, it is reasonable to entertain the hypothesis that these places lay in the real or imagined line of march of an invading Assyrian army. Unfortunately even those towns which can be identified and located seem not to be arranged along any one line. Thus the order of the names is of no help for cases where a name is unknown or corrupt. The fact that all recognizable places are in western Judah does help to eliminate some scholarly conjectures (such as Acco in v 10) from consideration.

Elliger sought to press beyond this point by proposing rather precise formal principles which governed the composition. He proposed that this poem consisted originally of bicola, each with a word-play on a place name, one name occurring in each bicolon. The text was not written continuously, as prose, but in a stichic arrangement. Then the outer right hand edge of the page was damaged, resulting in loss or damage to the first word in a number of lines. This theory has proved popular, and indeed would hold out promise of real progress with a difficult text, but it suffers from several grave difficulties (Karl Elliger, "Die Heimat des Propheten Micha," *ZDPV* 57 [1934]: 81–152). First, as especially van der Woude has pointed out (A. S. van der Woude, *Micah* [Nijkerk: Callenbach, 1976]), we have little evidence for anything but continuous writing of ancient Hebrew verse, and negligible attestation of the writing in poetic lines which Elliger's theory of a pattern of mechanical damage demands. A second point touches not only Elliger's theory but the procedures of many with this text. Although word play occurs here in abundance, yet fairly obvious puns occur in only about half of the sayings in the text as we have it, without emendation. Are we to compose some for the other lines, or is the situation perhaps like that in the "Testament of Jacob" (Genesis 49), where the sayings about Judah, Dan, and Gad contain obvious plays on the names, while other sayings about the tribes, including some that are intelligible, lack paronomasia? Isaiah's poem on the Assyrian advance seems to have just one pun (10:30) עֲנָתוֹת עֲנִיָּה. Genesis 49 and the similar portions of Judges 5 and Deuteronomy 33 also display lack of uniformity in the length of sayings about the tribes, and it seems unwarranted to posit that in Micah 1 there was originally a neat uniformity. Third, another, additional hypothesis to that of word play may help to explain why we do not always understand the text and have difficulty correcting it. Perhaps Micah at times uses traditional local tags and taunts about the towns he names. Since most of them were small, not famous even in Micah's time and certainly not in later periods, we may reasonably suppose that while Micah and his contemporary Judaean hearers would have grasped the force of the gibes, they would have become more and more unintelligible with the passage of time and the use of Micah's words in another region. A biblical example of this sort of saying may be Judg 5:14, apparently cited at Hos 5:8: "After you, O Benjamin" (אַחֲרֶיךָ בִנְיָמִין); the point escapes us. Thus sometimes the text may be correct even though we miss the point; or if it is corrupt, we need not necessarily seek for a play on words.

a   The LXX's οἱ ἐν Γεθ, "you in Gath," is interpretive; cf. οἱ ἐν Ακειμ in the following line. For the MT תגידו, the LXX's μεγαλύνεσθε most likely reflects תַּגְדִּילוּ since this Greek verb most often is used for a form of גדל, and since the reading is graphically close to the MT, the presupposed Hebrew verb would mean "do not behave insolently, exult" (cf. Lam 1:9 כִּי הִגְדִּיל אֹיֵב: for the verb the LXX has ἐμεγαλύνθη). Support is perhaps supplied by 1QpMi(14) frag ii,1 5, as read by Carmignac: בגודלי (J. Carmignac, "Notes sur les Peshârîm," *RQ* 3[1963]: 505-38). If correct, this would indicate that the commentator was playing on תגדילו rather than תגידו. In view of the fragmentary character of the text, however, this is very uncertain. Even so, I have adopted the reading on the assumption that at this time Gath is part of Judaean territory (cf. 2 Chr 26:6), lost to the enemy like other towns of western Judah; as other places are told to mourn, so Gath is told not to exult. This less familiar address to Gath was lost under the influence of 2 Sam 1:20. Paronomasia, if present at all, is just as good with this reading as the MT.

The MT is, however, not impossible; it would probably convey the traditional sense: "Don't let the enemy know of our loss" and would imply that Gath is thought of as foreign. The S *lā teḥdōn* ("do not rejoice") may be for תָּגִילוּ but is perhaps simply interpretive; Sebök, *Syrische*, plausibly suggests that the original S had *thwwn* ("do not make it known") which would equal the MT. This reading has been the basis for rather radical changes involving the Hebrew verb גיל and place names with the same consonants, none especially convincing (varieties in Nowack, Budde, "Das Rätsel," Sellin, and S. J. Schwantes, "Critical Notes on Micah 1:10–16," *VT* 14 (1964): 454–61).

The location of Gath is not definitely established, though the possibilities have been narrowed by recent study; see Peter Welten, *Die Königs-Stemple*, Abhand-

lungen des Deutschen Palästinavereins (Wiesbaden: Harrassowitz, 1969), 68–81, and Anson Rainey, "Identification" and "Gath" in *IDBS*. The attached sketch map shows the city at Tell eṣ-ṣafi, a leading candidate.

b   The MT (literally means "weeping do not weep") is grammatically suspect, infinitive absolute before the vetitive אַל and the corresponding finite form being rare (cf. 1 Kgs 3:26–27), though the construction infinitive absolute plus לֹא plus finite form is well-attested (Gesenius, Hebrew Grammar, ed. and rev. E. Kautzsch, tr. and rev. A. E. Cowley [Oxford: At the Clarendon Press, ²1910], para. 113 v.). Even more problematic is the fact that this colon does not continue the thought of the preceding (whether we render "Exult not in Gath" or "Tell it not in Gath") or prepare for the mourning gesture of the next line. Thus most have changed the saying to a positive injunction of some means. BHS is typical בְּכוּ אַף תִּבְכּוּ. One might note the conveniently ambiguous Ugaritic *'al*, which can introduce command or prohibition. However achieved, a command to weep seems to be appropriate.

Following the LXX οἱ ἐν Ακειμ others have sought in the infinitive absolute a garbled place name, such as Baka בָּכָא (Smith, Robinson, D. Winton Thomas, "The Root צנע in Hebrew and the Meaning of קדרנית in Malachi III, 14," *JJS* 1 [1948–49]: 182–88), the valley mentioned in Ps 84:6; the exact location is unknown but possibly near Jerusalem. This, or e.g., בְּכַבּוֹן (cf Josh 15:40; Bewer and Zeev Vilnay, "The Topography of Israel in the Book of the Prophet Micah (Hebrew)," *BJPES* [1939]: 1–19) provides a play on words, but the result is not especially satisfactory geographically or in sense. Often, if not always as Elliger maintained, there is only one place name per bicolon; such a consideration would strongly oppose searching for a parallel to "Gath." The LXX ἀνοικοδομεῖτε, "build up," points to תבנו rather than the MT תבכו.

c   This place name is otherwise unknown, and unparalleled in form, that is, in having ל between "house" and the following noun. The S and T do not reflect the preposition, probably they simply gloss over the difficulty. Simple עָפְרָה is a known place name, but the location of the two towns with this name, one in Benjamin and the other in Manasseh, is not appropriate for this passage. Robinson suggested that the personal name Ophrah in a Calebite genealogy (1 Chr 4:14) is connected with the place mentioned in Micah. The proposal in BHS בְּכַרְמֵי בֵית עפרה (whence?), only one of the many conjectures, has no textual support and can claim as an advantage only that it lengthens the first poetic colon—very weak grounds for adoption. The LXX καταγέλωτα, (twice) "derision" (?), for עפר is a translation attested elsewhere (3:7) for חפר but the intention of the LXX is most unclear (Vollers, "Das Dodekapropheton der Alexandriner (Schluss)," *ZAW* 4 [1884]: 3).

d   The K has "I (or 'you' feminine singular) have rolled," but the Q has "roll !" i.e., הִתְפַּלְשִׁי (feminine singular; cf. Mur 88 התפלשי; so 11 mss Kenn.). Read הִתְפַּלְּשׁוּ to agree with the plurals of this verse, as the LXX, S, T, and V. The combination of the verb פלש with "dust" or "ashes" is apparently ancient idiomatic or poetic use, cf. Ezek 27:30; Jer 6:26 and Ugaritic *'pr pltt* ("dust of wallowing") CTA 5 (67), 6. 15, in a context where El is mourning Baal's death.

e The phrase יוֹשֶׁבֶת שָׁפִיר requires a feminine singular verb, and consequently a feminine singular pronominal suffix; hence read לָךְ. The MT לָכֶם arises perhaps from the use of plurals in the preceding context and from the fact that the subject is a collective. This last point would account for the plural verbs of some Hebrew mss, the V, T, α′, and σ′. The LXX lacks any representation of עברי לכם. The text as translated can stand only if we assume that the point of the saying, mysterious to us, may have been clear to a contemporary. There is no good parallel for such a use as this of the imperative of עבר, and no etymological play is present as the text stands. Duhm's conjecture is the most popular, שׁוֹפָר יַעֲבִירוּ (or similar form of עבר in the Hiphil ("they will blow the trumpet for you"). Cf. Lev 25:9, ... וְהַעֲבַרְתָּ שׁוֹפָר תְּרוּעָה ("Then you shall send abroad the loud trumpet"). The suggestion of BH³, שְׁפִי, (pass over) "the bare heights," is unparalleled and implausible.

The location of Shaphir is unknown. Graetz (H. Graetz, *Emendationes in plerosque Sacrae Scripturae Veteris Testamenti libros*, ed. W. Bacher [Breslau: Schlesische Buchdruckerei, ²1895]) and Nowack have compared the Judaean city שָׁמִיר of Josh 15:48, for which Eusebius gives Σαφειρ. William Dever, "Iron Age Epigraphic Material from the Area of Khirbet el-Kôm," *HUCA* 40–41 (1969–70) 189, mentions Khirbet el-Kom or Tell 'Eitun as good possibilities, since the archaeological evidence at both permits the identification, but leaves the question open.

Some mss of the LXX add καθελῶ ("I will take down") at this point, after the equivalent of שָׁפִיר (καλῶς) and before "her cities" (עריה); the source of the reading is unknown.

f The MT עֶרְיָה בֹּשֶׁת ("naked, shameful thing") can yield the translation given here only by some forcing, and it is not clear whether this belongs to the preceding or following saying. In favor of joining it to the foregoing is the consideration that this would be a reference to exposure as punishment, a familiar OT idea, or to going into captivity naked, cf. Isa 20:4. Smith deletes it as a gloss, eliminating one syntactically awkward word. The LXX has no equivalent. Duhm's conjecture has proved popular: עִירָה תֵּשֵׁב, "She remains in her city, she has not gone forth, etc." A variation is מֵעִירָהּ (deleting בשׁת), "From her city has not gone forth, etc." Either of the foregoing may appeal to the LXX τὰς πόλεις αὐτῆς (for עריה). The S seems to have strained after acceptable sense.

g The sense may be "have not dared to come out to fight," or else the allusion escapes us. Zaanan, צאנן, is perhaps the same as צְנָן of Josh 15:37. There is a pun between the verb יצא, "go out," and the first consonants of the city-name. θ′ translates the name εὐθηνοῦσα "flourishing" which Ziegler ("Beiträge") plausibly supposes is by

equation with שַׁאֲנָן. Note 1 MS Kenn. and 4 de Rossi have שׁאנן.

The location is unknown; cf. especially Diether Kellermann, "Überlieferungsprobleme alttestament-licher Ortsnamen," *VT* 28 (1978) 423–32.

h The MT, if taken literally, means, "mourning of Beth Ezel. He takes from you his standing-place (?)," which is nonsense. The LXX does not reflect a different text, except possibly by the puzzling last phrase πληγὴν ὀδύνης ("blow of pain") (cf. the S *mḥōtāh* ["her stroke"]). BH³ suggests דְּמָעוֹת ("tears") for ὀδύνης but ὀδύνη is never otherwise the equivalent for any form of דמע, and the Hebrew phrase would be unparalleled. Conjectures such as BHS, "he is taken from the place of his standing" or "they take standing from you" and similar efforts, are more or less close graphically to the MT, but the expressions and the idea seem odd; מַעֲמָד or עֶמְדָּה or מַעֲמָד are used literally only of persons, never of cities, and no metaphorical use of this sort is attested. To secure intelligibility I read <סְפְדִי> מִסְפֵּד בֵּית הָאָצֶל יִקַּח מִמֵּךְ חֶמְדָּתֵךְ . For מִסְפֵּד with a cognate verb cf. Gen 50:10. חֶמְדָה and related nouns are used of anything dear to a man or people. Word-play is lacking in any form of text suggested to date (Rudolph's attempt is very weak).

The location is unknown.

i The MT has "because she writhed (in pain or labor) for good" (so also α′), which is unintelligible. It is rescued by Gordis (Robert Gordis, "A Note on טוב, *JTS* 35 [1934]: 186–88) by making טוב equal to Aramaic טָב ("greatly") but this sense seems not well established anywhere in biblical Hebrew and it is a desperate remedy here. Emendation to יִחֵלָה ("she waited"), accepted by many, may claim the support of σ′, ἤλπισεν, and θ′, ἀναμένουσα, and the T, *msābrā* (the LXX has ἤρξατο as if from הֵחֵלָה). With this emendation the text is otherwise in order, and has a play on the name of the town. Maroth, "bitter things," is the opposite of טוב, i.e., with the general sense "good." Here the play is sharpened if we recognize the sense "sweet" as in Cant 1:2–3, cf. Ugaritic *ṭb* ("sweet") and Akkadian *ṭābu* ("sweet"). In addition to emending the verb thus, many commentators go farther and read מה "how" at the beginning of the line; the LXX τίς suggests a spelling מִי חלה. An alternate is אֵיךְ, "how?" Either one is attractive. θ′ has εἰς ὕψος and he seems to have read מָרוֹם or רָמוֹת. The S has *dmerdat* ("who rebelled") which probably comes from etymologizing the name as if it were from מרי ("to rebel").

The place Maroth is not mentioned elsewhere and not surprisingly its location is unknown.

j The MT singular is acceptable, as is the plural of the LXX, S, and T (preferred by most). If a word-play is present, it involves a contrast between the שלם of Jerusalem, suggesting שָׁלוֹם ("welfare") and רַע ("evil, calamity"). It is very uncertain that the assonance of *YRd* and *YRwšlm* is significant, as has been thought. Robinson would emend to שַׁעֲרַיִם, a town in Judah, Josh 15:36, but there is no special appropriateness to justify such an implausible change.

k Imperative masculine singular is out of place before a

feminine subject, and most have preferred infinitive absolute רְתֹם, used as an imperative. רִתְמִי imperative feminine singular, would also involve slight change. The construction, literally "hitch the chariot to the horses" is compared by Rudolph to Latin *currum jungere equis*. A sense "hitch, harness" fits the context and is given by the T and the S, but the word occurs only here, and the sense is to some extent uncertain. The LXX's ψόφος ("noise") is unexplained. The play on words, as generally recognized, is between רכשׁ and לכישׁ.

The present translation of the second line as a relative clause without אֲשֶׁר, modifying Lachish, involves recognition that the switch to third person in such a clause is normal. There is no need to follow Budde ("Das Rätsel") in supplying an אַתְּ (so Nowack, Rudolph). Reversion to the second person in the third line is expected. The line makes sense as a taunt over Lachish for her vaunted military prowess, now proved ineffective and revealed as a sin. See the Introduction, 3., *Micah as Prophet of a New Age*, on horses and chariots as a burden on the poor, and as foreign to Israelite society, cf. Mic 5:9 (EV 10).

Almost universally Lachish is identified with Tell ed-Duweir; for recent bibliography see Boyd "Lachish," *IDBS*. A recent objection to the identification is by G. W. Ahlström, "Is Tell ed-Duweir Ancient Lachish?" *PEQ* 112 (1980): 7–9.

l It is probably out of place to seek a close logical connection between this and the preceding saying about Lachish, or to delete or alter the conjunction because of the lack of any obvious causal relation between the two (contra Elliger, "Die Heimat," BHS, and Rudolph).

m The second feminine singular is acceptable if a personified Zion is addressed, which is not unlikely. Some mss of the LXX and the V have a third person form (יֻתַּן or תֻּתַּן?). Many commentators have emended the MT to a plural or passive form (תִּתְּנוּ, נִתְּנוּ, יִתְּנוּ, יֻתְּנוּ) which comes to about the same thing. α', σ', and θ' have ὅτι δῶρα ("because gifts") which does not seem to agree with the MT and is unexplained.

n Hebrew שִׁלּוּחִים is used once again in this sense, 1 Kgs 9:16, also in connection with a town (Gezer): וַיִּתְּנָהּ . . . שִׁלֻּחִים לְבִתּוֹ אֵשֶׁת שְׁלֹמֹה. The word-play is usually thought to lie in giving "dowry" to מוֹרֶשֶׁת, which sounds like מְאֹרֶשֶׁת (מְאֹרָשָׂה absolute), cf. Deut 22:23f. The noun pattern is rather similar, but the two have only one root consonant in common!

Since Moresheth seems to be related to ירשׁ ("inherit, etc."), the name has often been explained as "possession of Gath," and taken to indicate proximity to Gath or some special relation between the two places (so Joachim Jeremias, "Moreseth-Gath, die Heimat des Propheten Micha," *PJB* 29 [1933]: 42–53; and Otto Proksch, "Gat," *ZDPV* 66 (1943): 174–91. Aapeli A. Saarisalo ("Topographical Researches in the Shephelah," *JPOS* 11 [1931]: 14–20) proposed that the Gath in this name is the common noun "press." The doubtful, but possible identification with *mu-uḫ-ra-aš-ti* of El Amarna 335:17 (mentioned with Lachish) complicates the etymological picture further.

Joachim Jeremias ("Moreseth-Gath, die Heimat des Propheten Micah," *PJB* 29 [1933]: 42–53) identified Moresheth-Gath with Tell ej-Judeideh, partially excavated by Bliss and Macalister in 1898–1900, with remains showing occupation during the time of Micah (F. J. Bliss and R. S. Stewart Macalister, *Excavations in Palestine during the Years 1898–1900* [London: Palestine Exploration Fund, 1902]). This identification has been accepted by Elliger, "Die Heimat," F.-M. Abel, *Geographie de la Palestine* II (Paris: Gabalda, 1938), and Peter Welten, *Die Königs-Stempel*, Abhandlungen des Deutschen Palästinavereins (Wiesbaden: Harrassowitz, 1969), and many others. In my opinion, Zechariah Kallai-Kleinmann, "Moresheth-Gath," *EM*, is justified in raising questions about the basis for it, stating that biblical references are inadequate by themselves, and that late Christian references to the location of the tomb of Micah are as unreliable as other late references to burial places of the prophets. It has been plausibly supposed that the "Gath" among the cities fortified by Rehoboam (2 Chr 11:8) was Moresheth-Gath. On Rehoboam's cities see Gustav Beyer, "Beiträge zur Territorialgeschichte von Südwestpalästina im Altertum," *ZDPV* 54 (1931): 113–70.

o As Ehrlich points out (Arnold B. Ehrlich, *Randglossen zur hebräischen Bibel*. V. [Leipzig: Hinrichs, 1912]), עַל exchanges with אֶל very frequently, and נָתַן עַל does occur, so that one need not emend to אֶל or לְ, though the change is slight. Those who emend the preceding verb to a passive "shall be given," taking the verb as addressed to Moresheth-Gath, emend here to "for you" (אֵלַיִךְ or עָלַיִךְ).

p It seems best to retain the plural of the MT, though the point of the line escapes us. The proposal that the reference is to the two Achzib's, one in Judah, one south of Tyre (Ehrlich, *Randglossen*) is to be rejected, not only because the Micah passage demands places in Judah only, but also because this would be an odd way of saying "the two Achzib's" in Hebrew. Easy emendations lie to hand: בֵּית (singular), "house," or בַּת ("daughter"), but the point is not thereby much clarified. BHS ישֶׁבֶת encounters the same objection, and is graphically implausible. A. Demsky ("The Houses of Achzib. A Critical Note on Micah 1:14b," *IEJ* 16 [1966]: 211–15) retains the MT, translating "the factories of Achzib are a loss to the kings of Israel"; this is based on a passage in Chronicles which permits the hypothesis that Achzib was the site of a royal industrial plant. This is attractive, but אַכְזָב is not just "a loss," but something that deceives or disappoints, which does not fit so well with "factories." Aharoni has published an ostracon from Lachish, dated to the end of the monarchy, whose last line is *lbyt 'kzy[b]* but the sense and significance of the whole is not clear (Yohanan Aharoni, "Trial Excavation in the 'Solar Shrine' at Lachish. Preliminary Report," *IEJ* 18 [1968]: 168–69).

q Again, the reason for the MT plural escapes us. It is scarcely a reference to the kings of the Northern and Southern Kingdoms (see on בָּתֵּי above). Emendation to singular "king" is widely favored (the plural could have arisen from dittography of the following *y*), but since we do not know what the line refers to, conjecture is exceptionally hazardous.

r   As in the preceding verse, we miss the precise point here, if the MT is retained, but the reason is apt to lie in our scanty knowledge of the history of Mareshah. For עֹד ("again") put first in this sort of prediction, see Hos 12:10 עֹד אוֹשִׁיבְךָ בָאֳהָלִים כִּימֵי מוֹעֵד. The LXX ἕως τοὺς κληρονόμους ("up to the heirs") presupposes no different text. The line may be taken as a question, and perhaps interrogative *h* should be prefixed. This depends on how יוֹרֵשׁ is translated; see note t below.

s   Construed as first common singular Hiphil of בוא (אָבִיא) as in many mss of Kenn. and de Rossi. The speaker is Yahweh. Since this seems to be a change from the previous, where it is assumed that the prophet speaks in his own person, many would read יָבוֹא ("will come") (Ehrlich, *Randglossen*, Budde, "Das Rätsel," et al., BHS, BH³). The word-play involves the assonance of *RŠ* in יֹרֵשׁ and מְרֵשָׁה; since the place name is elsewhere מָרֵאשָׁה (Josh 15:44, as if from רֹאשׁ), it is likely that there is no genuine etymological connection.

   Identification with Tell Sandaḥanna is now universally accepted; for bibliography and discussion, see Michael Avi-Yonah, "Mārēshāh, Māre'šāh (Hebrew)," *EM*.

t   Use of the article, if that is retained here, is either a way of referring to a well-known יוֹרֵשׁ, or idiomatic Hebrew use of the article where English does not use it, as הַפְּלִים Gen 14:3; cf. Gesenius' para 126r. Usage of the verb suggests a sense "dispossess, conquer" though the participle happens not to be attested in this sense (note, however, Jer 8:10). Understood thus, the line is an obvious threat. An alternate rendering "Shall I again bring an heir to you?" i.e., "Don't expect to have any heirs" is much less direct. יוֹרֵשׁ does occur in the sense

. . . הַבָּנִים אֵין לְיִשְׂרָאֵל "heir," 2 Sam 14:7 and Jer 49:1 אִם־יוֹרֵשׁ אֵין לוֹ . . . "Has Israel no sons? Has he no heir?" Also Isa 65:9 . . . וְהוֹצֵאתִי מִיַּעֲקֹב זֶרַע וּמִיהוּדָה יוֹרֵשׁ הָרָי "I shall bring forth from Jacob offspring, and from Judah one to inherit my mountains."

u   The line is grammatically and lexically impeccable, and contains the name of a place, Adullam, located perfectly for this context. Again, we miss the point, even in a general way. What is the "glory of Israel"? Why will it come "to Adullam"? Answers may escape us, but it is hazardous to emend, especially to eliminate the good place name! No word-play is apparent (Rudolph's proposal is fantastic). The S has *dammā l'ālam* which comes from a graphic error, a kind of haplography where עֹדלם עֹד becomes the very common עֹד עוֹלָם "forever." Emendation to עֹד עוֹלָם יֹאבֵד/יֹאבַד/אָבַד ("the glory of Israel shall perish forever") gives tolerable sense but is graphically improbable and eliminates the place name.

   Nothing in the history of Adullam—David's sojourn there during his flight from Saul is best known—serves as a key to the point here. The site is identified today as Khirbet eš-Šeḥ Madkûr.

v   One could think of wealth, military equipment (Isa 22:18), or multitudes of men, cf. Isa 5:13; 8:7; 16:14; and 17:3.

w   The LXX adds τῆς θυγατρός Ισραηλ.

x   No subject for these imperatives is expressed, and if a bicolon is intended, the first member is short. Jerusalem or Zion is presumably addressed, so some would supply צִיּוֹן; others lengthen the first line by adding (after וְגֹזִּי) עַל בָּנַיִךְ.

y   The LXX has τὴν χηρείαν σου ("your widowhood"); Ziegler explains this (*Sylloge*, p 386 [112]) as an extension of the normal sense: widowhood is "being bereft of hair," since the verb χηρείειν is often "be empty, desolate."

Commentary

This passage carries over from vv 8–9 the theme and imagery of mourning, and twice (12, 16) reaches the same climactic statement as v 9: the disaster touches Jerusalem. Aside from this double climax, there would probably not have been a detectable progression of thought even if the text were sound. As the text stands, its choppy, detached statements and shifting imagery seem to harmonize with a picture of confusion and disorder, and disintegration under enemy attack. This effect may have been intended. The towns of Judah go their separate ways to destruction or shame; the common factor is that this was somehow fated, woven into the very names of the towns, or local lore about them.

   Where an earlier passage had expressed personal grief (v 8: "I will mourn and wail"), there is an additional note of mockery and taunting here. The frequent imperatives of 10–16 seem at times to have this tone. This is

strengthened by the puns, at least to our taste, and by the allusions to local sayings about the towns, if these are indeed present (see Notes). In our somewhat homogenized American society we may forget how strong local, village rivalries may be. Actually in general times of disorder, peasants often use the chaos to settle old *local* scores. In a sense, and with words, Micah does something like that here, without destroying the dominant tone of mourning.

   Even if not every line contains a play on words (see Notes), puns are pervasive. Belief in a special significance of proper names was obviously widespread in ancient Israel, and there is no need to cite parallels (as from Amos, Hosea, Isaiah) for Micah's practise. Micah perhaps lays less theological weight on names than others have done. At least once the name indicates what did not happen to the town (Zaanan, v 11). No name is exploited for wide-sweeping, important theological purposes; their

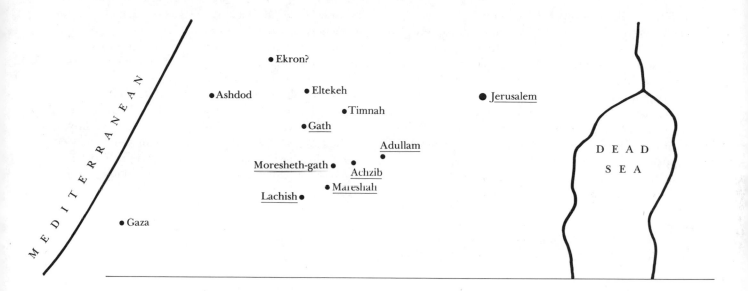

significance is local (contrast e.g., Shearjashub "a remnant shall return"). Micah does not assign new symbolic names.

The date of composition of this passage is disputed by scholars, though most think of a time shortly after the invasion of Sennacherib (701 B.C.), with its siege of Jerusalem and loss of Judaean towns. Since the poem is not so specific that it will fit *only* that time, there is some justification for other theories. Lindblom proposed the invasion of Sargon in 712[1], but the basis, problems connected with "Gath" in 701, met better by an earlier date, is not firmly based in the Micah text, or historically. More appealing is the proposal that this is a menacing lament *before* the Assyrian onslaught. It is well known that the lament form could be used ironically by the prophets before the disaster arrived, as Amos 5:1–2. All the same, the imperatives and other tenses ("they have gone into exile" [גָּלוּ], "has come down" [יָרַד]) of this passage fit Sennacherib's time most naturally. The cities that are known from Micah all lie in the area ceded by Sennacherib to the Philistines, which permits a natural understanding of v 16 "they have gone away from you into exile" (גָּלוּ). See Na'aman on the relation of Sennacherib's campaign to Micah.[2]

The accompanying map does not show places which are restored conjecturally to the text by some scholars, such as Kabbon, Giloh, and Baka. Also absolutely unlocatable places are not shown: Beth Leaphra, Shaphir, Zaanan, Beth Ezel, and Maroth. Those places shown have been identified plausibly or with certainty; see the Notes and Bibliography for details. Some names from Sennacherib's account of the campaign of 701 B.C. have been shown: Ashdod, Gaza, Eltekeh, Timnah, Ekron.

---

1   Lindblom, *Micha.*

2   N. Na'aman, "Sennacherib's Campaign to Judah and the Date of the LMLK Stamps," *VT* 29 (1979): 61–86.

■ **Against Those Who Steal Land**

The rich now have power to plot
against the poor and take their
land, but Yahweh will reverse
this and in future they will be
abased and cut off from any share
in the land.

2

1 Ah[a] you who think up evil
   And deeds[b] of wrong on your beds,
 Then perform it when day breaks[c]
   Because it lies within your power;
2 You who covet fields, and steal them,[d]
   Houses, and take them;
 Who oppress a man and his household,
   An owner and his property!
3 For these things, thus says the Lord,[e]
 I am going to devise evil against this family[f]
   From which you will not be able to remove your neck[g]
 Or walk upright,[h]
   For it will be an evil time.
4 On that day they[i] will sing a taunt-song about you
   And intone a lament,[j] saying:[k]
 "'We have been laid waste.[l]
   They are selling[m] the portion of my people.
 Alas, they take it from me![n]
   Our fields are allotted[n] to the apostate.'"[p]
5 Therefore[q] you[r] will have no one to cast the cord over
 your allotted land[s] in the assembly of Yahweh.

a   The LXX has ἐγένοντο which equals הָיוּ. For rendering
    of these lines as direct address, see Hillers, "Hôy and
    Hôy-Oracles," Freedman Festschrift, forthcoming.
b   The MT וּפָעֲלֵי ("and you who do [evil]") does not fit with
    the modifier "on your beds." Rather than delete the
    phrase as a gloss (Wellhausen and many), one could
    construe it as a plural construct of פֹּעַל "deed," cf. Isa
    59:6 פֹּעַל חָמָס which is parallel to מַעֲשֵׂי אָוֶן and Ezek 11:2
    הַחֹשְׁבִים אָוֶן וְהַיֹּעֲצִים עֵצַת. This explanation is preferred by
    Halévy and others since. Perhaps repointing to פֹּעֲלֵי is
    necessary, but Rudolph, citing the vocalization of פֹּעַל in
    Isa 1:31 and Jer 22:13, argues that no change whatever
    is necessary. For reference to plotting in bed, cf. Ps. 36:5
    (EV 4). J. T. Willis, "On the text of Micah 2, 1aα–β,"
    Biblica 48 (1967): 534–41, is an exhaustive discussion of
    the problem of this line; his own conclusion, that the MT
    refers to wicked dreams, is a curiosity.
c   The LXX's καὶ ἅμα τῇ ἡμέρᾳ "and when day comes" is a
    free translation.
d   This is not reflected in the S which is probably just a free
    translation. The LXX adds ὀρφανούς "orphans" (Hebrew
    יְתוֹמִים) which is a more or less appropriate addition, to
    supply an object for the verb.

e   The BH³ adds לְבֵית יִשְׂרָאֵל ("to the house of Israel"),
    which is quite unnecessary; the phrase of the MT is
    common and unproblematic. The S adds 'alāhā which is
    a free translation.
f   The order of the MT, with direct object following the
    indirect object, perhaps expresses an emphasis on the
    direct object, but is not so unusual as to suggest a
    corruption (contra Marti, Wolff, BH³, et al.).
g   This exact combination of words does not occur else-
    where, but the sense seems clear and the grammar
    unexceptionable; the assumed image is of evil as a yoke
    on a person's neck, cf. Isa 10:27.
h   The MT תֵלְכוּ רוֹמָה is a unique expression, perhaps
    meaning "act proudly," or perhaps continuing the image
    of a yoke. The LXX adds ἐξαίφνης ("suddenly"); the
    origin of which escapes us.
i   An indefinite singular equals "one" or "people," and is
    equivalent to plural or passive, cf. Isa 8:4 יִשָּׂא אֶת־חֵיל
    דַּמֶּשֶׂק ("They will take the wealth of Damascus" or the
    "wealth of Damascus will be taken"). Note the
    renderings of the V and the LXX (λημφθήσεται).

j Delete נהיה as arising from dittography, with most commentators. Hitzig defends נִהְיָה as a cry of despair: "it has been done!" but this is *ad hoc* and improbable. A supposed occurrence of נהיה "lament" in the War Scroll is cited by J. Carmignac, "Precisions apportés au vocabulaire de l'hébreu biblique par la Guerre des fils de Lumière contra les fils de ténèbres," *VT* 5 (1955): 349; Rudolph takes this as support for an older idea, that נְהִי נִהְיָה is a sort of superlative construction, meaning "a pitiable lament." But the Dead Sea passage (XVII 5) was misunderstood; it is actually a participle of *hyh*, cf. Yigael Yadin, *The Scroll of the War of the Sons of Light against the Sons of Darkness*, tr. B. and C. Rabin (London: Oxford Univ., 1962), and G. Vermes, *The Dead Sea Scrolls in English* (Baltimore, Penguin, 1965). The LXX ἐν μέλει ("in song") (cf. the V *cum suavitate?*) is probably an attempt to get sense from the MT.

k Read either וְאָמַר (cf. the S *wnĕ'mar*, Ehrlich, *Randglossen*, BH³, and BHS) or לֵאמֹר (Wellhausen et al.) introducing the direct speech that follows (whatever their Hebrew text, the LXX and the V interpret thus). There is no insuperable difficulty involved in a lament *over* an unfortunate which includes direct speech of the unfortunate, cf. Lamentations 1, where in the second half (from v 11) the third person form is largely replaced by first person; cf. also Lamentations 3. The additional, complicating feature here is that this is done in mockery. No basis exists for Rudolph's altering the introductory word to an imperative: "Say" or to "I will say."

l A unique Niphal perfect, first common plural with *u* (= *û*) instead of *ô* between stem and suffix (Gesenius' para. 67 u). Many have transferred this colon to the end of the little lament, or otherwise rearranged the lines, but such a procedure is exceptionally hazardous when, as here, the text of some lines can be restored only by conjecture.

m The MT "He (one) exchanges (sells)" is unintelligible. Ezek 48:14 uses מור in a prohibition of alienation of land allotted to the Levites and holy to the Lord. The sense here would be "our land is (unlawfully) being given to others." The LXX, however, has κατεμετρήθη ἐν σχοινίῳ ("is measured with a cord") which equals יִמַּד בַּחֶבֶל and this has been preferred by Wellhausen and others, cf. the S *bašwāytā npalleg* ("he will divide with a cord"). In any case the idea of a transfer of the promised land is in mind.

n "Alas" (אֵיךְ) is such a characteristic word in laments that it should not be emended away here. The sense of יָמִישׁ לִי is "(my property) gets away from me" i.e., "is no longer mine" (so approximately Rudolph). Admittedly מושׁ is not otherwise used of real estate, and the metaphor is unparalleled. The LXX καὶ οὐκ ἦν certainly reflects וְאֵין, but the remainder ὁ κωλύσων does not obviously point to מֵשִׁיב, as many commentators have assumed since Wellhausen. Such a use of κωλύω for שׁוב is otherwise only attested doubtfully at Isa 28:6. The sense "and there is none to return (it) to me" is, of course, well-suited to the context.

o As elsewhere in the immediate context, the second masculine singular may express an impersonal (passive) idea; pointing it as a passive, citing the LXX, is easy but not necessary.

p The MT "apostate" has seemed to many out of place. On the assumption that the lament has to do with the land's falling into enemy hands, perhaps to Assyria, "apostate" would be the wrong word, and some have preferred שׁוֹבֵינוּ "our captors." Others would delete the term as dittography (Robinson, Weiser). But the reference may be to assignment, in an eschatological future, of land to groups of people whom the wealthy and powerful of Micah's time would regard as religiously inferior; cf. Jer 31:22. The LXX τοῦ ἀποστρέψαι ("to turn away") seems to presuppose approximately the MT, as do σ' and θ', but the source of α' τοῖς γείτοσι ("to the neighbors") is puzzling.

q This seems to be the third conclusion following on the denunciation of vv 1–2. Only by drastic emendation (תְּנוּ of BH³) is it a continuation of the lament.

r The singular is unexpected after the preceding plurals, and many have preferred to read לָכֶם, supposing the MT results from haplography (see BH³ and BHS, following many others).

s The form of the MT, for which there is no exact parallel, can be construed thus: the instrument of division is named first (מַשְׁלִיךְ חֶבֶל), then the designation of the allotted land (בְּגוֹרָל), for which cf. Judg 1:3. Since גוֹרָל and חֶבֶל are practically interchangeable in phrases and clauses having to do with land-division, the text has seemed to some overloaded or conflated. Already the S inserts before "lot" the term "dividing," resolving the line into two parallel expressions; similar results are achieved by moderns, including BH³.

Commentary

Here begins a new section, as the book turns from an introduction that stressed the external threat to the people to the internal wrongs that lead to ruin. The address contains the indictment, which is then followed by a threefold sentence: the yoke saying (v 3), the mocking lament (v 4), and the saying about exclusion from the assembly of Yahweh. Because of this repetition of the concluding element, and because the theme of the oracle is continued in the following verses as well, there is real uncertainty as to the end of this element of the book.

32

The first part of the indictment stresses the deliberate, intentional nature of the crimes committed by the powerful. They lie awake and scheme, and eagerly carry out their plots when morning breaks. They do this because they can; they are conscious of their power and use it.

This attack is on a man's property. By whatever means (we are probably meant to think of their making loans and foreclosing) they "add house to house, field to field" as Isaiah put it in a very similar saying (5:8). But their actions constitute something more reprehensible than mere greed, for they are an assault on the basic structure of the people of God. This is signalled already in Micah's choice of words: "they covet" (חָמְדוּ). This recalls the commandment.[1] The economic and social ideal of ancient Israel was of a nation of free landholders—not debt-slaves, share-croppers, or hired workers—secure in possession, as a grant from Yahweh, of enough land to keep their families. "Each under his own vine and his own fig tree" summarizes the ideal. Other ideals, such as justice, mutual love and fidelity, a close-knit family, and so on, depended on achievement of this sort of economic security. If the family land was lost, little other economic opportunity remained. We do not know in detail the extent to which this was realized at any period in Israel's history, or by precisely what means and to what extent the ideal order was subverted. Alt's sharp distinction between the Jerusalem nobles, as the oppressing force, and the peasants of the countryside as the oppressed,[2] has no basis in this text, which does not make a distinction of this sort and allows for the participation of local magnates in land-grabbing. (The general theory of political relations between Judah and Jerusalem [a "personal union"] which Alt proposed has been convincingly refuted by Kallai.[3]

The speaker of the first doom is Yahweh. He will bring this "family" ("gang or crowd" [מִשְׁפָּחָה]; cf. Jer 8:3, "this wicked gang" [תַּמִּשְׁפָּחָה הָרָעָה הַזֹּאת]) under a yoke. For the image compare Isa 9:4; 10:27; 47:6; Jer 27:8;

28:14; and Ezek 34:27.

The second doom has the form of a mocking lament. It is unclear who is to be thought of as singing the lament; it seems best to imagine an impersonal "they will say." If the difficult text is correctly interpreted here, the "mourners" quote, in mockery, the wails of the dispossessed rich. When the land is taken away, it is they who will suffer expropriation of their ill-gotten land, and they will cry as if it were rightfully their own.

The speaker of the third doom is unidentified also. Perhaps we can best think of this as the prophet's own words. The scene presupposed is different. It is not a time of oppression, not a day of mourning, but a day when "the assembly of Yahweh" meets to allot lands. The measuring cord is used in such a division, along with lots. The covetous oppressors will have no share. Though the language is restrained and unexcited, in comparison to the preceding lament, this is the severest of the judgments. It cuts the rich off from future hope. No member of their line will, in time to come, stand in the assembly of Yahweh. Our ignorance of the role of land-division in ancient Israel is such that we do not know if Micah is speaking of a restoration of standing practice in ancient Israel, whereby common lands were regularly divided in a sacred assembly,[4] or to a visionary future, an eschatological assembly in which economic justice is restored by repetition of the primeval division (cf. Ezekiel 48). The latter seems more likely, but in either case, Micah speaks of the achieving of a social and religious ideal from which the covetous and their descendants will be excluded. The future "assembly of Yahweh" will consist of the oppressed; see Introduction, *3. Micah as Prophet of a New Age*. The view that this refers to a conqueror's redivision of the land is less probable; that would hardly have been thought of as a sacred act.

---

1   Even though the meaning of חמד in the commandment is disputed, see J.J. Stamm and M.E. Andrew, *The Ten Commandments in Recent Research*, Studies in Biblical Theology, Second Series, No. 2 (Naperville, Ill.: Allenson, 1967), 101–105, at least in Micah the traditional "covet" equals "desire" is appropriate.

2   Alt, "Micha 2, 1–5"

3   Zechariah Kallai, "Judah and Israel—a study in Israelite Historiography," *IEJ* 28 (1978): 251–61.

4   R. de Vaux, "'Le reste d'Israel' d'après les prophètes," *RB* 42 (1933): 526–39; Alt, "Micha 2, 1–5"; and Weiser.

■ **Enemies of the People**

The powerful are enemies of the people, but wish to retain the illusion that Yahweh will not punish them, and thus resist true prophecy. They deserve a prophet who would further delude them.

2

6 "Do not prophesy,"[a] is their prophecy.[b] "They shall not
     prophesy of these things.[c]
   Such reproaches will not come to pass."[d]
7 The house of Jacob says,[e] "Is Yahweh's patience exhausted?[f]
   Is this how he acts?
   Surely he speaks[g] of good[h]
   And the righteous walks with him."[i]
8 But it is you[j] who rise against my people as enemies.
   From the laborer[k] you strip his cloak;
   You take the garments off the captives in war.[l]
9 You drive the women[m] of my people out of her pleasant dwelling;[n]
   From her children[o] you take away my glory[p] forever.
10 "Get up and get out,"[q] you say, "You will not rest here."
   For[r] an unclean thing you do damage,[s] grievous damage.
11 If[t] a man possessed[u] of a deceiving spirit[v] lied[w] thus:
   "I will prophesy to you[x] of wine and beer,"
   He would be just the prophet[y] for this people.

Preliminary Note

This passage is corrupt or doubtful at so many points that even the general progression of thought is uncertain. Relying on such bits as are relatively clear, one may reasonably suppose that it begins with quotations of pious phrases from the religiously secure who oppose the prophets; then comes Micah's exposure of their crimes against society, and the bitter conclusion that only a prophet who would flatter their basest desires could please them. Here the most obscure parts have been interpreted to fit this general pattern, but frequently this can be done only by conjectural emendation or by rather forced construction of the existing text.

a This is plural; if correct, the pious reject not only the words of Micah, but any prophetic reproach; cf. Amos 2:12 וְעַל־הַנְּבִיאִים צִוִּיתֶם לֵאמֹר לֹא תִּנָּבְאוּ. Emending the text to the singular perhaps misses a point here (recently, Willi-Plein).

b Literally this means "they prophesy." If the text is correct, Micah repeats the word for ironic effect, to describe the speech of his adversaries. This rather implausible construction gains credibility if one reckons in the possibility that נטף (Hiphil) has a pejorative connotation: "Don't talk such drivel"—they drivel. But that is only a possibility and derives more from the supposed etymology (i.e., "drip, drool" becomes "prophesy," i.e., "drool in ecstasy"; the LXX and the S reflect

this etymology) than from usage. Mays' rendering: "'Don't preach,' they preach" neatly employs an English word favorable or neutral in some contexts, and unfavorable in others. A further question: why is the third person used here of those addressed, where "you" (plural) is used in what follows? Various emendations attempt to smooth out the abrupt shifts in person in this verse. On the whole passage, vv 6–8, see J. T. Willis, "Micah 2:6–8 and the 'People of God' in Micah," *BZ* 14 (1970) 72–87.

c If one may judge from v 11, *lamedh* is the appropriate preposition for "about," after הַטִּיף. If so, emendation is unnecessary (contra BH³, BHS).

d The Niphal of סוג ("will withdraw") seems inappropriate here, and the masculine singular form lacks a noun subject. Perhaps read תַּשִּׂיגֵנוּ equals תַּשִּׂיגֵנוּ (cf. similar exchange of these verbs in Job 24:2 and Mic 6:14); this would be Hiphil imperfect of נשׂג with ס for שׂ; cf. a' καταλήψη ("you will overtake") which equals תַּשִּׂיג/תַּשִּׂיג. The subject would be כְּלִמּוֹת ("reproaches"). Cf. Isa 59:9 וְלֹא תַשִּׂיגֵנוּ צְדָקָה. The object ("us") need not be expressed, cf. 1 Sam 30:8; Ex 15:9; and Ps 7:6 (EV 5). For הַסִּג of the coming-true of a word see Deut 28:15 and Zech 1:6. Joseph Reider, "Etymological Studies in Biblical Hebrew," *VT* 4 (1954): 276–95, retains the MT and arrives at a rendering "they shall not forge speeches" but only by unconvincing use of Arabic meanings for

Hebrew words.

e The MT, giving the only occurrence of Qal passive participle of אמר, is thereby suspect, and in general it has proved difficult to fit this clause into the context. Read אָמַר, making the line a parenthetic reference to the speaker of this section, Jacob. Compare the contexts where אָמַר יהוה interrupts a sentence or series of sentences, e.g., אֵין שָׁלוֹם אָמַר יהוה לָרְשָׁעִים 48:22 Isa or Isa 54:1–2. Smith reads הָאוֹמֵר, citing the LXX ὁ λέγων, but the result is implausible Hebrew. Rather similar is Ps 124:1–2 לוּלֵי יהוה שֶׁהָיָה לָנוּ יֹאמַר־נָא יִשְׂרָאֵל לוּלֵי יהוה cf. Ps. 129:1–2.

Because the following clause is a question, many have wished to construe the ה of הָאָמוּר as interrogative, most commonly with a change to הָאָרוּר ("Is the house of Jacob accursed?" [thus Sellin and many others]). But the coordinate questions . . . אִם . . . הֲקָצַר are complete by themselves and do not require a preceding question. Van der Woude reads הֶאָמִיר (cf. Deut 26:17–18), supposed to mean "the house of Jacob affirmed," or "He (i.e., Yahweh) affirmed (what has been undertaken by) the house of Jacob," but neither fits the context without reading in a great deal.

f The LXX παρώργισε ("provoked") is probably not equal to הִקְצִיף but a translation suggested by the context.

g The first person is out of place where the people are speaking. A change to the third person דְּבָרָיו is preferred by most commentators, citing the LXX οἱ λόγοι αὐτοῦ.

h If the preceding change is accepted, most likely the verb must be singular יֵיטִיב with Yahweh understood as the subject. The exact expression "he makes his words good" is unparalleled; similar are Deut 5:28; 18:17. His "ways," reading דְּרָכָיו (Budde, ["Micha 2 und 3," ZAW 38 (1919/209): 2–22], Sellin, Nowack), involves no great change, but is not a significant improvement.

i The word order does not permit the AV translation "to him that walketh uprightly." Read וְעִמּוֹ הַיָּשָׁר הֹלֵךְ and cf. the LXX μετ' αὐτοῦ, and for the whole expression see Gen 5:22, 24. Even so the expression would be unusual and the text may be more deeply corrupt. A commonly accepted emendation is עִם עַמּוֹ יִשְׂרָאֵל "with his people Israel," supposing עמו to have been lost by haplography.

For the LXX εἰσι καλοὶ . . . πεπόρευνται, R has ἠγ]αθυναν μ[ει .. πορευόμ]ενον, thus R equals the MT in number. For the MT הֹלֵךְ see Mur 88 הלך.

j The MT "And yesterday" gives no sense. Read וְאַתֶּם "But you." Elsewhere in this book oracles frequently begin with w plus personal pronoun, expressing a strong adversative: 4:8, 12; 5:1; cf. 3:8 (וְאוּלָם אָנֹכִי "But I . . ."). At this point in the oracle such a shift seems in place, and this emendation is favored by most commentators since Wellhausen. Beyond this point much greater uncertainty arises. Following Wellhausen at most points, read: וְאַתֶּם עַל עַמִּי לְאֹיֵב קָמִים (so, approximately, many others ["But you are not my people"]). וְאַתֶּם לֹא עַמִּי is favored by Budde, "Micha 2 und 3," Sellin, and others. The LXX follows the MT closely with ἀντέστη for יְקוֹמֵם. R has, perhaps significantly, [. . . αντέ]στησαν.

k The MT, if taken word for word, reads: "from opposite

the cloak glory (or, a mantle[?]) you strip," which is impossible. Since אֶדֶר is not the usual term for a cloak, and to avoid emendation, G. W. Ahlström, "'eder," VT 17 (1967): 1–7, postulates several other senses ("buckle; girdle"), but not quite convincingly. Emend the MT to מַעֲמֵל שַׂלְמָה/אַדֶּרֶת תַּפְשִׁיטוּן with the two terms for cloak regarded as a double reading, i.e., the MT incorporates ancient, equivalent senses. The general sense, that the rich take the garments of the poor, is easy to parallel in the law and the prophets (Exod 22:25–26; Deut 24:10–13; and Amos 2:8), and in the Yabneh-yam letter (KAI 200). Another emendation, commonly accepted, achieves the same general sense: מֵעַל שְׁלֵמִים אַדֶּרֶת etc.: "From those who are peaceful the cloak, etc." (Wellhausen et al.). The LXX τὴν δοράν αὐτοῦ ἐξέδειραν ("his hide they have flayed"), takes אַדֶּרֶת in the Aramaic sense "skin" as does the S; see A. Büchler, "אֶדֶר = Fell in LXX zu Micha 2,8," ZAW 30 (1910): 64–65. R has [. . . περιβ]όλαιον ἐξεδύσ[ατε . . .] ("you took off the robe") which equals the MT.

l Again, if taken word for word, the MT reads: "from those who pass by (in) security, returned of war" which gives no acceptable sense. Read מֵעֹבְרִים בֶּגֶד שְׁבִי מִלְחָמָה. The participle is appropriate in this sort of prophetic indictment. For תעביר בגד cf. Jonah 3:6 וַיַּעֲבֵר אַדַּרְתּוֹ מֵעָלָיו. The rich are enemies of the people, in the prophet's mind; the poor are their captives, and captives were as a matter of course stripped and left with at best the most meagre clothing; cf. Deut 21:13 שִׂמְלַת שִׁבְיָה. Isaiah 20 gives a vivid example. Other commentators, since Wellhausen, have accepted שְׁבִי for the meaningless שׁוּבֵי (also BH³ and BHS), but have tried in one way or another to preserve בֶּטַח. Still others, following the LXX συντριμμὸν πολέμου ("destruction of war") have read מֵעֹבְרִים לְבֶטַח שֶׁבֶר מִלְחָמָה which is supposed to mean "You bring to the secure the destruction of war," which seems very unidiomatic.

m The LXX has διὰ τοῦτο, which may equal לָכֵן, but is scarcely correct in any case. For the MT "women" the LXX has ἡγούμενοι ("leaders") as if for נְשִׂיאֵי, but "women" is preferable.

n The singular is appropriate here if one assumes the prophet has in mind two things, the individual women of Israel, and בַּת עַמִּי, the nation personified as a woman. In dispossessing women and children—widows and orphans—from their houses, the rich are like enemies driving off a captive people from its pleasant dwelling, taking away its glory, i.e., all that was involved in being the people of God in the promised land. Cf. Isa 35:2 for both senses of הֲדָר. The common emendation of בית and of the suffixes (to plural) agreeing with "women," is only a slight change, but perhaps unnecessary. The LXX, S, and V, with plural, have surely only done what most moderns have. The change of בית "house" to בְּנֵי "children" (Wellhausen and others) can be supported by 1:16 for the occurrence of the phrase, but the sense is suspect, being the reverse of the normal atrocity: children are driven from mothers (or Mother Zion) rather than the reverse.

35

o The LXX διὰ τὰ πονηρὰ ἐπιτηδεύματα αὐτῶν equals עַל־מַעַלְלֵיהֶם, a corruption of the MT by haplography. Of the rest of the LXX to this verse, ὄρεσιν αἰωνίοις, is clearly from הַרְרֵי עוֹלָם which represents a change of *d* to *r*, but the verb forms ἐξώσθησαν and ἐγγίσατε are unexplained.

p הָדַד is explicable here without searching for a form of חָדַר (BHS).

q If addressed to the women, the masculine is a slight difficulty. Perhaps עוֹלְלֶיהָ was in mind, or note the LXX has the singular, ἀνάστηθι καὶ πορεύου for קוּמִי) ולכ(י. In the following clause the LXX adds σοι ("for you"), probably just a free translation.

r Perhaps, remaining in the picture of land-grabbing, the MT is defensible as meaning "You damage the land"; cf. Isa 13:4–5 . . . צְבָא מִלְחָמָה: בָּאִים מֵאֶרֶץ מֶרְחָק . . . לְחַבֵּל כָּל־הָאָרֶץ. cf. Cant 2:15 מְחַבְּלִים כְּרָמִים. By driving off the women and children from their property, they render the land טָמְאָה ("unclean"). It is as if the people were in exile in their own land, which has become an אֲדָמָה טְמֵאָה. This interpretation can claim only a certain plausibility, and the variety of roots and senses involved in Hebrew words from the root חבל makes the sense here unusually uncertain. On חֶבֶל נִמְרָץ whose exact sense is very uncertain, cf. 1 Kgs 2:8 קִלְלַנִי קְלָלָה נִמְרֶצֶת ("he cursed me with a terrible curse"). This seems to render unnecessary the correction of the adjective to נֶחֱרָץ (Grätz, *Emendations,* Marti and BH³). By changing טָמְאָה to מְאוּמָה or מְעַט מְאוּמָה, one may render, "For a trifle you take a pledge, a terrible pledge" (Budde, "Micha 2 und 3," and others), but מְאוּמָה by itself does not mean "a trifle" and the addition of מְעַט is no small insertion.

s The LXX has the passive διεφθάρητε, which cannot be eliminated from consideration.

t Mur 88 has לא, apparently negative, which results from misunderstanding the passage; however, it could be an alternate spelling of the conditional particle, cf. e.g., the K of 2 Sam 18:12 and the lexicons for other examples. For the MT הוֹלֵךְ . . . לוּ the LXX has κατεδιώχθητε οὐδενὸς διώκοντος ("you are pressed hard with no one

pursuing"), which is a stab in the dark, perhaps influenced by Prov 28:1. The LXX seems to have only one term ψεῦδος for "lying," to render וָשֶׁקֶר כֹּזֵב, but is so obviously groping for sense at this point that the omission must be regarded as probably insignificant. The V "would that I were not a man having the spirit but rather speaking falsehood" is a similar wrestling with the sense; the text equals the MT.

u The MT gives this as a modifier of אִישׁ, which has been followed here. רוּחַ וָשֶׁקֶר is then an adverbial modifier, cf. הֹלֵךְ צְדָקוֹת ("walking in righteousness") Isa 33:15 cf. Prov 6:12. It is equal to Jer 23:14 וּבִנְבִאֵי יְרוּשָׁלַ͏ם רָאִיתִי שַׁעֲרוּרָה נָאוֹף וְהָלֹךְ בַּשֶּׁקֶר . . . ("And in the prophets of Jerusalem I have seen a horrible thing: they commit adultery and live by falsehood . . ."). Since Wellhausen many have preferred to make coordinate clauses by reading perfect הָלַךְ ("If a man walked . . . and lied"). Little difference in sense is involved. Hitzig pointed to 2 Sam 18:12 as a case of לוּ plus participle in a conditional clause, but to admit that construction here would produce disharmony in tense between coordinate conditional clauses, since כִּזֵּב is perfect.

v This is literally, "wind/spirit and falsehood." With Rudolph one may see here a hendiadys. Or one might emend to read רוּחַ שֶׁקֶר, cf. 1 Kgs 22:22 . . . אֵצֵא וְהָיִיתִי רוּחַ שֶׁקֶר בְּפִי כָּל־נְבִיאָיו ("I will go and be a lying spirit in the mouth of all his prophets").

w As construed here, this is the verb of the *lû*-clause, expressing a contrary to fact condition in the present or future, with וְהָיָה as the apodosis. The reason for the emendation offered in BH³ and the sense intended escape me.

x The following reference to "this people" perhaps suggests that a plurality of persons is intended, so לָכֶם has been preferred by some, but this is unnecessary.

y This noun, and the verbal use of הַטִּיף in v 6, have influenced the title of an adversary of the Qumran sect, who is called מַטִּיף כֹּזֵב and closely related terms. IQpMi 1. 3 has the form מַטּיף, which may be a kind of pun on the usual title; see Milik, *Midrash,* 412–15.

Commentary

The charges of crimes against the weak link this with elements in chap 2 and 3; the resistance of the rich to the prophetic word may be read as a reaction to Micah's harsh words in the preceding oracle.

The people resist prophecy of Micah's type, a familiar reaction, cf. Amos 2:12, "But you gave the Nazirites wine to drink, and commanded the prophets: 'Do not prophesy'" (וַתַּשְׁקוּ אֶת־הַנְּזִרִים יָיִן וְעַל־הַנְּבִיאִים צִוִּיתֶם לֵאמֹר לֹא תִּנָּבְאוּ). See also Amos 7:13. Van der Woude supposes that here as elsewhere in the book the false prophets speak (see on 4:9 for fuller discussion), but the context seems to make clear that it is the rapacious rich who are objecting to Micah's words. The rich do this in the name

of piety; as Rudolph puts it, they quote Scripture against the prophet, for the reference to Yahweh's patience recalls what must have been familiar to all (Exod 34:6, "Yahweh, Yahweh, a god merciful and kind, patient and abounding in covenant love and fidelity" [יהוה יהוה אֵל רַחוּם וְחַנּוּן אֶרֶךְ אַפַּיִם וְרַב־חֶסֶד וֶאֱמֶת]). "Do not prophesy" is plural, thus directed against more than Micah alone (if one may press a detail in a textually difficult passage). Though especially the rich are in mind, the speakers represent the people (v 11, "this people" [הָעָם הַזֶּה]). Perhaps it is a situation where oppressor and oppressed alike regard prophecy as irreligious.

Expanding the image of the rich as the enemy, Micah describes how they strip clothing off their captives, and

36

drive people off the land in which Yahweh had promised them "rest," a theologically important term for undisturbed enjoyment of God's gift of the land. Perhaps in fact the rich had seized garments taken in pledge (Amos 2:6), and robbed widow's houses. In so doing they gain power in the land, but at the same time defile it, making it an unclean thing (Num 35:34; Deut 21:23).

The concluding observation is in part a contemptuous restatement of their relationship to prophecy: they could get along with a prophet who spoke of wine and beer. Micah caricatures prophesies of plenty, such as Joel 2:24, "And the threshing-floor shall be full of grain, and the vats overflow with new wine and oil" (וּמָלְאוּ הַגֳּרָנוֹת בָּר) or Amos 9:13, 14 "The mountains shall drip sweet wine, and all the hills shall (וְהֵשִׁיקוּ הַיְקָבִים תִּירוֹשׁ וְיִצְהָר)

flow with it . . . they shall plant vineyards and drink their wine" (וְהִטִּיפוּ הֶהָרִים עָסִיס . . . וְנָטְעוּ כְרָמִים וְשָׁתוּ אֶת־יֵינָם . . . . . .). Jeremiah used the image in a similar way in 13:12, "Every jar will be filled with wine" (כָל־נֵבֶל יִמָּלֵא יָיִן). As Jeremiah's words had ominous intent, symbolic of the drunkenness to come on the people, so Micah's words conceal a threat: you will create for yourselves prophets who, filled with a lying spirit, will make your blind folly worse (similarly already Theodore of Mopsuestia).

■ **The Shepherd-King and His Flock**

Yahweh, as shepherd-king, will
gather his flock safely into the
fold, and lead them in triumph.

2

12   I will surely gather[a] all[b] of Jacob;
         I will assemble the survivors[c] of Israel.
      I will put them together[d] like a flock in a fold,[e]
         Like a herd inside its pen[f] it will resound[g] with people.
13   [h]The One who Breaks Out has gone up before them.
      They have broken out and gone on their way.
      They have made a breach and gone out of it.
         Their king has gone on before them;
         Yahweh, at the head of them.

a   The LXX συναχθήσεται is passive and third person;
    parallelism requires the MT first person active.
b   With most commentators (cf. the LXX) read כֻּלּוֹ. The
    MT second person may have arisen because this initial
    clause of the oracle could be read as beginning with a
    vocative. The following third persons rule out the MT
    reading. There is a stylistic feature, place name followed
    by "all of it," which is very old. Cf. Ugaritic (17 [2 Aqht]:
    V:21, 31) *tk . ḥqpt . il . klh* ("toward divine Memphis, all
    of it") and Jer 13:19 הָגְלָת יְהוּדָה כֻּלָּהּ, cf. Isa 14:29, 31,
    פְּלָשֶׁת כֻּלֵּךְ.
c   The S has *šarbeh*, "the generation of," which is a free
    translation.
d   The LXX adds τὴν ἀποστροφὴν αὐτῶν which was prob-
    ably influenced by the rather common ἀποστρέφω τὴν
    ἀποστροφήν for שׁוּב שְׁבוּת/שְׁבִית, as at Ezek 16:53.
e   Though we know nothing special about sheep of Bozrah,
    an Edomite fortress city, the MT is not in itself nonsen-
    sical, for Isa 60:7 refers to "flocks of Kedar" and "rams
    of Nebaioth." But whereas in Isaiah the mention of a
    specific place is in order in a context having to do with
    the tribute of foreign lands, here the emphasis is on
    unity, hardly characteristic of any local variety of sheep.
    The parallel *dōber* suggests a common rather than a
    proper noun. Hence most adopt Wetzstein's reading
    (reported in Franz Delitzsch, *Biblischer Commentar über
    den Propheten Jesaia* [Leipzig: Dörfling und Franke,

[5]1897], p 705 n. 1) בְּצִירָה ("in the fold"), from *ṣîrāh*,
cognate with Arabic *ṣira*. Cf. the V *in ovili* and the T
ḥuṭrā' ("sheepfold"). The Hebrew word is supposed by
some to be an alternate form of טִירָה Gen 25:16 "fenced
encampment" but this is phonetically difficult. *a'* (from
Syh) *bglylt'* ("in a round place") may have known a
meaning "fold, fenced-in place" but σ' and θ' ἐν
ὀχυρώματι ("fort") translate as if from בצר ("fortify").
f   Read הַדֹּבֶר ("the pen" [perhaps add the *w* to the
    beginning of the following verb]), with the LXX, S, T,
    and V.
g   The MT is a third or second person feminine plural and
    does not fit; the root is uncertain (הֵמֶם/הוּם/הָמָה).
    Perhaps תֶּהֱמֶה (subject צֹאן, feminine) is to be read, or
    given the consonants of the MT, it could be construed as
    a third feminine singular energic (independent energic,
    i.e., not having an object suffix); in either case, it would
    give the sense translated here. On *hmh m-* cf. Zech 1:17,
    "Once again my cities shall overflow with prosperity"
    (עוֹד תְּפוּצֶינָה עָרַי מִטּוֹב), and "for abundance of inhabi-
    tants" (מֵרֹב אָדָם) Zech 2:8. I do not know the source of
    the LXX ἐξαλοῦνται, "they leap forth," or of the S
    dmagnay ("which is made to lie down").
h   The translation has deliberately been made as literal as
    possible, and the MT retained; for the sense of this, see
    the Commentary. To הַפֹּרֵץ cf. Isa 14:8 הַכֹּרֵת ("the
    hewer").

Commentary

All agree that this hopeful passage interrupts the context
of condemnation and doom in which it is set. Not only is
the intent at odds with the context, but there is no
connection by catchword, and no thematic continuity,
since the shepherd-flock image is not found in adjoining
passages. Condamin held that 2:12–13 had been acciden-

tally transposed from following 4:7,[1] but the evidence is weak, and such suggestions mostly seem to point to the problem. If, as has been proposed (see Introduction, *4. The Form of the Book of Micah*), this passage concludes a major section of the book having the general pattern: doom, then grace, it must still be acknowledged that there is no logical or natural continuity with the foregoing.

The present exposition attempts to avoid being over-specific about these lines, a quality found in many other interpretations which may vary widely in other respects. Aside from the familiar linguistic difficulties in these verses, it is hard to tell where the image of shepherd and flock leaves off, or whether it is present with equal prominence throughout. Also, the actions of a shepherd's life, which shape the imagery derived from it, are not necessarily sequential or unique, but repeated and cyclical; at various times the shepherd leads, heals, gathers, feeds, and protects, and having done these things may repeat any or all of them.

The speaker at the beginning is Yahweh himself, whereas in the second verse (13) he is spoken of in the third person, a stylistic feature shared by the very similar oracle in 4:6–7. He promises to gather the nation, called "Jacob" in keeping with traditional poetic usage. The vocabulary is very similar to that of 4:6–7, including the term "survivors" (שְׁאֵרִית).[2] The great multitude of people within the fold, in this ideal future, seems to be indicated by the phrase "it will resound with people," but the text is rather uncertain.

If the picture of a flock continues through v 13, as is often held, the united flock is released from the pen and marches out, with God as the leader. This has the advantage of striving for a consistent reading, but encounters some difficulties. "Breaking out" of the fold is not a desirable thing for sheep to do, certainly not something a shepherd would do for a flock. Note Mishnah Baba Qama 6,1: "If it breaks out by night . . . and goes out and does damage" (נִפְרְצָה בַלַּיְלָה . . . וְיָצְאָה וְהִזִּיקָה). Some

understand the "Breaker" to be a title of God as the divine bell wether, but this departs from the picture of the shepherd-king, and offers an unparalleled and downright bizarre conception.

An alternate view is that with the change in speaker at v 13 comes abandonment of the flock-shepherd image, so we may read the verse as a less figurative depiction of God's rule, and especially his military leadership, in the ideal future. The unique title הַפֹּרֵץ is perhaps related to use of the verb פרץ in passages describing the unpredictable outlashing of divine energy occasionally referred to elsewhere, as in 2 Sam 5:20 "Yahweh has broken out on my enemies like onrushing flood waters" (פָּרַץ יהוה אֶת־אֹיְבַי לְפָנַי כְּפֶרֶץ מָיִם); cf. Exod 19:22; 2 Sam 6:8; Ps 80:13; and 89:41 (EV 40). With Yahweh at their head, his people also will break through all restraints and obstacles, and march in triumph. Hos 2:2 (EV 1:11) conveys a similar thought.

Thus understood, the passage is too general to be an unmistakable reference to any set of historical circumstances. Quite commonly, this has been taken to be obviously exilic or post-exilic; Mays divides into two parts, both post-exilic. The arguments for this position, summarized by Smith, are unimpressive, the strongest being that these verses presuppose the dispersion of the people. But the loss of the Northern Kingdom in 722 and the large deportations by Sennacherib in 701 might easily have suggested in the eighth century that the flock of God was in need of gathering. On the other hand, the attempts by Schmidt[3] and Sellin to read this as a rather exact *description* of events of 701, where the people of Judah were packed into Jerusalem under siege, and then broke out, is over-specific on the other side, and wide of the mark. Cramming of a besieged people into Jerusalem would hardly be described as Yahweh's gathering of his flock, and one would not speak of release from Jerusalem as "going up," for one "went up" *to* Jerusalem.

If the oracle is of a more general, non-specific nature, there is nothing decisive against thinking it early or even

---

1   Albert Condamin, "Interpolations ou transpositions accidentelles?" *RB* 7 (1902): 379–97.

2   On this term and the related literature see Werner E. Müller, *Die Vorstellung vom Rest im Alten Testament,* ed. Horst Dietrich Preuss (Neukirchen: Neukirchener, 1973).

3   Hans Schmidt, *Micha*, SAT, Abteilung 2, Band 2, *Die grossen Propheten* (Göttingen: Vandenhoeck &

Ruprecht, ²1923).

by Micah, if one allows for positive, visionary elements in his thought; the position of these verses in the book remains unexplained.

From very early—in fact since Ibn Ezra—this passage has been believed by some to be the words of the false prophets of Micah's time. Most recently this view is held in an elaborated form by van der Woude. But Margolis already observed: "It is not likely that the false prophets concerned themselves with the events following the downfall of the nation, which contingency they were most emphatic in denying."[4]

---

4   Max L. Margolis, *Micah* (Philadelphia: Jewish Publication Society, 1908).

■ **The Courts as Cannibals**
The heads and judges, though
responsible for justice, prefer
wrong to right, and devour
the weak. One day the judges will
have to call on Yahweh, and he will
not answer.

3

1 And he will say:[a]
   Hear,[b] O heads of Jacob,[c]
     Judges[d] of the house of Israel!
   Is it not your duty to know justice,
2 You haters of right and lovers[e] of wrong?[f]
   Who rob their skin off them,
     And the flesh from their bones,[g]
3 Who[h] eat the flesh of my people
     And strip the skin off them,
   Break their bones and serve them up[i]
     Like flesh[j] in a pot
     And like meat inside a kettle—
4 Then[k] they will cry to Yahweh,
     And he will not answer them
   But hide[l] his face from them at that time[m]
     Just as they have done evil deeds.[n]

a The LXX καὶ ἐρεῖ is for וְאָמַר, cf. the S. Perhaps this is an
editorial addition linking this oracle to the preceding.
The MT וָאֹמַר ("and I said") has been defended as a
remnant of a longer, perhaps narrative context (Budde;
"Micah 2 und 3," Sellin, Weiser), which is possible, but
encounters the objection that though this verb form
often introduces the prophetic *response* to a message
from God (e.g., Amos 7:2; Isa 6:5, 8, 11; and Jer 1:6), it
never introduces this kind of oracle. More likely, then,
the first person form of the MT is a change from the
original third, reflecting an interpretation of the oracle
as the prophet's word (in the light of 3:9 and the rest of
the chapter). Similar confusion is present at Isa 40:6 with
וָאֹמַר for וְאָמַר.

J. T. Willis' article ("A Note on ואמר in Micah 3:1,"
ZAW 80 [1968]: 50–54) is an exhaustive survey of proposals on this problem; his own view, that "and I said" is
a redactor's addition to emphasize the break between
chaps 2 and 3, is improbable. In Mays's opinion, Micah
introduced this phrase himself to link 2:6–11 and 3:1–4,
"to show that they were spoken to the same addressees,"
which is not strictly true, since there is no reason to think
that chap 2 is addressed to judges and magistrates. Van
der Woude retains the first person and makes this oracle
a response and rebuttal to the hopeful message of 2:12–
13, which is supposed to have been spoken by the
pseudo-prophets. Fuller discussion of van der Woude's

general view is given at 4:9; note that here, 3:1–4 is
scarcely a reply to 2:12–13, though it contrasts with it.
In making this textually dubious word "die entschei-
dende Interpretationshilfe" for chap 3, Lescow lays a
very shaky foundation (see Theodor Lescow, "Redaktionsgeschichtliche Analyse von Micha 1–5" *ZAW* 84
[1972]: 46–85).

b The LXX and S add "this"; they are influenced by v 9.
c The LXX has "the house of Jacob," cf. mss Kenn. and de
Rossi; influenced by v 9. α' and θ' are reported to have
"house" also, but in Ziegler's opinion the reading is due
to the LXX's influence, see *Beiträge*, p 367 (*Sylloge*, p 93).
d The LXX here and in v 9 has οἱ κατάλοιποι ("remaining
ones"), which is an unexplained rendering. Rudolph's
proposal that קָצִין was associated by the translator with
קָצֶה "end" is ad hoc. See also commentary.
e The LXX ζητοῦντες ("seekers"), if a translation of אהב, is
paralleled (doubtfully) only in mss at Prov 8:17, and note
that all occurrences of forms and derivatives of אָהֵב in
the Twelve are rendered by forms of ἀγαπᾶν including
Mic 6:8 (except for the lovers of the faithless woman in
Hosea, who are ἐρασταί). Thus the LXX may represent
מְבַקְשֵׁי; the expression to "seek" wrong (to harm someone) is more common than to "love" wrong (only Ps
52:5; [EV 3]; for the former, Num 35:23; I Sam 24:10;
25:26; I Kgs 20:7; Ps 71:13, 24; and Esth 9:2). The MT
is preferable because it has the rare form.

f   Q רָע and K רָעָה are variants indistinguishable in sense.

g   Commentators have been troubled by lack of antecedents for the pronouns "their" and "them" and the resemblance in sense to 3b and c. Some have been content to put 2b after v 3 (Lindblom, *Micha*, reading וְגָזְלוּ; Weiser, reading גָּזְלוּ), or after 5a "my people" (Nowack, Duhm, Sellin, Marti, reading הַגּוֹזְלִים). Wellhausen and others delete as a doublet of 3b and c, or a gloss. Others delete other things: Rudolph "and strip the skin off them" of 3b; Ehrlich, *Randglossen*, and Lindblom, *Micha*, still other variations. The MT, supported by the versions, is retained here, in this way: 1) the antecedent of the suffixes "them," "their" is understood to be "Jacob" and "the house of Israel"; 2) this syntactic progression is recognized—vocatives after an imperative (v 1), then participles continuing the vocative (v 2), followed by a switch to relative clauses continuing the vocative (v 3) with third person, finally, judgment pronounced, with second person abandoned for third person. The elements of this pattern are discernible in *hôy*-oracles, where the participles commonly used are vocatives, often continued by a third person(note Isa 5:8, 11); the conclusion often reverts to second person, but may be in third person. Amos 6:1–7 illustrates the pattern well; cf. Isa 5:13–14; 5:24, and see Hillers, "Hôy and hôy-Oracles," Freedman Festschrift, forthcoming. On the order, note that the three elements "flesh . . . skin . . . bones" in v 3 occur, in that order, in Lam 3:4; cf. Job 19:20.

h   The LXX has ὅν τρόπον connecting vv 3 and 4. This might reflect כַּאֲשֶׁר, usually rendered ὅν τρόπον in the

Twelve and elsewhere; decidedly inferior to the MT. The LXX more likely read אֲשֶׁר, cf. 5:7 and Zech 11:13, in which case the reading is little different from the MT, though the LXX seems indefensible as a translation.

i   The MT וּפָרְשׂוּ as if from פרשׂ ("spread out") gives no satisfactory sense, so the verb is taken as פרס ("divide" [as does the LXX]). Since "divide" does not seem especially characteristic of what is done to meat inside a pot, "serve up" is tentatively proposed here, since פרס is used of doling out bread in Isa 58:7 and Lam 4:4. The object "them" (referring to the people) is supplied from the context. See also Th. Nöldeke, "Mene tekel upharsin," *ZA* 1 (1886): 414–418.

j   With the LXX ὡς σάρκας read כִּשְׁאֵר along with many commentators.

k   For the LXX οὕτως ("so") see on v 3 above.

l   The MT וְיִסְתֵּר is a jussive form without jussive sense; cf. Gesenius' para. 109k.

m   This is deleted by Smith, Marti, and others as disturbing the meter or as repetitive misunderstanding in a temporal sense (Ehrlich, *Randglossen*, and Ina Willi-Plein, *Vorformen der Schriftexegese innerhalb des Alten Testaments*, BZAW 123 [1971]). But meter and parallelism here are not strict, and אָז may well have a temporal sense, though not technically eschatological. "At that time" serves to make אָז more explicit; cf. "on that day" 2:4.

n   The LXX adds ἐπ᾽ αὐτούς, which may be for עֲלֵיהֶם. Perhaps one could explain this on the basis of dittography but עֲלֵיהֶם is really different from מַעַלְלֵיהֶם.

Commentary

This oracle is linked to what follows, verbally (3:1 with 3:4, 7, 9), and thematically, as a pronouncement of judgment on the ruling classes. The links to the preceding are less obvious, and have been less noticed, perhaps because commentators have been content to identify 2:12–13 as a salvation-oracle intrusive in a collection of genuine oracles of Micah. But note the correspondence of "Jacob . . . Israel" (2:12; 3:1) and "with Yahweh at their head" (2:13) and the address to the "heads" of Jacob and Israel (3:1); this is something between a mere verbal echo or catchword and a comment on various kinds of leadership. After the picture of saving rule by Yahweh the picture of misrule by his deputies comes as a foil. The "then" and "at that time" of 3:4 are drawn into the picture of the future salvation begun in 2:12–13. Whatever the true origin and sense of ואמר (see Note), the LXX "and he will say" makes the dependence of chap. 3 on 2:13 explicit (perhaps the odd translation by the LXX

of "remnant" for קְצִינֵי is further attempt to stress the continuity with 2:12, where καταλοίπους is used for שְׁאֵרִית "remnant").

The "heads" and "judges" of vv 1, 9, and 11, are the men responsible for administering justice in the community. They were probably family and clan heads. As Knierim notes, the fact that they are linked in vv 9–12 with priests and prophets shows that they have a kind of sacral function (Exodus 18).[1] Though it is undeniably true that the king is not mentioned here or in any indictment for perversion of justice in Micah, this does not, unfortunately, permit any conclusion as to the prophet's attitude toward Hezekiah (or other kings he knew). Isaiah (1:10–20, 21–23; 3:14) and Amos (2:6–7; 5:7, 10–13) also delivered severe indictments addressed to "judges" in the plural, not singling out the king, but this does not of course define their relation to an Ahaz or Jeroboam II, which we know of only on the basis of other passages. It is fairly common, in protests by peasants or

---

1   Rolf Knierim, "Exodus 18 und die Neuordnung der mosaischen Gerichtsbarkeit," *ZAW* 73 (1961): 158–59; cf. J.R. Bartlett, "The Use of the Word ראש as a

Title in the Old Testament," *VT* 19 (1969): 1–10.

other lower orders, for the deprived and oppressed to believe the king to be innocent, ignorant of their plight and surrounded by evil ministers.

In calling the nation "Jacob" and "house of Israel" Micah continues an old religious tradition, and a poetic one, for "Jacob" is the A word to "Israel" as the B word in poetry, from ancient times, thus in Num 23:7, 10, etc.[2] Mic 3:9 shows that these titles were applied by the prophet to the Southern Kingdom, centered at Jerusalem, but that does not necessarily define the sense here in v 1, or place the passage with certainty after the fall of Samaria. The point is that the leaders identify themselves as heads and judges of the people of God, and the prophet accepts and exploits this identification.

The charge that they are "haters of right, and lovers of wrong" is unique in precisely this formulation, and thus unusually pointed. There are, however, close parallels in the eighth century prophets, so that the idea was current in Micah's time. Amos 5:15 is a positive formulation of the ideal for judges: "Hate wrong and love right, and establish justice in the gate"; cf. Prov 5:12; 8:13, Ps 45:8 (EV 7); 97:10, and Isa 61:8. The reversal of this ideal in practise is denounced in Isa 5:20: "You who call wrong right and right wrong" and Amos 5:10: "They hate anyone who gives reproof in court"; cf. Job 34:17.

What these judges "hate" and "love" is טוב and רָע, that is "good" and "bad" as these general terms relate to the courts, hence "right" and "wrong" or "justice" and "injustice." The association of Hebrew "hate" and "love", in legal contexts, provide the progression to the term "rob." Just as a good judge "hates" profiting by his decisions (Exod 18:21 and Prov 28:16) so the besetting sin of unjust judges was "love" of a bribe (Isa 1:23; cf. Mic 3:11; 7:11, etc.), making them "partners with thieves" (גַּנָּבִים; Isa 1:23), who may be said to "rob of

their rights the poor of my people" וְלִגְזֹל מִשְׁפַּט עֲנִיֵּי עַמִּי (Isa 10:2, NJPS).

The greed of the judges is such, and so great is its baneful effect on the weak, that they can be said to rob the skin and flesh from their victims. In itself only hyperbole for their rapacity and cruelty, this expression leads over to a figure of cannibalism: the judges eat their prey, cracking the bones (presumably for the marrow) and tearing off the hide (as inedible, but of value). The closest parallel is the charge against the shepherds (rulers) in Ezek 34:2–3: "Should not shepherds feed the sheep? You eat the fat, you clothe yourselves with the wool; you slaughter the fatlings; but you do not feed the sheep" (cf. Isa 9:19 and Zech 11:9). The evildoers of Ps 14:4 equals 53:5 (EV 4) "devour my people as they devour bread." The final detail, the meat in the kettle, is paralleled in a different context in Ezekiel 11, and graphically in Ezekiel 24. Cf. also Hab 3:14 "to devour the poor in secret" (לֶאֱכֹל עָנִי בַּמִּסְתָּר).

Abruptly the prophet speaks of a time to come when the judges will be in trouble. Then they will call on Yahweh, but he will not answer them (this is the reverse of the promise of salvation of Isa 58:9, "Then you shall call, and the Lord will answer"; cf. Jer 11:11). He will hide his face because of their evil deeds. After the vivid indictment, this announcement of judgment is colorless and conventional (Prov 1:28; Job 35:12; Deut 31:17, 18; and Jer 33:5). Yet it amounts to saying that they will have no god, since "calling" and "answering" is used so often to describe the normal, desirable relation of worshipper and deity (Zech 13:9; Isa 58:9; Jer 33:3; Job 13:22; 14:15; and Isa 65:24).

---

2 "A word" and "B word" are convenient terms for words traditionally used in the first and second lines of a pair of poetic lines in parallelism.

■ **False Prophets and a Real Prophet**

Those prophets who give oracles
for profit will suffer loss of
word and vision, but Micah is full
of unfailing power.

3

5   Thus says Yahweh:
     "Woe to you[a] prophets,
        You who mislead my people.
     You cry peace[b] when you bite with your teeth,
        But if a man does not put[c] something in your mouth
           You prepare holy war[d] against him,
6   Therefore it will be night[e] for you, not vision;
        And darkness[f] for you, not prophecy.[g]
     The sun will go down on the prophets
        And the day grow dark on them.
7   Then the seers will be frustrated,
        And the mantics helpless;
     All will cover the upper lip,[h]
        When there is no response from God."[i]
8   But[j] I am full of power, of the spirit of Yahweh,
        And of judgment, and of strength,[k]
     To tell Jacob his rebellion,
        And Israel his sin.

a   After the introductory "messenger-formula," where does
    the word of Yahweh begin? Surely v 6 which uses the
    word "you" two times is direct address, but לָכֵן ("there-
    fore") is an improbable beginning for an oracle, and עַמִּי
    ("my people") suggests that the word of Yahweh begins
    earlier (Sellin's עַם יהוה ["people of Y."] and George's עַמּוֹ
    ["his people"] deal with the latter problem, but not the
    former). Here הַמַּתְעִים has been construed as vocative,
    which is grammatically possible (cf. Amos 2:7; 5:7; 6:13;
    and Isa 42:18 for occurrence at the beginning of an
    oracle). Yet one expects at least a הוֹי, if not a "Hear, O
    prophets" or the like, so perhaps something is missing
    from the text at the beginning of the oracle. Nowack,
    following Budde, "Micha 2 und 3," proposed הוֹי for עַל; I
    have preferred to read הוֹי עַל "Woe to you prophets,"
    supposing a haplography from *yhwh hwy. For the con-
    struction cf. Jer 50:27 and especially Ezek 13:3, which is
    a very close parallel to the conjectured reading.

b   The LXX adds ἐπ' αὐτόν ("to him"); this is probably
    introduced from the following sentence to clarify the
    statement.

c   The LXX may have read a different grammatical form,
    and α', σ', and θ' may have the plural, but see Ziegler,
    "Beiträge," p 367 (Sylloge, p 93).

d   The Hebrew literally means to "sanctify war," whereas
    the LXX ἤγειραν means to "stir up." To the LXX trans-
    lators the use of the Hebrew technical idiom may have

    seemed unsuitable for a private matter (Rudolph), or just
    un-Greek.

e   The Hebrew lacks a verb; none need be supplied (contra
    Wellhausen), cf. Jer 50:35–38.

f   The LXX σκοτία (ὑμῖν ἔσται), which probably reflects
    וַחֲשֵׁכָה ("darkness") is preferred by almost all commen-
    tators as yielding a syntactical parallel to the preceding
    colon. The MT וְחָשְׁכָה ("and it will be dark") is reflected
    in R κα]ι σκοτασθ[ήσεται υμ]ειν which may confirm that
    the third feminine singular was idiomatic in this ex-
    pression. Possibly the MT arose as syntactically easier, or
    more prosaic.

g   The Hebrew is מִקְסֹם, an infinitive; it is pressing parallel-
    ism too far to repoint to מְקַסֵּם as Marti and others have
    done.

h   The LXX καὶ καταλαλήσουσι κατ' αὐτῶν ("and they will
    speak against them") is quite different, probably due to
    the misunderstanding of an idiom unfamiliar to the
    translator.

i   The LXX ὁ εἰσακούων αὐτῶν is perhaps for אֲלֵיהֶם, לָהֶם,
    or אֱלֹהֶם.

j   The LXX ἐὰν μὴ ("if not") does not necessarily imply אִם
    לֹא; in Amos 7:7 the LXX thus renders כִּי אִם ("unless,
    except"), and the LXX in general uses a variety of ren-
    derings for the relatively infrequent אוּלָם. Note the
    transliteration at Gen 28:19 and the conditional (ἐὰν δὲ)
    at 1 Kgs 20 (LXX 21):23.

k   The list is usually thought to be overloaded and unbalanced metrically. Some would delete כֹּחַ "power"; many more eliminate the phrase אֶת־רוּחַ יהוה not only because of its length, but 1) as a gloss (Marti, Sellin, and many others); 2) because the spirit of Yahweh cannot be listed along with the attributes created by it (Rudolph); 3) because it alone has אֵת (Smith and Robinson deal with this Gordian knot by deleting the אֵת); and 4) as prosaic. It is noted that if genuine, this reference to the spirit of Yahweh would be unique in the pre-exilic prophets. But the line seems metrically adequate, being by accents 4 plus 4 (or 2 plus 2, 2 plus 2); by syllables 10 plus 10.

None of the terms supposed to be "glossed" by "the spirit of Yahweh" is obscure. The prophet as man of the *spirit* may be attested elsewhere in Micah; see 2:11. The expression is not anachronistic, cf. 2 Sam 23:2 and Isa 30:1. Nor is it especially theological—it might be thought of as rather primitive.

Commentary

This passage, clearly marked off from the foregoing by the "messenger-formula," rare in Micah (only otherwise at 2:3), is nevertheless thematically related to earlier elements. It resumes the indictment of crowd-pleasing prophets of 2:11, and it is closely tied to a major theme of the oracle against the judges, whose cannibal rapacity is echoed by the petty greed of the prophets. There are verbal echoes as well: "my people" (עַמִּי, vv 3 and 5); "he will not answer them" (v 4) and "there is no response from God" (v 7); the nation is "Jacob and Israel" (vv 1 and 8). The equipment of the true prophet includes "judgment," the quality sought in vain from the judges (v 1). Most of these themes are picked up in the culminating oracle which follows, 3:9–12.

Formally, vv 5–8 are much like 1–4. Each opens by calling on certain people to hear, and in the description of the hearers lies the charge against them, so that the sentence follows directly. Unusual is the prominence given to the prophet's conviction about himself. 1:8–9 is similar in that the prophet gives his personal reaction to his own preceding oracle of doom, but at that point he expresses solidarity with the people, even as a sinful people. Here the "I" is set off from the other prophets, and from the people as well. Taken together, these two passages express in brief the tension that the man Micah experienced in his calling, a theme expanded at length by Jeremiah.

The language of the charge against the prophets is vivid and compressed. "You bite with your teeth," in this context, seems to refer principally to the prophets' appetite, perhaps proverbial in Israel, which may be read from Amaziah's contemptuous "Eat bread there" addressed to Amos (Amos 7:12). But the phrase conveys overtones of animal ferocity, recalling the cannibal figure of 3:3. As the oracle goes on, it seems that what Micah depicts is not so much the prophets in their grandest capacity as national leaders, but as venders of petty oracles consulted by the common people. If paid (fed) adequately, they will say: "Peace! All is well."[1] But if left hungry they screw themselves to the highest pitch of spiritual dignity and "sanctify war" against their customers. Though the expression "sanctify war" recurs (Jer 6:42 and Joel 4:9), it is not clear what precise role the prophet played in making an upcoming conflict "holy," since ritual preparations not involving prophets were an important part of achieving the desired consecration. But a variety of activities connected prophets to war;[2] especially the advice to the king: "Go into battle."

If we understand the imagery correctly, the prophets are venal in little things. Unlike the gruesome judges, they appear as pests, not monsters. Precisely in this reduction of their ancient role—recall "By a prophet Yahweh brought Israel up from Egypt"—lies their misleading of the people. By self-seeking they have made themselves powerless.

The punishment that is announced may seem in this case the obvious outcome of the crime, or not even an "outcome" in the sense of what follows, but the immediate logical accompaniment. We think of them as conscious frauds, or at least as self-deceived. Yet the extended description of the night and darkness in which

---

1   Mays notes that Jeremiah and Ezekiel used "There is no peace" as a slogan against the prophetic opposition (Jer 6:14; 8:11; 12:12; 30:3; Ezek 13:10 and 16).

2   Duane L. Christensen, *Transformations of the War Oracle in Old Testament Prophecy* (Missoula: Scholars Press, 1975), 15.

the prophets will be helpless because there is no divine response, shows that Micah recognizes the reality of visions and dreams and does not deny these seers at present the possession of some sort of prophetic charisma. This will be withdrawn, however, and they will feel its absence. They will experience a famine of the word of God, as described in Amos 8:11–12.

The figure of darkness, night, and sunset exploits the specific associations of dark with inability to see (cf. Isa 29:18) and the more general associations with what is ominous and threatening. As Rudolph has pointed out, here and in v 11 no pejorative sense is present in forms of קסם. Whatever the sense elsewhere, here קֹסֵם is another word for "prophet," and the verb most likely means "to do what a prophet does" without specific reference to use of any technical means. Here "divination," and "divine" would be misleading as translations. It is not technique that is condemned, but the sale of prophecy.

To cover the upper lip, or mustache, was a gesture of mourning (Ezek 24:17, 22) and a sign required of a leper (Lev 13:45). It is symbolically congruent, then, with another association of "night," namely death and exclusion from society. A close verbal parallel to 3:7 is Zech 13:4, "Every prophet will be ashamed of his vision" (יֵבֹשׁוּ הַנְּבִיאִים אִישׁ מֵחֶזְיֹנוֹ).

The striking feature of Micah's list of those qualities and gifts with which he is filled is their scope and grandeur. He claims "power" and "might," which are rather general terms but often associated with military prowess. He has the spirit of Yahweh, the charismatic gift associated with various kinds of leadership in ancient Israel. Most strikingly, he has "judgment," the gift or authority for judgment, an area associated earlier in the chapter to the "heads" and "chiefs," and claimed in another passage for the king, Ps 72:1 and 1 Kgs 3:9. With good reason this list has been compared to the attributes of the Messiah-figure of Isaiah 11. It recalls also the various roles filled by Moses. If in fact, at least in later periods, the role of the prophet was mostly that of communicator of the divine word, Micah could nevertheless enunciate a view of the office as embracing other roles or taking precedence over them.

Micah is called to declare to the nation their rebellion and sin. (Cf. Isa 58:1, "Declare to my people their transgression, to the house of Jacob their sin" [וְהַגֵּד . . . לְעַמִּי פִּשְׁעָם וּלְבֵית יַעֲקֹב חַטֹּאתָם] In the context of this chapter and the preceding chapters, the rebellion lies in the abuse of divinely delegated power by those in political and religious authority. The judgment will, of course, strike the whole nation.

■ **Zion Shall Be Plowed as a Field**

In Jerusalem all the machinery of
a rule of God is present, yet all
has been perverted and those
responsible still think Yahweh
is with them! Therefore the
symbols of His presence, city and
temple, will be destroyed.

3

9   Hear this, heads of the house of Jacob,[a]
   Judges[b] of the house of Israel,
Who abhor justice
   And pervert all that is right,
10 Who build[c] Zion at the price of bloodshed,
   Jerusalem at the cost of wrongdoing![d]
11 Her heads judge for bribes
   And her priests give instruction for pay,
     While her prophets give oracles for money.
All the while they rely on Yahweh, and say,
   "Surely Yahweh is in our midst;
     No harm shall come upon us."
12 Therefore[e] on your account
Zion shall be plowed as field,
   Jerusalem shall become ruins,[f]
     And the temple mount shall belong to the wild animals.[g]

a   Comparing 3:1a, where "house" is absent from a similar
   clause, and appealing to meter, Sellin and Rudolph
   would delete. But the additon of זֹאת ("this") may be
   regarded as producing a tripartite line, perhaps 2 plus 2
   plus 3, so the MT may stand.
b   The LXX has κατάλοιποι ("remnant"); see on 3:1 above.
c   The MT singular participle בֹּנֶה is inexplicable, except
   as a chance error. Whether the LXX, S, T, and V attest
   a Hebrew reading בֹּנַי may be doubted, because a translator is compelled to render as plural in this context. The
   infinitive absolute בָּנֹה (Paul Kleinert, *Obadja, Jona,*
   Micha, Nahum, Habakkuk, Zephanha, Theologisches-
   homiletisches Bibelwerk, ed. J. P. Lange [Bielefeld &
   Leipzig: Velhagen and Klasing, ³1893], Ehrlich, *Rand-*
   glossen, and Rudolph) is an ingenious repointing to
   preserve the MT, but stylistically most improbable; even
   more so is Willi-Plein's נְבֶנָה or בְּנֵיה (Ina Willi-Plein,
   Vorformen der Schriftexegese innerhalb des Alten Testaments,
   BZAW 123 (1971).
d   There is no need to restore a second verb from Hab
   2:12 (so Robinson).
e   "Thus says the Lord" is in place in the narrative of Jer

   26:18, but not required or especially appropriate here
   (against Budde, "Micha 2 und 3," Nowack, Sellin).
f   The MT has עִיִּין, while the more common עִיִּים stands in
   Jer 26:18, cf. mss Kenn and de Rossi and Ps 79:1 . . .
   שָׂמוּ אֶת־יְרוּשָׁלַם לְעִיִּים. The MT is a dialect variant of the
   masculine plural.
g   The MT here and at Jer 26:18 has לְבָמוֹת יַעַר ("wooded
   heights") with plural after singular "mount." The
   versions have probably smoothed this out (the LXX is
   especially unreliable as to singular and plural in the
   Twelve). Ehrlich, *Randglossen,* first proposed "wild
   animals" from בַּהֲמוֹת יַעַר of 5:7 and 1 ms Kenn לבהמות.
   A parallel, both in the phrase and in the zeugma (using
   the same verb in two slightly different constructions)
   occurs in Mal 1:3. For parallels in extra-biblical texts and
   a fuller discussion, see Delbert R. Hillers, *Treaty-Curses*
   and the Old Testament Prophets. Biblica et Orientalia 16
   (Rome: Pontifical Biblical Institute, 1964): 44–54.

Commentary

Themes announced in the first three chapters are gathered here, in a quantity that makes a detailed exposition unnecessary. There are close ties, not always recognized, to the following oracle, which will be enumerated in commentary on 4:1–5; the remarks here will only prepare the ground.

The opening address to the "heads" and "judges," and the charge that they actually abhor justice, recall the beginning of this chapter. Though the prophet brings the court of law to the fore as the center of injustice, he leads over into the idea of a general abuse of power within the society with: "(who) pervert all that is right." "Justice" and "right" then mean all sound relations within the people of God.

Their authority and activity is centered at Jerusalem, and is associated with "building" the city.

It seems impossible to suppose that Micah does not have the royal court in mind. As a result, the fact that he does not use the word "king" here is somewhat problematic, especially in view of the picture given by the Deuteronomistic historian of Hezekiah as especially active in building and in cultic matters. But one feature of some millennial movements is a naive belief that the highest authority (often the king) is good and kind, however evil the regime; see on 3:1–4.

Building Zion with blood is not so mundane a crime as putting up one's own fine town house there (Weiser et al.). Building the holy city, its fortifications, palaces, and temple, is a divine prerogative (Ps 51:20 [EV 18] and 102:17 [EV 16]), transferred in the visible kingdom to the ruler. As such, the action is potentially holy and right, as is judging, giving of priestly instruction, or prophecy. Abuse of the sacred is, however, the worst of transgressions. We know from the archaeological record that a great deal of building was in fact going on in the Jerusalem of Micah's time; see Introduction, 3. *Micah as Prophet of a New Age.* Micah evidently regarded this as a kind of sacrilege, because it is done at the cost of blood.

We must not restrict the sense of "at the price of blood" to fatal accidents during construction. Only poetic style separates "bloodshed" from "wrongdoing." They must be regarded as a kind of hendiadys, and refer to oppression of the weak by the mighty, which Micah attacks again and again and which he views as amounting to the taking of life for profit.

Judges ("heads"), priests, and prophets sit in Jerusalem and sell their wares; justice, religious teaching, and the inspired word of God are all for sale. The sin of the priests is commented on by Mal 2:9, "you show partiality in your rulings" (NJPS) (וְנֹשְׂאִים פָּנִים בַּתּוֹרָה). Weingreen has argued plausibly that the sense here is "her priests give judicial directives for a price," that is, take bribes to pervert the rules of religious conduct.[1] The charge against the prophets resembles that of 3:5. Note that it is not their technique (יקסמו) which is attacked, for קָסַם is for Micah apparently a neutral term for "give an oracular response." It is the prophets' venality which excites his anger. For a similar oracle, see Zeph 3:1–4.

The final folly of the people is reliance on God and his sacred place, in the face of such guilt. For "lean on" equals "rely" see Is 31:1; 10:20; 2 Chr 13:18; and 14:10 (EV 11).

The famous prophecy of the destruction of Jerusalem is cast in readily intelligible form. That Zion should be plowed as a field, and become ruins, echoes the oracle on Samaria, 1:6. That wild animals should live in the deserted city is a frequent theme in biblical literature, thus Isa 13:19–22; 34:11–17; Zeph 2:13–15; Jer 50:39, and also in other ancient Near Eastern literature[2] A passage from the first Sefire treaty (Sf I A 32–33, from ca. 750 B.C,) illustrates the use of this threat, and also the sequence: the city becomes a ruin-heap (*tl*, תל or עִי), and then is infested by wild animals: "And may Arpad become a mound to [house the desert animal and the] gazelle and the fox and the hare and the wild-cat and the owl and the [ ] and the magpie."[3]

1   J. Weingreen, "The Title Moreh Sedek," *JSS* 6 (1961): 162–74.

2   Hillers, *Treaty Curses,* 44–54.

3   Ibid., p 44.

■ **The Kingdom to Come**

**In the ideal future Yahweh's
earthly dwelling will be
transfigured, and he will rule
over all peoples from Zion,
bringing justice and peace to
the world and security to his
people, who now can only wait
in hope.**

4

1 The time will come[a] when the mountain[b] of Yahweh
    Will stand firm[c] over the mountaintops,[d]
      And it[e] will be lifted up above the hills.
    Then peoples will stream[f] to it[g]
2   And many nations[h] will come, and say,[i]
    "Come, let us go up to the mountain of Yahweh,
      To[j] the house of the God of Jacob,
    That he may teach us[k] of his ways,
      That we may walk in his paths."
    For out of Zion[l] shall come instruction,
      And the word of Yahweh from Jerusalem.
3 And he shall decide disputes between many peoples
    And arbitrate for mighty nations, far-off nations,[m]
    So that they will beat their swords into plowshares,
      And their spears into pruning-hooks.
    One nation will not raise[n] the sword against another,
      And they will no longer train for war.[o]
    Each man will sit under his own vine
      And under[p] his own fig tree, with none to disturb them,
    For the mouth of Yahweh Sebaoth has spoken.
5 "Though every nation walks in the name of its own god,[q]
    We will walk in the name of Yahweh our God forever and ever."

Preliminary Note.

Variants between the MT of Mic 4:1–4 and Isa 2:2–4 have
been recorded here, but sometimes without comment, since
some are of such a nature that there is little if any basis for a
preference.

a   בְּאַחֲרִית הַיָּמִים is not necessarily a late expression; see E.
Lipiński, "באחרית הימים dans les textes préexiliques," *VT*
20 (1970): 445–50 and the bibliography there.

b   This translation agrees with the LXX of Micah; the MT
of Micah and Isa 2:2 add בֵּ ("of the house of"
[Yahweh]), which could well have been added under the
influence of 3:12 or 4:2. The LXX of Isa 2:2 has τὸ ὄρος
τοῦ κυρίου καὶ ὁ οἶκος τοῦ θεοῦ (cf. α', σ', and θ' [Syh] θεου
"God" for "Lord" ad Mic 4:1), a conflate reading which
points to early variants of the introductory line.

c   Isa 2:2 puts נכון before יהוה. The Micah text is perhaps
superior in poetic style, with the נכון clause followed by
the נשא clause. The LXX of Mic 4:1 has a double rendering of נכון (ἐμφανὲς . . . ἕτοιμον), the first introduced
from Isa 2:2.

d   IQIs[a] lacks the article. Rudolph and H. Wildberger "Die

Völkerwallfahrt zum Zion Jes. II 1–5," *VT* 7 (1957): 62–
81, favor construing *b* as *beth essentiae*, translating "as
chief of the mountains." But the common רֹאשׁ (singular
or plural) הָהָר (singular or plural) seems everywhere to
mean "mountain-top(s)." The expression here seems to
combine two ideas: the mountain will be unmovable
(נכון) and high, the latter made explicit in the following
colon. Cf. John Kselman, "A Note on Isaiah II 2," *VT* 25
(1975): 225–27, for a suggestive, though to me unconvincing, treatment of this verse.

e   The MT of Micah has הוּא; this is missing in Isa 2:2.

f   This translation is based upon the understanding of וְנָהֲרוּ
as related to נָהָר "river," which is explicit already in α'
and σ'. H. Wildberger, "Die Völkerwallfahrt zum Zion
Jes. II 1–5," *VT* 7 (1957): 62–81, supposes that this may
be a reinterpretation of the "river" that flows from Zion
(Ps 46:5), but this seems fanciful, since the direction of
flow is reversed. NJPS "shall gaze on it with joy,"
associates the verb with "light" and verbal uses in Isa
60:5; Jer 31:12,; and Ps 34:6 (EV 5).

g   Micah has עָלָיו but Isa 2:2 has אֵלָיו (IQIs[a] עלוהי). With the
sense of the rare verb in doubt, there is no firm basis for

h   Isa 2:2 and 3 "all the nations . . . many peoples." So many
    mss of Micah, the S, and T.

i   Marti and Nowack (cf. BH³) would delete as a prosaic
    gloss. But this is in keeping with prophetic style (see
    Introduction).

j   Isa 2:3 has אֶל, but Micah has וְאֶל.

k   The LXX καὶ δείξουσιν and IQIsᵃ וירונו ("and they will
    teach us"), perhaps arises from transposition of letters
    out of ויורנו.

l   A close parallel in construction is Isa 37:32.

m   This is not in Isa 2:4; it is deleted by many commentators
    as disturbing the meter, which may be true, and as a
    gloss, which is scarcely correct since it does not explain
    anything in the context. (Rudolph's "that will happen
    only in a long time" is fanciful). In light of the expression
    "far-off nation" (גּוֹי רָחוֹק) Joel 4:8 (EV 3:8); Jer גּוֹי מִמֶּרְחָק

5:15 (cf. Jer 31:10 and the adjectival use of the prepo-
    sitions in Isa 5:26 גּוֹיִם מֵרָחוֹק and Jer 23:23 אֱלֹהֵי מֵרָחוֹק),
    I propose that the Micah text is a conflation of variants
    גּוֹיִם עַד רָחוֹק and גּוֹיִם עֲצֻמִים, neither obviously superior.

n   Micah has יִשָּׂא, and Isa 2:4 has שָׂא; either one is accept-
    able.

o   NJPS adopts a different nuance, "they shall never again
    know war," citing Judges 3:2. The present translation is
    based on Ps 18:35 (EV 34) (same as 2 Sam 22:35) and Ps
    144:1; cf. 1 Chr 5:18. Micah uses the form יְלַמְּדוּן, and
    Isa 2:4 has יְלַמְּדוּ.

p   For the LXX καὶ ἕκαστος ὑποκάτω ("and each under") cf.
    2 Kgs 18:31 and Isa 36:16.

q   The LXX has τὴν ὁδόν αὐτοῦ ("its own way"); the MT is
    preferable because it is unique.

Commentary

The contrast between this view of Zion and the Jerusalem to be "plowed like a field" has seemed to some to
amount to a contradiction. In Wellhausen's unlovely
phrase it is a poultice stuck on the wound left by chapter
three. But whatever view one takes of the relation of this
vision to the rest of the book, all will agree that it has
been placed strategically, for (to cite only the most
obvious) it continues the topic of Jerusalem from chap. 3
and leads into the Zion prophecies of chap. 4. The
authorship, and the relation to Isaiah 2, are dealt with in
a separate section following these comments. In the
exegetical comments that now follow, detailed explanation of the ties between this section and 3:9-12 is undertaken, primarily to bring out more clearly the sense and
emphases of the passage in its present context rather
than to argue the question of authorship. The questions
are related, however, and if an unforced reading
discovers a detailed congruence of 4:1–5 with the rest of
the prophecies, and if the sense of this vision is illumined
and deepened in turn, authorship by Micah may appear
less improbable than is usually thought.

The phrase "The time will come" (Hebrew, "at the end
of days"), i.e., "in the future," places the vision in an
indefinite future (cf, 2:4; 3:4; 4:6; and 5:9), which fits
with the mysterious, mythical transformation of political
and even geological conditions involved in the vision.

The first and fundamental element in the vision is a
transformation of the earthly dwelling of God. The
earthly center of his rule, which involves some kenosis at
best (Zion is not even as tall as the neighboring Mt. of
Olives), and the extreme of humiliation in its destruction, will appear as it is in sacred reality. This is expressed through emphasis on its character as divine

mountain. Canaanite gods, like the Olympians and other
deities, lived on sacred mountains which were actual
earthly mountains, yet centers of cosmic rule. Israelite
religion followed this in assigning to Yahweh a mountain,
Zion, which was the site of his temple and at the same
time his cosmic abode. In the time to come, Zion will
appear "over the mountaintops" and "lifted up above the
hills"—its appearance will then correspond to its nature,
now hidden. This initial note of unreality, of fantasy, is
deliberate and sustained through the vision to its paradi-
siac close.

The response to this transformation is world-wide and,
one is made to feel, automatic. Ancient people, even the
nations, were not irreligious so much as misguided, in
Israel's view. They were ready to pay homage at all kinds
of sacred places where a god was thought to have mani-
fested himself. When the mountain of Yahweh's house is
decisively lifted up, all peoples will "stream" there, a
word which perhaps implies the inevitability of their
response, though the term is rare and somewhat obscure.

"Go up" is the common term for pilgrimage to Jerusalem. It is worth noting that its character as a pilgrim
center must have been the most fundamental characteristic of Zion for Israelites as a whole, thus also for the
villager Micah. Three times in a year all male Israelites
were to go up there, in the developed form of the rule.
Only the Jerusalem priests and people knew Zion directly
as a center of daily cult and personal worship, whereas its
early and primary significance for the countryside was as
a pilgrim center.

The nations come for "instruction." It has been
argued, with some force, that this is not a clear reference
to conversion of the nations. They are not said, unambig-
uously, to become part of Yahweh's people (contrast Isa

19:25) and the expression "of his ways" (מִדְרָכָיו) perhaps implies something less than total acceptance of the Torah. Rudolph aptly compares the coming of foreigners as well as Greeks to the Delphic oracle. On the other hand, the result is that the nations "walk in his paths," and the coming of universal peace, so that a rather fundamental change is in mind.

The speech of the nations concludes at this point, and the prophetic voice takes up. Resuming the theme "instruction" from the foregoing, two other components of the rule of God are added: the "word of Yahweh" and "justice". Word of Yahweh here is not wholly synonymous with "instruction" (Torah) but a complement to it. As Grether[1] has shown "word of Yahweh" is in the overwhelming number of cases used of the *prophetic* word, so that the probability is that here too it refers to the message that comes from the prophet. Yet neither priest nor prophet is mentioned in this vision of a reconstituted world order, and the judging and arbitrating is done by Yahweh himself. This is a pointed and, we may say, intentional contrast to the perverted Zion depicted in 3:9–12, where these three functions have failed, where the chiefs do not judge right, nor priests teach, nor prophets divine (v 11). The contrast between the present and the future Zion is thus drawn not only in general terms, but in specific details.[2] This correspondence is at least significant for the positioning of this passage, and perhaps also for the authorship: they might have been framed with 3:9–12 in mind. They do not erase the indictment, they confirm it, for if the functions of authority continue, the functionaries disappear. It is Yahweh who teaches, prophesies, and judges in the new Zion.

The following lines, which are too familiar and immediately striking to require comment, are doubtless a traditional description of change from war to peace; the image is reversed in Joel 4:10 (EV 3:10): "Beat your plowshares into swords, etc."[3] After the mention of the plowshare, as Mays notes, the line about the vine and the fig tree follows naturally. This last, missing in Isaiah, is certainly traditional, for nearly identical phraseology occurs in 1 Kgs 5:5 (Eng 4:25); 2 Kgs 18:31; and Isa 36:16. Yet there is a particular appropriateness in its occurrence in Micah. It is not simply a synonym for security, but for security of a particular kind: secure in possession of land, one's own land ("each man . . . his own . . ."), for a long time (vines take at least three years to become productive, fruit trees even longer). Such a peasant ideal would be quite congruent with Micah's thought. Brueggemann discusses at length the social significance of this passage, and writes: "there is here no desire to claim this oracle for Micah in the eighth century, but to observe that such an interpretation fits well with Micah's strictures against the surplus-value practice of the royal economy."[4]

The section closes with a kind of divine "Amen": "for the mouth of Yahweh has spoken." To this is added, as a congregational response to the prophetic vision, the statement of an interim resolution: this all lies far in the future, since the nations show no sign of turning to Yahweh. Sustained by hope, we will live faithful to our God if it takes forever. It is going too far to say that this contradicts the vision,[5] but it does seem likely that it is a liturgical addition to a prophetic word, of undetermined date.

Micah or Isaiah, or neither?
The occurrence of substantially the same verses in two prophetic books is not absolutely unique in the Old Testament (Obad 1–10 is substantially the same as Jer 49:7–22), yet is sufficiently unusual to merit discussion, and must affect our understanding of the relation of this passage to the thought of Micah or Isaiah. The history of scholarly discussion of this question of authorship given here is a sketch based on the more detailed treatment in Wildberger's commentary on Isaiah.[6] Compare also the

---

1   Oskar Grether, *Name und Wort Gottes im Alten Testament*, BZAW 64 (1934).

2   This point is stressed by Eduard Nielsen, *Oral Tradition*, Studies in Biblical Theology, 11 (Chicago: Allenson, 1954), 92.

3   Incidentally, this illustrates a feature of ancient economy that might escape those in a more affluent society; scrap metal was normally reused, not thrown out, and obsolete war weapons were readily convertible.

4   Walter Brueggemann, "Vine and Fig Tree: A Case Study in Imagination and Criticism," *CBQ* 43 (1981): 188–204.

5   So Rudolph.

6   Hans Wildberger, *Jesaja*, BK 10/1 (Neukirchen-Vluyn: Neukirchener Verlag, 1972): 78–80.

summary offered by Cannawurf.[7]

Until the middle of the 18th century, the traditional view remained unshaken; the passage was considered authentic in both Isaiah and Micah. Then the logical alternatives began to be explored: first, that the prophesy was by Isaiah and borrowed from him by Micah; then, that the passage was by some anonymous third person, on whom both Isaiah and Micah drew. Naegelsbach[8] defended authorship by Micah, whereas Stade[9] (1881) held that the vision was the contribution of an anonymous post-exilic prophet, hence not even known to either eighth century prophet. Wildberger himself argues for the authenticity of this passage in Isaiah,[10] thus returning to an early critical view and illustrating thereby, that the discussion has not reached a final conclusion, and is not apt to. This sketch is very incomplete, but there seems to be little point in compiling a scorecard of those scholars who have favored the various options.

Arguments against Micah's authorship are given in a succinct summary by Mays, whose order is followed here. First, the vocabulary and style of 4:1–4 have no parallels in oracles that can be assigned to Micah with confidence. Second, the message has no place in the mission of Micah as defined by his genuine oracles and his statement of vocation (3:8) and is clearly a direct contradiction of 3:12, the prophecy for which he was remembered a century after it was uttered. Third, the elements of the Zion theology included here, the concept of a positive relation between Yahweh's reign and the nations, and the idea of the peaceful pilgrimage of other peoples to Zion, are exilic or post-exilic. In the course of the discussion, an additional area has been explored, namely the relation between the text-form in Micah and that in Isaiah, but, as Wildberger states, no useful conclusion for authorship would emerge even if one could establish which book preserves a more original text, since a borrower's book could happen to have been treated more kindly in textual transmission than the text of the book from which it was copied. The issues as listed by Mays, then, are those that most deserve discussion.

As to the argument from vocabulary ("style" in this context is hopelessly vague), we confront the familiar case, especially in the prophetic literature, that the size of our sample, either of oracles indisputably by Micah or the passage in question, is less than ideal. But is it even correct to say there are "no parallels" as Mays does? Even "the mountain of the Lord's house" (3:12; 4:1) is a kind of parallel in vocabulary; Gray[11] spoke of a catch-word arrangement at this point in Micah. There are other parallels in important terms, as pointed out in the notes: 3:11 ישפטו parallels 4:3 ושפט and 3:11 יורו parallels 4:2 ויורנו. At this point argument from vocabulary turns into argument about what is a significant parallel, thereby revealing the somewhat unsatisfactory nature of the criterion.

As to the relation of this passage to Micah's message, it is stating the obvious to say that Micah thought of it as his vocation to denounce sin. Yet is 3:8 an all-inclusive statement of what he felt impelled by God to proclaim? Even if it were a kind of programmatic call account we might doubt it, but coming as it does at the end of a polemic against prophets whose vice is venality, the most prominent feature of Micah's assertion is its contrastive character rather than any all-embracing, exhaustive self-definition. As argued in the Introduction, Jeremiah 26 is also far from restricting the compass of Micah's thought to condemnation.

Nowack already made the point against Stade that a vision of a future glorious Zion was not incompatible with condemnation of present conditions. Movements of protest in human history have rather commonly been accompanied by visions of an ideal future, sometimes of the most impractical kind, and this is not hard to understand psychologically. That Jerusalem was not unimportant or indifferent to Micah we know from 1:2, 3, 5,9, 12; 3:1 (cf. 9) and especially 3:10–12. To test the validity of calling 4:1–4 a *contradiction* of 3:12, write a contradic-

7   E. Cannawurf, "The Authenticity of Micah IV 1–4," *VT* 13 (1963): 26–33.

8   As noted by Wildberger, *Jesaja.*

9   Bernhard Stade, "Bemerkungen über das Buch Micha," *ZAW* 1 (1881): 161–72.

10   Wildberger, *Jesaja.*

11   George Buchanan Gray, *The Book of Isaiah,* I–XXXIX, I.C.C. (Edinburgh: T & T Clark, 1912), 41–48.

tion of 3:12; it would have to be something like "Jerusalem will not fall, etc."—something very different from 4:1–4.

A history of Zion theology whereby Micah 4:1–4 would fit only in an exilic or post-exilic phase is only one possible writing of that history. Recent restudy of this question, especially by J.J.M. Roberts[12] has made it probable that the major elements of the Zion tradition were developed long before the eighth century, under the United Monarchy.

In sum, it would be fatuous to suppose that one could at this date settle the question of the authorship of Micah 4:1–5. On the hypothesis of this commentary, the Micah book arises in connection with a movement of revitalization; three possibilities seem to fit such a hypothesis: 1) the passage is by Micah, part of his vision of the new age; 2) the passage is by Isaiah and was added to Micah as *fitting* with authentic elements of his thought; 3) that the passage is from an anonymous prophet, either earlier or contemporary, and was incorporated as harmonious with the rest of the Micah book.

---

12   J.J.M. Roberts, "Zion Tradition," *IDBS* and "The Davidic Origin of the Zion Tradition," *JBL* 92 (1973): 329–44.

■ **The Kingdom of the Survivors**

**Yahweh the shepherd-king will
gather and restore his flock,
and rule over these survivors from
Zion.**

4

6   On that day, Yahweh said,
     "I will gather in the one who limps[a]
        And collect the one who has strayed,
           And the one I did harm.[b]
7   Then I will make the one who limps[c] a remnant,
        And the far off one[d] a populous nation."
     Then Yahweh will rule[e] over them on Mount Zion,
        From now and forever.

a   צֹלֵעָה is used of sheep also in Zeph 3:19 (with the identi-
     cal parallel term). The idea seems to be that the injured
     sheep becomes separated from the flock and needs to be
     "gathered."
b   The LXX has ἀπωσάμην ("whom I rejected, thrust
     away"); it is probably a free rendering rather than a
     variant. There is no need to suppose that this third colon
     is incomplete (Sellin supplies a verb, "I will heal").
c   The sign of the accusative is written above the line in Mur
     88.
d   If the unique MT form is correct, it may be a Niphal of a
     denominative from הָלְאָה ("far off"); the LXX, S, and T
     are compatible with this understanding. Many commen-

tators have preferred וְהַנִּלְאָה ("the weary one" [following
Graetz, *Emendationes*]) or הַנַּחֲלָה ("the sick one" [Well-
hausen]), cf. Ezek 34:4 for forms of חלה used of sheep;
the V is compatible with either emendation. A rather
close parallel to this verse, with its association of
"remnant" and "mighty nation" is Gen 45:7, as pointed
out by R. de Vaux, "Le 'reste d'Israël' d'après les
prophètes," *RB* 42 (1933): 526–39.

e   Elliger (BHS) would remove the shift in construction by
     reading וּמָלַכְתִּי ("and I will rule") but the MT involves no
     real difficulty.

Commentary

The theme of this oracle is a continuation of the earlier
portion of chap. 4, but the passage is clearly set off from
the foregoing by a new introduction ("On that day") and
by a formula of quotation ("Yahweh said"). The theme of
kingship is resumed in the next passage (v 8) and succeeding oracles through 5:5, and the extent to which
portions of this section should be thought of as separate,
or as elements of one or more larger compositions is
difficult to decide. "From now and forevermore" is often,
but not always (Ps 113:2 and 125:2) the conclusion of a
composition.

This oracle applies to the future, "that day," a time
after catastrophe. The people, for the adjectives apply
not to separate groups, but to the whole, is wounded,
strayed, and removed far away (see Notes for other
possible translations). Yahweh himself is the one who has
done this harm to them. But he will gather them to-

gether and make of them a "remnant," that is, a group of
survivors who carry the hope of continued and renewed
life in them. This idea is expanded in the promise that
they will become a "populous nation." Then Yahweh
himself will rule over them from Zion.

Most commentators assign this oracle to exilic or post-
exilic times because it seems to presuppose the exile and
uses "remnant" in a positive, hopeful way expecially
characteristic of late writers (e.g., Isa 11:12–16 and Zeph
5:18–20). Such a reading of the passage, suggested by its
present position (following on 3:9–12), seems less obviously correct when the passage is taken in isolation,
bearing in mind that its present position is mostly due to
catchword principles. By itself, the poem refers to
catastrophe and and exile, but though the fullest experience of these came in the sixth century, Micah and his
contemporaries would have experienced the loss of most
of Israel's territory and of much of her populace, the fall

of Samaria, the invasion of Judah, and a siege of Jerusalem. This could have been sufficient cause to speak of the people as "limping" and "driven away." Sellin's attempt to be very precise about just which events in Micah's time fit this oracle is unconvincing because the figurative language resists a pedantically precise reading. Yet the general picture of a scattered, ravaged flock is not anachronistic for Micah's day. The term "remnant" or "survivors," is an old one; to turn it to a positive sense, almost a title of honor, could be the work of a very brief time.

To the picture given in this passage, compare, from Ahab's time, 1 Kgs 22:17 "I saw all Israel scattered on the mountains, like sheep that have no shepherd." In the treaty between Ashurnirari V of Assyria and Mati'ilu of Arpad (754 B.C.), a principal rite sealing the pact is described in these words "If Mati'ilu sins against (this) treaty made under oath by the gods, then, just as this spring lamb, brought from its fold, will not behold its fold again, also, Mati'ilu, together with his sons, daughters, officials, and the people of his land [will be ousted] from his country, will not return to his country, and not behold his country again."[1] No relation between treaties and prophetic thought is being argued at this point, but only this, that national catastrophe, including exile, was well-known by personal experience or that of other nations, in Micah's day, and was connected even ritually with imagery of removal of a lamb from its fold.

---

1   Erica Reiner, ANET³, p. 532.

■ **Restoration of Sovereignty
as at First**

**The human, earthly expression
of divine rule from Zion will be
restoration of the empire of
David.**

4

8
**To you,ᵃ tower of the flock,ᵇ
Strongholdᶜ of Zion,ᵈ
To you shall come and arriveᵉ
Sovereignty as at first,ᶠ
Ruleᵍ by Jerusalem.ʰ**

a   This is a *casus pendens,* emphasis of one clause-member
by putting it first, outside the clause structure, to be
resumed within the clause by a pronoun (עָדֶיךָ).

b   The Hebrew is מִגְדַּל עֵדֶר. This is a place name in Gen
35:21, the location being at a little distance from
Jerusalem (cf. Mishnah Shekalim 7, 4), so that the phrase
here has been taken to refer to that place, and to be a
proper name. But עֹפֶל "stronghold" seems to be in
apposition to it and in the context there is reference to
Zion and Jerualsem, so that the phrase is more likely a
reference to the fortified city of David, not any separate
part. Even if it is a proper name, the sense is transparent,
and the phrase continues the flock picture from the
preceding.

c   Hebrew עֹפֶל, "hill or citadel," cf. Isa 32:14, is in later
texts the name of a portion of the ancient fortified city,
on the Eastern hill of Jerusalem (2 Chr 27:3; 33:14; Neh
3:26–27; and 17:21), and may already in Micah's time
have been the name of a specific portion of the city. If
so, it serves here as a designation for the whole city, by
synecdoche, cf. "Zion." The LXX, S, V, and apparently
T have connected the word with אֹפֶל "darkness, gloom."

d   Hebrew בַּת, literally "daughter," has been omitted from
the translation here and also with "Jerusalem," as serving
primarily rhythmical purposes.

e   The sequence of synonymous verbs, the second common
in Hebrew, the first in Aramaic, has led commentators to
delete one or the other. But stylistically this is an accepted, apparently even valued, feature of Hebrew
poetic diction, especially in unbalanced (Qinah) meter.
See Delbert R. Hillers, *Lamentations,* Anchor Bible Vol
7A (Garden City, N.Y.: Doubleday, 1972), on 1:6 and
cf. Lam 2:15b, 16b; 3:2, 5, 11; 3:43; and 3:12. Lam 3:2
is especially close in form to the present passage.

f   Cf. Isa 1:26 . . . וְאָשִׁיבָה שֹׁפְטַיִךְ כְּבָרִאשֹׁנָה וְיֹעֲצַיִךְ כְּבַתְּחִלָּה.

g   The LXX adds ἐκ βαβυλῶνος ("from Babylon"). This
seems to reflect a gloss מִבָּבֶל, representing the applica-
tion of these words to an exilic or post-exilic situation,
when the Davidic line survived in Babylon, and royalist
hopes might center around a figure like Zerubbabel.

h   If the pointing is correct, מֶמְלֶכֶת is a construct before a
prepositional phrase (Gesenius' para. 130). The idea is
not "rule *over* Jerusalem" but "rule belonging to Jerusalem," exercised from or by Jerusalem. The concept is
similar to that in 4:2. Thus it is unnecessary to change to
"rule over the house of Israel" (Wellhausen et al.). There
is no good reason for thinking that this whole colon is a
gloss (Marti, Willi-Plein, *Vorformen*).

Commentary

"Zion" and "Jerusalem," and the idea of rule, are obvious
ties to the foregoing. Less obvious is the use of "flock,"
which continues an earlier metaphor. This theme is
developed in succeeding passages, to 5:8. There is a
verbal link of "and you" (וְאַתָּה) with 5:1, and a resonance
between "as at first" and "from of old, from olden times,"
which confirms understanding of the passage as referring
to the Davidic empire.

This passage does not necessarily presuppose the
disappearance of the dynasty, or even the captivity. It
would fit with the circumstances of a kingdom where the

territory has been much reduced, as in Hezekiah's day. If 5:1–4 is about the return of David (as argued below), this passage would harmonize with this sort of messianism, which may be entertained by the disaffected even during the reign of an actual king.

Cazelles understands this and the hopeful prophecies that follow as having arisen during the time of intense diplomatic activity after the death of Sargon, when Merodach-Baladan was briefly on the throne of Babylon (2 Kings 20).[1] But no specific promising situation is required to engender this sort of "millenial" hope.[2]

1   H. Cazelles, "Micah," *Encylopaedia Judaica* (New York: Macmillan, 1971), XI, cols. 1480–83.

2   Cf. H. Cazelles, "Histoire et géographie en Michée IV 6–13," *4th World Congress of Jewish Studies,* Papers I (Jerusalem, 1967): 87–89.

■ **Human Failure and Divine Help**

**The city is in distress and
hopelessness, her king powerless;
the trouble will get even worse
as she goes off into captivity,
but there she will experience
Yahweh's deliverence.**

4

9   Now[a] why are you crying out?[b]
Is it that you have[c] no king,[d]
  Or has your counsellor perished,
    That pains like labor pains have come over you?[e]
10   Writhe and gasp,[f] O Zion, like a woman in labor,
For now you will go out of the city
  And camp in the open.
Then you will go to Babylon;
  There you will be delivered,[g]
    There Yahweh[h] will free you from the enemy's hands.

a   The LXX has καὶ νῦν ("and now"). This slight variant is of some potential importance because וְעַתָּה joins elements of discourse, and does not introduce new independent units, according to the detailed study of André Laurentin, "wᵉʿattah-kai nun, Formule caractéristique des textes juridiques et liturgiques (à propos de Jean 17,5)" *Biblica* 45 (1964): 168–97 and 413–32. But in the present case there is little basis for preferring either reading.

b   The text is doubtful at this point. The verb תָּרִיעַ is not well-attested in the sense "cry in distress" (only doubtfully Isa 15:4), and the cognate noun is also poorly attested. The ancient versions give different, rather fanciful renderings. The LXX's ἔγνως perhaps reflects a defective spelling of תדעי. Ehrlich, *Randglossen*, proposed תָּרֹעִי רֹעַ ("Why do you suffer so?") cf. Prov 11:15. But none of these is clearly superior to the MT, which seems defensible, especially in light of Jer 8:19, which also refers to an outcry.

c   The LXX's σοι is probably just a rather free rendering.

d   In view of יוֹעֲצֵךְ ("your counsellor") Rudolph would read מֹלֵךְ "counsellor," but this presses the parallelism too hard.

e   The MT has this feminine suffix but 4QMi(?)(168) has [החזיקכה], thus masculine.

f   The meaning is uncertain, and the text may not be correct. Versions differ markedly and perplexingly. The LXX has the apparently double reading ἀνδρίζου καὶ ἔγγιζε ("act the man and draw nigh"), which has not been convincingly explained. Various emendations yielding a sense of "cry out, sigh," or the like have been proposed, none especially close to the MT graphically. If גֹחִי is correct, the sense of "burst out, let go" (used of waters, and of men in ambush) may be extended here to the people's leaving, "bursting out" of the city, or to the outcry of a woman in labor. Julius Lewy, "Lexicographical Notes," *HUCA* 12–13 (1937–18): 97–101 would construe the form as an imperative of גנח, attested in post-biblical Hebrew in the sense of "groan," but the form is dubious, since it is hard to account for loss of *nun* in this position. Horgan, *Pesharim*, p 263 construes גֹחִי as Qal imperative of נגח ("push"). Allen compares the extreme emotional and physical reaction to impending trouble depicted in the topos "Reaction to Bad News," discussed by Delbert R. Hillers, "A Convention in Hebrew Literature: The Reaction to Bad News," *ZAW* 77 (1965): 86–90. Cf. also O. García de la Fuente, "Notas al texto de Miqueas," *Aug* 7 (1967): 145–54.

g   The LXX's ῥύσεταί σε, ("He will deliver you"), was probably influenced by the following clause.

h   The LXX adds "your God."

Commentary

There are thematic and verbal ties to what precedes and what follows: the theme of kingship, the distress and deliverance of Zion. These are sufficient to explain the placement of this oracle within chapter four. It is, nevertheless, a self-contained unit, with its own little drama of distress and deliverance, and in some ways it can be misleading to connect it too closely with its context, especially the preceding, an example being in identifying the "king" of v 9.

On one reading, the "king" of v 9 is Yahweh. This conception is present in the near context, v 7, and there is a rather close parallel to the thought and form of this verse in Jer 8:19, "Is Yahweh not in Zion? Is her king not in her?" (הֲיהוָה אֵין בְּצִיּוֹן אִם־מַלְכָּהּ אֵין בָּהּ . . .). With this identification, the thought goes: The people are reproached because they have forgotten that their heavenly king is in their midst, and are in panic. The principal difficulty seems to be that unexpectedly the prophet goes on to say: your fears will be justified, for you must pass from the present distress to a worse one.

An alternate, perhaps superior, reading is to think of the "king" as the human king of Judah. The people are reproached, almost taunted, for being in panic in spite of the presence of their vaunted king and counsellor. Note the similar group of ideas in Isa 19:11–17, directed at the Egyptians. The deepening of the catastrophe follows naturally, not paradoxically. She will go from siege into captivity. If this passage is from the time of Micah, it would be the most direct attack on the king of Judah—Hezekiah, presumably—in the book.

There is an obvious obstacle in assigning this passage to the time of Micah, in the reference to Babylon. A reference to exile, or deliverance from exile, would fit well in the time of Samaria's fall, but naming of Babylon is not easily imaginable at this time. To be sure, Babylon existed at this time, and as a lively, stirring power. But Assyria was the power that threatened the west, and attempts to defend "Babylon" as appropriate for Micah have the character of a tour de force. An obvious solution to the difficulty is to suppose this is a late oracle, actually from the time of Jeremiah, which has been inserted here. A third possibility is to suppose that an oracle from Micah's time has been altered, made contemporary. "Babylon" would be a substitution for a different place-name, perhaps Ashur, with the alteration at the end of the oracle being more extensive. This sort of view had the allegiance of Y. Kaufmann who calls it ". . .one of the few instances in the whole corpus of prophecy of a genuine revision in the light of later events."[1]

---

1   Yehezkel Kaufmann, *The Religion of Israel*, abridged and tr. Moshe Greenberg (Chicago: University of Chicago Press, 1960), 352.

■ **The Defeat of the Nation**

When the nations finally
assemble against Zion, they
are actually being gathered by
God's plan, as sheaves to the
threshing-floor; Zion will
thresh them out and dedicate
their wealth to God.

4

11 Now many nations have assembled against you,
  Thinking:[a]"Let her be polluted.[b]
  Let us[c] have a look at Zion."
12 But they do not know Yahweh's designs,
  Or understand his plan:
That he has gathered them
  Like sheaves to the threshing floor.
13 Arise and thresh, O Zion,
  For I will make your horn iron
    And your hooves bronze.
So you can trample many peoples,
  And devote[d] the gain from them to Yahweh,
    Their wealth to the lord of the whole earth.

a The MT has האמרים (defective). According to J. Strugnell, "Notes en marge du volume V des 'Discoveries in
the Judaean Desert of Jordan'," *RQ* 26 (1970): 163–276,
4QpMi should be restored האו[מרים] (plene), with 3 mss
of Kenn.

b This translation follows the MT; see Commentary for
defense. The S clearly implies the same text; the T "she
will be guilty" and σ′ κατακριθήσεται ("she will be condemned") (*Syh tthyb*) are probably free renderings of
תחנף, in view of the Syh to Jer 3:2 and Ps 105:38. But
the LXX ἐπιχαρούμεθα ("we will exult over") and α′ "she
will fall into anger" and the V *lapidetur* ("let her be
stoned/ assailed") show no obvious relation to the MT.

Robinson, following the LXX, reads נשמח; Ehrlich,
Randglossen, reads תחרב, Wellhausen תפחד, and Sellin
תחסף ("may she be bared"), cf. Isa 47:2.

c The Hebrew subject is "our eyes," spelled plene עינינו in
the MT; apparently עיננו was in the Vorlage of the S and
the V (the T is ambiguous). Since sound and sense are
the same, there is little basis or necessity for a choice.

d The verb-ending -ti of the MT is commonly first common singular, but that is inappropriate here, so either
the MT has preserved an uncommon, but attested,
variant form of second feminine singular, or the MT is
to be corrected to -t, the usual spelling. All versions have
second feminine singular.

Commentary

This oracle, though complete in itself, fits well in chap. 4
as far as the theme is concerned. It pictures Zion surrounded by hostile enemies but finally triumphant by
God's help. Also the catch-word וְעַתָּה ("and now") links
this section with vv 9–10 preceding and v 14 following,
and possibly also (by assonance) with וְאַתָּה ("and you") of
4:8 and 5:14.

The idea that all nations gather against Jerusalem is a
stock element of the "Zion Tradition," as delineated in
recent scholarly writing; See J.J.M. Roberts, "Zion
Tradition," *IDBS*, and "The Davidic Origin of the Zion
Tradition," *JBL* 92 (1973): 329–44, with bibliographies.
Roberts lists these parallels: Isa 14:32; 17:12–14; 18:1–

6; 29:1–8; 31:4–9; Ezek 38–39; Joel 4:9–21; Zech 12:1–
9; 14:3, 12–15; Ps 46:7–12 (EV 6–11); 48:5–9 (EV 4–8);
and 76:4–10 (EV 4–9). Of these Joel 4:9–21 (EV 3:9–21)
is close to the present passage, in that it uses harvest
imagery, v 13 reads: "Put in the sickle, for the harvest is
ripe. Go in, tread for the wine press is full" (שִׁלְחוּ מַגָּל כִּי
בָשַׁל קָצִיר בֹּאוּ רְדוּ כִּי מָלְאָה גַת . . .). Note also Zech 12:6:
Judah will be "like a flaming torch among sheaves"
(וּכְלַפִּיד אֵשׁ בְּעָמִיר) a phrase that invokes the picture of dry
grain on the threshing floor.

That Zion should be "polluted" or "profaned," a
notion that has been thought incongruous as spoken by
her enemies, is appropriate here if we suppose that the
Israelite attitude is projected on the attackers. Israel

believed that bloodshed or other wrongdoing defiled her land (Isa 10:6; Jer 3:1, 9; and Num 35:33), severing her relationship with God unless atonement was made. Here the enemies voice Israel's fears: "She is polluted," hence open to attack. "Let us gloat over Zion" is literally "let our eye(s) look on Zion." The expression seems to be the equivalent of רָאָה בּ meaning "to see, with joy, victory over" (one's enemy). Note Mic 7:10 and Ps 54:9, cf. Lam 2:16.

God has a concealed plan in permitting this assault on Zion. The terms "design" and "plan" (עֵצָה, מַחֲשָׁבָה) occur elsewhere as poetic parallels: of a king's plan, Jer 49:30; contrasting man's purpose with God's, Prov 18:21; of God's plans, as here, Jer 49:20; 50:45; and Ps 33:11. The earliest datable reference to the plan of God seems to be Isa 5:19, "the plan of the Holy One of Israel" (עֲצַת קְדוֹשׁ יִשְׂרָאֵל), which uses a characteristic term of the first Isaiah. Jer 29:11 also expresses the idea that God's plan may be unkown to man: "I know the plans I have in mind." Though God's plan may be good (Jer 29:11 and 40:6), in the present context the emphasis is on the sudden reversal of the heathen's high hopes. One might almost render "Yahweh's plot."

The nations are to be like sheaves on the threshing-floor, that flat, hard area where the grain is separated from the stalks by any of various processes of cutting or trampling. Since the threshing-floor was often at the gate of an ancient town, it is at least appropriate to see here a congruity: the enemy at the gate is like sheaves on the threshing-floor.

God the harvester will use Zion as the beast (probably a great heifer, cf. Hos 10:11) which will tread on the sheaves. Though the idea of trampling on one's enemies is sufficiently common in the Old Testament, the specific image of the grain harvest is relatively rare. For an early allusion, cf. Amos 1:3 "Because they threshed Gilead with iron sledges." Closer to Micah are Jer 51:33 "Babylon is like a threshing-floor; it is time to tread her" (בְּבֵל כְּגֹרֶן עֵת הִדְרִיכָהּ) and Isa 41:15 "I have made you a sharp threshing-sledge . . . you will thresh the mountains, etc." Supposed Ugaritic parallels, none very impressive, are gathered by Bordreuil,[1] and Gottlieb.[2]

In the actual threshing the hooves do the work. Reference to the horns, and to the metals iron and bronze, illustrates what I have termed "conceptual imagery," where the reference to concrete objects is not to call up a picture in our minds (certainly not of an animal threshing with its horns), so much as to invoke concepts of strength, for which the horn is proverbial, and hardness, exemplified by iron and bronze.[3]

The final couplet refers to an aspect of the ban (חֵרֶם) connected with holy war. All animate things, thus all the people of the hostile nations, will be killed without sparing anyone. Deut 20:16 "You must not let anything live" (לֹא תְחַיֶּה כָּל נְשָׁמָה). But the indestructible booty of gold, silver, and other metals, though not to be appropriated by Israel is to be "devoted" to God. At Jericho (Josh 6:24), "they burned the city in fire, with all that was in it. Only the silver and the gold and the bronze and iron things they put into the treasury of the house of Yahweh." Isaiah 34 illustrates projection of the destructive side of the ban into the future, and Hag 2:6–7 parallels the idea of the wealth of nations coming to the God of Israel.

The title "Lord of the whole earth" for God is relatively rare; it occurs in Josh 3:11, 13; Ps 97:5; Zech 4:14; and 6:5.

1 Pierre Bordreuil, "Michée 4:10–13 et ses parallèles ougaritiques," *Semitica* 21 (1971): 21–28.

2 Hans Gottlieb, "Den taerskende kvie Mi IV 11–13," *Dansk teologisk tijdsskrift* 26 (1963): 167–71.

3 Delbert R. Hillers, "Dust" forthcoming in the Pope Festschrift.

■ **A Fragment: Humiliation of the King**

4

14 **Now you are gashing yourself with gashes:**[a]
"He has laid[b] siege[c] to us.
 With a staff they are striking the cheek
 Of the judge of Israel."

a The fragmentary form (see Commentary) makes it exceptionally difficult to be certain even as to the existence of textual or linguistic problems, to say nothing of their solution. Probably Zion is being addressed, as in 4:9 and 11, for note עַתָּה or וְעַתָּה in each. Since the city of v 14 (EV 5:1) is under siege, it seems necessary to think of Zion, and not "Beth-Gader" (Augustin George, "Michée [Le Livre de]," *DBS*. vol. 5 [Paris: Letouzey et Ané, 1955]: cols 1252–63 and A. van Hoonacker, *Les douze petits prophètes*, Études Bibliques [Paris: Gabalda, 1908]), however plausible textually, and to dismiss the idea that it is the besiegers who are being addressed (Ehrlich, *Randglossen*). But בַּת גְּדוּד "daughter of gashing," if not impossible, seems without good parallel as an epithet of a city (as the phrase is construed by Weiser, Sellin, Rudolph, for example). Mays compare Jer 10:17 יֹשֶׁבֶת בַּמָּצוֹר but since this does not involve the word בַּת "daughter of," the parallel to the present phrase is inexact. S. J. Schwantes' defense of "O daughter of troops" does not seem actually explained by his otherwise correct references to Israel's military organization; see "A Note on Micah 5:1 (Hebrew 4:14)," *AUSS* 1 (1963): 105–07. Hence it seems best to follow Well-

hausen's popular emendation הִתְגֹּדְדִי תִּתְגֹּדְדִי, without insisting on every detail. גרד is indeed used of gashing, with reference to a common funerary practice. An alternate emendation is based on the LXX's ἐμφραχθήσεται θυγάτηρ Εφραιμ ἐν φραγμῷ (approximately, "a daughter shall be blockaded by a blockade"), which suggest the root גרד, so that Robinson proposed תִּתְגָּדְרִי בְגָדֵר ("You are enclosed with a wall"). The sense fits the context and the reading is graphically close to the MT.

 The words that follow are taken here as the cry of the city, without introductory word; "and saying" is implied.

b Many have preferred a plural to the MT singular, citing the S, T, and V.

c Mays suggests "siege-rampart," citing such as use of מָצוֹר in Deut 20:20.

Commentary

This seems to be a fragment that, when complete, would have had the same sequence of ideas as 4:9–10, 11–12. The kingdom is in great distress, but is to take heart from a promise of divine intervention. Only the beginning has been preserved. It is not only the incompleteness of thought that suggests this conclusion, but the fact that a new unit begins at 5:1, with the characteristic וְאַתָּה and a new addressee, Bethlehem. Willis contributes a valuable compilation of opinion on this and 5:1–5, but he overstates the case when he calls these associated bits a

"unit."[1]

 Whenever the loss took place, whether before the catch-word collection was made or in transmission of the collection, the result is that a picture of a humiliated "judge of Israel" now stands before a promise of the future king, 5:1–4. No logical bridge is present, but a thematic continuity exists.

 Noth shows that the evidence for identifying the "judge" in this passage is inconclusive. Most have thought of it as a title of the king, where others have taken it as a collective: "judges of Israel." Noth himself argues for the

1 J.J. Willis, "Micah IV:14–V 5—A Unit," *VT* 18 (1968) 529–47. Cf. also J. Coppens, "Le cadre littéraire de Michée V: 1–5," *Near Eastern Studies in* *Honor of William Foxwell Albright*, ed. Hans Goedicke (Baltimore and London: John Hopkins, 1971), 57–62.

persistence of a premonarchic office of "judge" down through the time of the monarchy, comparing Deut 17:8–13.[2] Beyerlin has argued that here the title refers specifically to the king of Judah,[3] an identification that is certainly appropriate in the context.

A search for a precise set of circumstances to match this fragment is not apt to be fruitful. The general idea of a city in despair fits many historical cases, cf. 1:16. Reference to siege fits the time of Micah, when the Assyrians invaded, or the Babylonian onslaught of a later time. Just what is meant by the smiting of the "judge" is uncertain, since it is surely to some degree metaphorical, cf. Ps 89:39–45 (EV 38–45). For references to smiting the cheek, see 1 Kgs 22:24; Job 16:10; Ps 3:8 (EV 7); and Lam 3:30.

---

2   Martin Noth, "Das Amt des 'Richter Israels'," *Festschrift A. Bertholet* (Tubingen: J.C.B. Mohr, 1950), 404–17.

3   W. Beyerlin, *Die Kulttraditionen Israels in der Verkündigung des Propheten Micha,* FRLANT 54 (Göttingen: Vandenhoeck & Ruprecht, 1959), 20–21.

■ **Return of the King of Peace**

**Yahweh will bring about a rule
of peace for the united people
under a ruler from Bethlehem,
David come back again.**

5

1   **From you, Bethlehem Ephrata,[a] least[b] of the clans of Judah,
      From you he will come[c] to be ruler for me[d] over Israel
        Whose rising[e] is of old, from ancient times.**
2   **Therefore he will give them over[f] until the time
        When the mother[g] has given birth.
    Then the remainder[h] of his brethren will return
        To the children of Israel,**
3   **And he will stand[i] and rule[j] by the might of Yahweh,
        By the majestic name of Yahweh his God.[k]
    They will remain[l] . . ., for then[m] he will be
        Great to the ends of the earth;**
4   **And he will be the One of Peace.[n]**

---

a   The LXX βηθλεεμ οἶκος τοῦ Εφραθα (R και συ οἶ[κος βηθλεεμ ε]φραθα) probably is an accommodation of the LXX to the MT, preserving οἶκος as a translation of the original and transposing it. The LXX has led T. Roorda, (*Commentarius in Vaticinium Michae* [Leipzig: Weigel, 1886]), followed by Wellhausen and many others, to take בית אפרתה as original and בית לחם as a (correct) explanatory gloss; Marti compares the LXX at Josh 15:59. This would be more convincing if Beth Ephrata were elsewhere attested. In favor of the MT, note that two Bethlehem's are known, one in Judah and a less well-known one in Zebulon. Though the Bethlehem in Judah is closely associated with Ephrat(ah), the two are not identical, even though not all details of the historical relation are known (Ephrata may be a district or clan name). Therefore a double name, Bethlehem Ephrata, could have served to signal the close relation of the two entities, and to distinguish this Bethlehem from the other. The MT is metrically balanced if Ephrata is retained (3 plus 3).

Matt 2:6 (βηθλεεμ γῆ Ἰούδα) "Bethlehem in the land of Judah" is not wide of the mark as an explanation, but it is not a good basis for insertion of אֶרֶץ in the Micah text (contra Robinson). On the NT passage, see Krister Stendahl, *The School of St. Matthew* (Uppsala: Almqvist and Wiksells, 1954) pp 99–101; and Robert H. Gundry, *The Use of the Old Testament in St. Matthew's Gospel*, Supplements to Novum Testamentum, Vol. XVIII (Leiden: Brill, 1967), 91–93.

b   Delete לִהְיוֹת ("to be") of the MT as ungrammatical, having arisen by dittography from the second poetic line; so Hitzig, Wellhausen and others. The MT has

been defended by Joseph Fitzmyer, "l⁰ as a Preposition and a Particle in Micah 5,1 (5,2)," *CBQ* 18 (1956): 10–13 by taking ל as equal to מִן, but even a reading מִהְיוֹת would be unsatisfactory. Even Isa 49:6, the only occurrence of מִהְיוֹת, is not a perfectly identical construction, and a sense "too little to be . . ." is not really what the context requires. See the objections of O. Loretz, "Fehlanzeige von Ugaritismen in Micah 5,1–3," *UF* 9 (1977): 358–360.

Matt 2:6 οὐδαμῶς . . . εἶ has been understood as reflecting a reading לֹא הָיִיתָ. It might be simply an interpretation of the MT. In any case the sense is inappropriate.

A translation as superlative fits the topos: cf. 1 Sam 9:21, where the divinely chosen king comes from the smallest tribe. "Least" is also supported by the LXX and indirectly by Matt 2:6. Many, following Hitzig, would read הַצָּעִיר, but though the article would be normal in this construction if it were prose, it is doubtful that we can insist on it in poetry.

c   A nominal subject for the third person verb יֵצֵא is lacking, nor is there an antecedent. A word may have fallen out after יֵצֵא. The T already supplies "the Messiah," Sellin suggests " king," while others suppose that "to me" conceals יֶלֶד "a child" (Schmidt, Rudolph, BHS). It seems preferable to account for the incompleteness by supposing that this is a quotation (see Commentary).

d   This seems to be lacking in the S. In the Hebrew, the לִי stands before the main verb "will come," not with the infinitive "to be." The present translation is adopted for the sake of English style. The first-person element in sayings concerning divine choice and "bringing out" of the king (people, etc.) is pervasive. 2 Sam 7:8 "I took you from the pasture, from following the sheep, to be commander over my people, over Israel." Cf. 1 Kgs 8:16; Deut 4:20; and 1 Sam 16:1 כִּי־רָאִיתִי בְּבָנָיו לִי . . . מֶלֶךְ literally, "For I have seen among his sons a king for me." The sense of our passage is close to "From you I will bring forth one to be." It is unnecessary to suppose that לִי conceals a corruption. J. T. Willis, "ממך לי יצא in Micah 5:1," *JQR* 58 (1967–68): 317–22, is an exhaustive review of opinion on the phrase, but his own view, that a ruler will come forth and submit to Yahweh, is implausible.

e   מוֹצָאָה a noun related to יצא "go out" is too rare a word to permit a more precise rendering on the basis of usage; this is, in effect, the only occurrence. "Rising" is based on thematic consideration. Aage Bentzen, *King and Messiah* (London: Lutterworth, 1955), p 17, compares Ps 19:7 (Ev 6) and Luke 1:78 (ἀνατολή) and suggests that in קֶדֶם there is a pun on "East" and "old."

f   "He" is taken to refer to Yahweh, but it is unnecessary to add the divine name, as does Sellin.

g   Hebrew lacks the article, but in poetic usage this does not necessarily imply indefiniteness (see Commentary).

h   If עַל is taken to be in place of אֶל, which would be the normal preposition in the expression "return *to*," the sentence in isolation is grammatical. Semantic and contextual considerations suggest that the sense, as reflected in the present translation, though acceptable, is strained and unnatural, and permit conjecture as to a more original form of the statement (see Commentary). Note the LXX αὐτῶν ("their") for the MT "his."

i   The sense of ועמד here is uncertain; is it "take a stand" in order to perform the following action, or "appear" (equal to וקם), cf. Dan 11:3 "then a mighty king shall appear" (וְעָמַד)? The LXX adds καὶ ὄψεται apparently

from וראה a variant of ורעה.

j   Literally, this means "shepherd"; the LXX adds τὸ ποίμνιον αὐτοῦ ("his flock"), which is an interpretive expansion.

k   The LXX has τοῦ θεοῦ αὐτῶν ("their God").

l   A literal rendering of the MT, which is perhaps supported by Ps 125:1 and Joel 4:20 (EV 3:20) (but these both have "forever," and are of places, not people, so that the sense "be inhabited" lies close). The text may be incomplete, lacking בֶּטַח ("secure") or the like. Schmidt is perhaps right in principle in adding "each under his own vine and under his own fig tree." Perhaps however there is a corruption involving a dittography from יֵשׁוּבוּן of v 2. The LXX has ὑπάρξουσι ("they will begin, arise, be at hand"); the S has *wnetpnon;* and the V translates, *et convertentur,* coming from וְשָׁבוּ "they will return."

m   עַתָּה of the immediate future, cf. e.g., Mic 7:10.

n   This is a royal, quasi-divine title; cf. Isa 9:5 (EV 6) שַׂר שָׁלוֹם ("Prince of Peace") and the divine titles with *d* (*dû*) in Ugaritic, as *dpid* ("the Merciful One"), cf. Cross, *Canaanite Myth,* pp 18–20. Such an interpretaton was proposed for this passage in 1907 by Eerdmans (according to Smith); it is expounded, with rich detail, by Kevin J. Cathcart, "Notes on Micah 5,4–5," *Biblica* 49 (1968): 511–14. Contrast, however, Kevin J. Cathcart, "Micah 5,4–5 and Semitic Incantations," *Biblica* 59 (1978): 38–48.

Commentary

The broad topic of the rule of God over his people and the world links this passage with 4:1–4. The specific problem of the human king and restoration of "the former kingdom" which pervades the rest of chap. 4 here finds its culmination. As a catch-word, the וְאַתָּה of 5:1 echoes 4:8 and resembles וְעַתָּה of 4:11 (4:9 and 14 [EV 5:1] have עַתָּה without וְ).

At points the language of the oracle is obscure. This is no doubt partly deliberate; the prophet adopts a mysterious tone as appropriate to his subject. But the obscurity also arises from two additional features. In my opinion, the prophet is at points alluding to, or quoting, traditional material which we no longer possess. Moreover, the eighth century oracle has been reworked later in an exilic situation. As a result we may probably regard it as a prophecy of Micah, but we cannot restore the original form with complete confidence, or understand it at all

points.

Bethlehem is significant in two ways, as the town from which the great David sprang, and as a place very tiny to have produced so great a man. The story of David's origin from an obscure town was no doubt true, but emphasis on it is in part due to a fondness on the part of Old Testament writers for the theme: reversal of fortunes, rags to riches. Thus when Samuel told Saul he would be king, Saul replied (1 Sam 9:21): "Am I not a Benjaminite, from the least of the tribes of Israel? And is not my family the humblest of all the families of the tribe of Benjamin?" Similarly Gideon says: "How can I save Israel? My clan is the poorest in Manasseh, and I am the youngest in my father's house" (Judg 6:15). The theme gave pleasure as a satisfying narrative element, while at a religious level it expressed the working of divine power contrary to human capabilities or expectations. The term "clans" (אַלְפֵי) refers to a basic and ancient feature of

Israelite social organization, the "thousands," the troops raised from each tribal subdivision (מִשְׁפָּחָה) for military purposes. It recalls the pre-monarchic times of Moses, Joshua, and the judges, and thereby throws hearers of this prophecy back to the time before the coming of the first king.[1]

From Bethlehem will come someone to be a "ruler." This term was perhaps chosen as less definite and prosaic than "king," more shadowy and suited to prophecy. Perhaps the preceding line and following lines are quoted from an older poem or poems depicting the coming of the Davidic dynasty. The Balaam oracles give an example of the kind of thing that is cited. Writing under the monarchy, the narrator of the Balaam story casts his tale back to the time of the conquest, and into the mouth of Balaam he puts the artfully mysterious prediction—transparent in sense to his hearers—"a star shall come forth out of Jacob, and a sceptre shall rise out of Israel."

Since the language of this oracle is somewhat veiled and indefinite, two lines of interpretation are open. Either the prophet is speaking of a new Messianic king who will be born of the old line, or he is talking about the reappearance of David himself. Schmidt[2] has collected many examples of the myth of the returning king, and others could be added from accounts of "millennial" movements in world history. Some weight might be given to the stress on the coming from Bethlehem, original home of the line, and not from Jerusalem, but this too is susceptible of more than one reading.

In either case, it is likely that by this messianic prophecy the prophet implies a rejection of the current ruler, as has been argued recently by Rohland.[3] To be sure, it can be read as a reminder to the monarch of his glorious origins and future, or as a prediction of the great future of someone to come from his line. But on the whole it seems more natural to take the oracle as referring to someone other than the ruling king, and thus by implication as a rejection of the Judean king.

The ancient "rising," or origin, of the king is his descent from a ruling house that began nearly three centuries before Micah's time, with David. Or, if we are to think of David himself redivivus, the emphasis is on David as a figure from remote antiquity. At the same time, there is a strong flavor of myth here, for "of old" has the suggestion "primeval, from the beginning, as an order of creation."

At present, however, he (presumably Yahweh) will give them over—probably an obscure expression for "deliver into tribulation." The time when the mother has given birth is similarly mysterious, recalling the obscurities of Isaiah 7. "Mother" ("she who bears" [יוֹלֵדָה]) has no definite article in the Hebrew. Since this is poetry, that may mean that the word refers to an unidentified person or persons ("a mother," "parturient women") or to a definite figure "the mother," known to the prophet and his hearers though not specified here. Thus the sense of the temporal expression could range from: "a brief time—only as long as a pregnant woman carries a child" or even "as long as a woman is in labor" to "until the time when the designated mother (now living? herself in the future?) will bear him," which does not emphasize the time so much as the person. If the initial reference is to the coming again of David, more likely this obscure section refers to a preliminary time of anguish, rather than the birth of the messiah, but the language is veiled enough to leave the question open. Mays and Lescow[4] argue for approximately this conclusion, in different ways.

As it stands, and as translated here, the next line (2b) predicts the reunion of a scattered Israel, a thought paralleled in Micah (2:12 and 4:6–7, cf. Jer 3:18) and in itself not inappropriate to a time when the Northern kingdom had been lost and many had gone into exile out of Judah, in Sennacherib's invasion. But the phrase "remainder of his brethren" is very strange. "Remainder" should mean those left in the land, not the exiles; cf. Zech 14:2 "And the remainder of the people shall not be

---

1   Walter Harrelson, "Nonroyal Motifs in the Royal Eschatology," *Israel's Prophetic Heritage*, edd. Bernard W. Anderson and Walter Harrelson (New York: Harper, 1962), pp. 155–59, stresses very strongly the pre-monarchic elements in this oracle.

2   Hans Schmidt, *Der Mythos vom wiederkehrenden König im Alten Testament*, Schriften der Hessischen Hochschulen, Universität Giessen, Jahrgang 25, Heft 1 (Giessen: Töpelmann, 1925).

3   Edzard Rohland, *Die Bedeutung der Erwählungstraditionen Israels für die Eschatologie der alttestamentlichen Propheten*. Diss. Heidelberg, 1965.

4   Theodor Lescow, "Das Geburtsmotiv in den messianischen Weissagungen bei Jesaja und Micha," *ZAW* 79 (1967): 172–207.

destroyed out of the city" (וְיֶ֫תֶר הָעָם לֹא יִכָּרֵת מִן־הָעִיר).
And in what sense have the exiles left the children of
Israel (as distinct from the land of Israel) that they should
return? What does אֶחָיו mean? The people of the
kingdom were scarcely thought of as the brothers of the
monarch. Sellin was probably correct to see in יֶ֫תֶר אֶחָיו a
royal title "He who surpasses his brothers," comparing
Gen 49:3 "exceeding in rank and exceeding in honor"
(JPS; said of Reuben) (יֶ֫תֶר שְׂאֵת וְיֶ֫תֶר עָז), cf. 26 "the elect
of his brothers" (of Joseph) נְזִיר אֶחָיו. Instead of "will
return" one might conjecture (יֵשֵׁב) "will rule, sit en-
throned." The whole line would be: "Then he who
surpasses his brothers will rule the children of Israel."
This is plausible in outline, if some details are problematic (can יֵשֵׁב עַל mean "rule"?), enough to make it likely
that the present form of the line is a rather awkward
reworking of an old text, in the interest of finding the
idea "return." This would stem from an attempt by the
exilic community to appropriate this oracle for their own.

The force of "stand" וְעָמַד is unclear. Does it mean
"arise," or "take a stand," or "endure"? Any of these is
appropriate here. "Rule" is Hebrew רָעָה which also
means "tend a flock," and thus touches lightly on the
shepherd-king motif. The rule is by human agency, for
the king is separate from God and under him, but
through the king flow divine power and majesty. "And
they will remain. . ." is baffling in its incompleteness; see
Textual Notes. The dominion of the king is universal,
like David's (cf. Ps 2:8, "And the ends of the earth as
your possession" (וַאֲחֻזָּתְךָ אַפְסֵי־אָרֶץ . . .), and ultimately
like the divine rule, cf. 4:2. The universal peace of the
divine kingdom is reflected in the title of the Messiah:
the One of Peace.

■ **Imperial Dream**

When Asyria attacks the empire
of Israel, Israel can deal with
the threat easily, by raising
up subject chiefs who will ravage
Assyria and deliver Israel.

5

4   As to Assyria,[a] when they come into our land,
   When they tread on our ground,[b]
We will raise[c] against them seven[d] rulers,
   Eight[d] Aramaean chiefs.[e]

5   These then will rule[f] Assyria[g] with the sword,
   The land of Nimrud with a dagger.[h]
They will deliver[i] us[j] from Assyria
   When they come into our land,
      When they tread on our territory.

Preliminary Note.

Commentators have proposed many changes in the wording or arrangement of this passage in order to make it follow on the preceding. The Targum already seems to make efforts in this direction. But if זֶה שָׁלוֹם of 4a is taken as a title of the messianic king, as is done above, and if 4b–5 is recognized as dealing with a separate, though related, subject (see Commentary), it becomes unnecessary to seek to tie 4b–5 more closely to the preceding. Changes introduced by commentators to link this passage to the foregoing, then, are not even cited here; Rudolph provides much data along this line for those interested.

a   Mays asserts that "In the present MT 'Assyria' stands outside any expected syntax," but actually it is rather common for the subject of a temporal/conditional clause beginning כִּי to precede the conjunction; see the examples in Francis Brown, S. R. Driver, and Charles Briggs, *A Hebrew and English Lexicon of the Old Testament* (Oxford: Clarendon, 1907, reprint 1952), p 473.

b   Reading בְּאַדְמָתֵנוּ cf. the LXX ἐπὶ τὴν χώραν ἡμῶν. The MT בְּאַרְמְנוֹתֵנוּ ("our palaces/fortresses") could easily have arisen by scribal error. Cathcart's vigorous defense of the MT is nevertheless unconvincing; see "Micah 5,4–5 and Semitic Incantations," *Biblica* 59 (1978): 38–48. Wellhausen's בִּגְבוּלֵנוּ (as in v 5) does not account for the MT.

c   The LXX has καὶ ἐπεγερθήσονται "will be raised, rise up"; The Hebrew equivalent is uncertain, perhaps Qal וְקָמוּ. Sellin supposed הִתְקוֹמְמוּ.

d   "Seven" followed by "eight" (as is known from Ugaritic) is an indefinite number but fairly large (not "two or three"). Cathcart, "Micah 5,4–5," notes the parallel in the Arslan Tash incantation, as also the occurrence there of the verbs יבוא and ידרך, but these are insufficient to establish that the style of Micah 5 is related to a tradition of incantations.

e   The MT אָדָם "mankind" has been accepted by commentators as satisfactory, either in the sense "princes over men" or "from mankind," i.e., "mortal rulers," but both yield a very feeble sense. In addition, Hebrew usage make the phrase suspect, for in several hundred occurrences of אָדָם no closely comparable phrase occurs. Prov 15:20 and 21:20 כְּסִיל אָדָם "foolish man" and Gen 16:12 פֶּרֶא אָדָם "wild ass of a man" are somewhat similar, but not very close. Read instead אַדִּם and compare Ezek 32:30 נְסִיכֵי צָפוֹן "the princes of the north." Akkadian *nasiku* (perhaps from Aramaic נְסִיכָא) is used of Aramaean chiefs in neo-Assyrian and neo-Babylonian inscriptions. For a discussion of the term see J. A. Brinkman, *A Political History of Post-Kassite Babylonia 1158–722 B. C.* Analecta Orientalia 43 (Rome: Pontifical Biblical Institute, 1968), 273–75. The word, which Brinkman translates "sheikhs," was used of the heads of a people, a land, a city, or even a river. The LXX δήγματα, "bites," is as if the word were from נשך "bite."

f   This translation assumes that the verb is from רעה; others explain it as from רעע "break"; cf. Ps 2:9 תְּרֹעֵם. The LXX and S imply תִּרְעֵם. Cf. Max Wagner, *Die lexikalischen und grammatikalischen Aramaismen im alttestamentlichen Hebräisch,* BZAW 96 (1966): 107.

g   The MT has "land of Assyria"; אֶרֶץ is most easily understood as an insertion. The shorter reading, which fits parallelistic style better, is attested in the LXX, but has R τὴν γῆν Ασσουρ which reflects the MT.

h   The MT בִּפְתָחֶיהָ "in its entrances/gates(?)" is unsatisfactory in sense and as a parallel to "sword." פְּתִיחָה "dagger" (approximate; exact sense unknown) occurs in Ps 55:22 (EV 21) and the verb פָּתַח is used with חֶרֶב Ps 37:14 and Ezek 21:33. Some such sense can claim the support of various minor ancient versions: the Ach, Sa, α′, and ε′. A plural form is also possible, as are variants in suffix. The

LXX, T, and S seems to struggle with the text.

E. Lipiński's attempt in "Nimrod et Aššur," *RB* 73 (1966): 27–93, to show that "land of Nimrud" is literarily secondary in this passage is rather obviously carried out in service of his theory that "Nimrod" equals "Marduk," to which an eighth-century parallelism of "Nimrod" to "Ashur" would be an embarrassment.

i   This is read as a plural, with Marti and others. The MT has singular, perhaps influenced by vv 1–3, which speaks of a single ruler to come, or perhaps the singular is a copyist's error. The bulk of the passage favors plural.

j   The pronoun is supplied from context; it is not necessary

to change the Hebrew text, since הִצִּיל is not necessarily followed by an object, note Zech 11:6; Isa 31:5; 1 Sam 17:35, and the frequent absolute use of אֵין מַצִּיל.

Commentary

As the text stands (see Note) there is little direct continuation of the theme of the new David announced in the preceding oracle. Here the people, in first person plural, speak of joint action ("we will raise") when the Assyrian comes against "our land." Yet the theme of invasion successfully repelled picks up ideas from 4:9–14 (EV 5:1), and thus 4b–5 is "Davidic" in the sense that it speaks of conditions and policies appropriate to an empire as large as David's. There are a few possible verbal links with the foregoing; "and he will rule" (וְרָעָה) with 4: "shepherds" (רֹעִים) and 5: "these then will rule" (וְרָעוּ), and 3: "land" (אֶרֶץ) with 4: "our land" (אַרְצֵנוּ) and 5: "land" (אֶרֶץ) and "our land" (אַרְצֵנוּ).

In the time of David, Israel's empire was conceived as reaching, ideally, from the Euphrates to the boundary with Egypt, and to some extent this ideal was realized. Israel could think of herself as adjoining Mesopotamia, but protected from that side by subject Aramaean states. In later times, down to the fall of Damascus, the successors to the Davidic empire, confronted by threats to their land by Assyria from the ninth century on, could think of their security as lying in alliance with the Aramaean states that lay in between. Whatever the real strength of the states between her and the Euphrates (Israel might at times not even be *primus inter pares*), Northern and Southern kingdoms could cherish an old conception of the extent of "our land" and the function of the Aramaeans as her tools.

"When the Assyrian comes into our land" in this ideological context means "when the Assyrian army crosses the Euphrates." Israel will in such a situation "raise up" the intervening subject states, who will conquer and rule Assyria with the sword, i.e. military might and violence. Thus Israel will be saved.

On the view that Micah was associated with a movement of revitalization and protest, this rather mundane "imperial dream" would have formed part of his view of the good time to come, a restoration of conditions already destroyed by the Assyrians. Elements of such a vision persist into later periods of Israel's history. "Assyria" could be read as a name for Babylon, or the Seleucid empire, or any enemy of the kingdom of God. But this peculiar formulation of hope for a renewal of the kingdom seems most likely to have its origin at a time when the original imperial situation was still fresh in mind.

■ **The Irresistible Survivors**

**The descendants of Jacob will
dominate all enemies, sudden
and uncontrollable as dew,
irresistible as a lion.**

5

6   **Then the descendants of Jacob, among the nations,**[a]
         In the midst of many peoples, shall be
     Like dew coming[b] **from Yahweh,**
         Like showers[c] **on the grass,**
     Which does not wait for any man,
         Or stay for any human.[d]
7   **Then the descendants of Jacob, among the nations,**[e]
         In the midst of many peoples, shall be
     Like a lion[f] **among the beasts of the forest,**[g]
         Like a young lion in a flock of sheep.
     If he comes along he tramples and tears his prey,
         And none can save.
8   **Your hand will be exalted**[h] **over your foes,**
         and all your enemies will be exterminated.

a   The two sayings joined here have much the same form, but there may be doubt as to whether to aim at an even greater similarity by textual reconstruction, and if so, how this should be achieved. Here "among the nations" (בַּגּוֹיִם) has been added (so Marti, Nowack, Robinson) because the LXX and S have this; it is present in v 7; parallelistic style, used elsewhere in these sayings, is often characterized by a short first member, paralleled by a longer second element; terms in synonymous parallelism are vulnerable to loss in transmission, a kind of reduction to prose. Of course formal similarity can also be achieved by elimination of the elements in v 7 that are not in v 6, namely בַּגּוֹיִם, but this cannot claim any support in the textual tradition. It deserves mention that Ehrlich, *Randglossen*, deleted the second of the parallel terms in v 7 עַמִּים to achieve maximum *dissimilarity*.

b   This verb is to be supplied here for the sake of English; Hebrew does not require it. The LXX πίπτουσα ("falling") seems to have arisen to supply the same sort of need.

c   The LXX has καὶ ὡς ἄρνες "and like lambs"; Ziegler, "Beiträge," p 386 (*Sylloge*, p 92), plausibly supposes this is

for כרבים <כרים which he identifies as a corruption of כרביבים by haplography. But כרים could be a genuine form, cf. Delbert R. Hillers, "Amos 7,4 and Ancient Parallels," *CBQ* 26 (1964) 221–25, for occurrences of the shorter form *rb* ("rain") in Ugaritic and Hebrew.

d   The LXX reads μὴ συναχθῇ μηδεὶς μηδὲ ὑποστῇ ("not one is gathered up or waits"); the translator has apparently taken the first verb, *yqwh*, as *yiqqāweh* ("be collected").

e   This is omitted by Sellin, Augustin George, "Michée (Le livre de)," *DBS*, Vol. 5 (Paris: Letouzey et Ané, 1955) Cols. 1252–63, Weiser.

f   The MT has כאריה; Mur 88 בארית is a copyist's error.

g   The LXX ἐν τῷ δρυμῷ probably reflects no different text. The S *d'ānā* ("of the flock") is an inner-Syriac error for *d'ābā* ("of the forest"), influenced by the parallel; cf. the similar development in Mic 7:14.

h   The MT תָּרֹם implies a wish "may your hand, etc." The text may, however, be read as imperfect; the LXX and V use future tenses. Perhaps the triumphal note of the preceding context is more likely to have continued with a statement of conviction rather than hope.

Commentary

Though this passage is only loosely joined to what comes just before it, it does have close thematic ties to the section about the future beginning in 4:1. To "survivor" or "remnant" compare the same term in 4:7; the parallel pair "nations/many peoples" recurs in 4:1–3. The translation "descendants" for שְׁאֵרִית is meant to bring out the positive side of the term, which is intended here, as in 4:7.

"Among the nations. . .in the midst of many peoples" does not imply the scattering of Israel, but the gathering of the nation at one focal point, as in 4:1–3 and 6–7;

Israel is surrounded by the nations.

The sense of the two similes, especially the first, is disputed, but this is in part because commentators have relied on conventional modern associations with "dew" (that it is spread far and wide, that it is beneficial). This leads to a reading of the passage as a blessing on the gentiles; scattered Israel will be "a blessing and benediction to humanity" . . . "as the dew refreshes the morning landscape, and as showers cause the grass to grow," so will Jacob be, in the words of Wolfe;[1] cf. Weiser. But these notions do not lie down comfortably beside the lion simile which follows. Smith badly confuses matters by making this a simile about grass, in defiance of the grammar of Hebrew similes, where "dew" has to be the thing compared, and of Hebrew associations with "grass," which were not those of Carl Sandburg. Rudolph and McKeating aptly compare 2 Sam 17:12, where a royal council is plotting the overthrow of an enemy, and the suggestion is made: "We shall light upon him (David)

as the dew falls upon the ground." This establishes the possibility of a hostile sense for a dew simile. The explanation given in v 6 further specifies the aspect under which dew is viewed: its fall is beyond human control or resistance.

The lion simile complements the dew simile. Like dew from heaven, the lion is irresistible, among either wild or tame beasts.

In the last verse the speaker is an anonymous voice addressing the people. Victory over their enemies, even their utter destruction ("cutting off", cf. Gen 9:11) is promised.

---

1   Rolland E. Wolfe, "The Book of Micah," *IB* VI (New York and Nashville: Abingdon Press, 1956), 897–949.

■ **The Preparatory Purging**

In time to come Yahweh will
take away from his people every
foreign element; then he himself
will vindicate their cause with
the nations.

5

9	An oracle of Yahweh:
	On that day I will take away the horses from your midst
	And destroy your chariots.
10	I will take away the cities of your land
	And tear down your fortresses.
11	I will take your incantations away from you,
	And youᵃ will have no soothsayers.
12	I will take away your carved images
	And the standing stones from your midst,
	So that you no longer worship the work of your hands.
13	I will pull down the Ashera's from your midst
	And destroy your idols,ᵇ
14	And I will bring vengeance, in wrath and anger,
	On the nationsᶜ who were disobedient.

a The MT has לָךְ; the LXX has ἐν σοί "in you," probably
just free rendering, but note one ms Kenn בָךְ.

b The MT עָרֶיךָ "your cities" is an odd parallel for אֲשֵׁרֶיךָ
and repeats "cities" of v 10. A sense "idols" is appropriate, and can be achieved by reading עֲצַבֶּיךָ, with Marti
and many others. Cf. 2 Chron 24:18, where "Asherah" is
followed by עֲצַבִּים. Sellin achieves a similar sense with
צִירֶיךָ "your images," cf. Isa 45:16. J. T. Willis, "The
Authenticity and Meaning of Micah 5:9–14," ZAW 81
(1969): 353–68, following earlier scholars, arrives at a
sense "idols" by appealing to a Ugaritic *ʿr, supposed to
equal psl "image," but the Ugaritic word appealed to
(first by Theodor H. Gaster, "Notes on the Minor

Prophets," JTS 38 [1937]: 163–65) is now recognized to
have nothing whatever to do with idols; ǵr is a verb. For
an alternate suggestion, translating עריך as "your temple
quarters," see L. R. Fisher, "The Temple Quarter," JSS,
Vol. 8, No. 1, 1963, 34–41.

c Some have rejected this whole verse as inappropriate;
for the same reason Bewer proposed change of הַגּוֹיִם to
הַגֵּאִים (equals הַגָּאִים) "the proud." The V has in omnibus
gentibus.

Commentary

The phrase "in that day" links this with the preceding
predictions, and thereby helps determine its meaning.
Whereas in itself the oracle is largely negative in tone,
the context of the future glorious time makes it appear as
the reverse side of the fabric: being deprived of cities,
horses, and the rest prepares for a time when God will
rule unchallenged through his Messianic king. Within
the general understanding of Micah presented in this
commentary, this passage was originally a formal renun-
ciation of inauthentic, foreign elements as a prelude to
the Messianic age.

There is no close tie to the following; instead a new
major section begins at 6:1.

An impressive formal unity is secured by a simple
device: first singular forms (all waw-consecutive with the
perfect, four from the same root) begin eight of the cola.
The same principle of construction is employed in Jer
51:20–24 ("I will shatter" [וְהִפַּצְתִּי] eight times, plus other
first-person forms). In a number of parallel texts "I will
take away" (וְהִכְרַתִּי) occurs, though not repeated as a
constructive device. Zech 9:10, "And I will cut off the
chariots from Ephraim, and the horses from Jerusalem,
and the bow of war will be cut off" (וְהִכְרַתִּי־רֶכֶב מֵאֶפְרַיִם
וְסוּס מִירוּשָׁלַם וְנִכְרְתָה קֶשֶׁת מִלְחָמָה . . .), is especially similar
to Micah in content, and also forms part of a prophecy of
hope (note the last words of the verse, "and he will speak
peace to the nations" [וְדִבֶּר שָׁלוֹם לַגּוֹיִם . . .]). Zechariah 9

may be dependent on Micah; other texts with similar phraseology are contemporary with Micah, thus Amos 2:3 "and I will cut off her judge from her midst" (וְהִכְרַתִּי שׁוֹפֵט מִקִּרְבָּהּ ...) (cf. 1:5). In a different way Isa 2:6–8 is close in sense and words. Note also Isa 9:13 (EV 13); Lev 26:30; Zeph 1:4; Nah 1:14; and Zeph 13:2.

In the time to come, Yahweh will take away military equipment, divination, and illegitimate cultic apparatus, each in its way an illegitimate object of trust by the people, inauthentic and foreign to its true nature. The polemic against reliance on fortifications and military equipment, especially horses, is old and widespread in Israel. Thus Hos 14;4, "Ashur will not save us; we will not ride on horses." (אַשּׁוּר לֹא יוֹשִׁיעֵנוּ עַל־סוּס לֹא נִרְכָּב). The same context refers to "bowing down to the work of one's own hands." Compare also Isa 31:1, "Ah, you who go down to Egypt for help, relying on horses, and trusting on a multitude of chariots, and on great numbers of horsemen, never looking to the holy one of Israel." (הוֹי הַיֹּרְדִים מִצְרַיִם לְעֶזְרָה עַל־סוּסִים יִשָּׁעֵנוּ וַיִּבְטְחוּ עַל־רֶכֶב כִּי רָב וְעַל פָּרָשִׁים כִּי עָצְמוּ מְאֹד וְלֹא שָׁעוּ עַל־קְדוֹשׁ יִשְׂרָאֵל ...). Note also Deut 17:16; Ps 20:8 (EV 7); 33:17; and Hos 1;7. In Jer 5:17 trust in fortified cities is explicitly condemned, and cf. Hos 10:13–14.

Divination is also to be removed in that day. The precise reference of the parallel terms כְּשָׁפִים and מְעֹנְנִים is unknown to us, nor is it made explicit in this or parallel texts *why* divination is illegitimate. We may reasonably suppose, however, especially on the basis of evidence concerning divination in other societies, that divination in its various forms (hepatoscopy, augury, etc.) presupposed and attempted to exploit an order of reality and power to which even the gods were subject.[1] In Israel such a conception would be felt to run counter to belief in Yahweh as the only source of power and help. At a less philosophical level, divination was identified as foreign, not native to Israel.

Images also lead the worshipper away from Yahweh. Note Isa 17:7–8 "On that day a man will look to his maker . . . He will not look to altars his own hands have made . . . or the Ashera's or incense altars." (בַּיּוֹם הַהוּא יִשְׁעֶה הָאָדָם עַל־עֹשֵׂהוּ . . . וְלֹא יִשְׁעֶה אֶל־הַמִּזְבְּחוֹת מַעֲשֵׂה יָדָיו וְהָאֲשֵׁרִים וְהַחַמָּנִים . . .). Steles, or standing stones, were used in various ways in ancient Israel, and in early times at least some of these uses were regarded as legitimate. In the present context, the steles are evidently regarded in their strictly cultic use, where they "marked the cultic immanence of the deity",[2] and hence they are condemned along with "images," which had much the same function. It may well be that such a condemnation of steles is a sign of the lateness of this passage, which is closely paralleled by 26:1. These idols are "the work of your hands," a designation common in Old Testament polemic against idolatry. Sometimes the theme is expanded to depict in detail the whole laborious process humans might use to make an idol (Isa 44:9–20). "Asherim" were wooden cult-symbols of a principal goddess of the Canaanites, Asherah. As such, they were rejected by Yahwists. If "cities" is retained here, this verse recurs to a theme mentioned earlier, but since such a reading is rather awkward, some word for "idols" is to be preferred; this would complete and to some extent summarize the foregoing.

Without these foreign, false sources of trust, Israel's protection will be carried out by her God. Mendenhall, distinguishes between punitive vindication (vengeance) and defensive vindication, where an injured person's rights are upheld.[3] Here the reference is to punitive vindication. Israel's rights have already in the past been violated by other nations, but she cannot and should not avenge herself. Instead the supreme power will step in to vindicate her rights by punishing her adversaries.

This passage has been assigned a late date by some on the basis of the ideas contained. Opposition to steles (מַצֵּבוֹת) and the theme of vengeance against the nations are most common in late compositions. Willis has an exhaustive review of opinion on this issue, his own conclusion being that the passage is to be associated with

---

1 See J.P. Vernant, et al, *Divination et rationalité* (Paris, Seuil, 1974), and the review by Giorgio Buccellati in *OrAnt* 16 (1977): 239–40.

2 Carl F. Graesser, "Standing Stones in Ancient Palestine," *BA*, 35 (1972): 34–63.

3 George E. Mendenhall, *The Tenth Generation* (Baltimore: Johns Hopkins, 1973), pp 77–88.

the reform of Hezekiah.[4] It seems doubtful that this is tenable in detail; we do not know of any opposition by Hezekiah to horses and cities, for example! In principle, however, the passage seems congruent with the times of Hezekiah, and the situation of Micah and villagers in Judah, who prior to the onset of the Messianic time look for a purging of the nation. Judgment on the nations is announced in the first sentence of the book (1:2), and though rare in early writings, the theme of vengeance on the nations is perhaps not unthinkable in an oracle of Micah.

4   J.T. Willis, "The Authenticity and Meaning of Micah 5:9–14," *ZAW* 81 (1969): 353–68.

■ A Covenant Lawsuit: The Whole Duty of Mankind

In a covenant lawsuit the prophet recites the righteous acts of Yahweh, which leave the people no excuse for infidelity; to their offer of ritual performance comes the charge: do justice, love kindness, and walk wisely with your God.

6

1 Hear now what Yahweh is saying:[a]
   "Up, plead before[b] the mountains!
      Let the hills hear your voice!"

2 "O mountains,[c] hear the suit of Yahweh,
      And you, primeval streams![d]
   For Yahweh has a suit against his people,
      With Israel he wishes to contend."

3 "My people, what have I done to you
      Or how have I troubled you?[e]
   Testify against me!

4 For I brought you up[f] out of the land of Egypt,
      And redeemed you from the slave-house.
   I sent before you Moses,
      Aaron and Miriam with him.[g]

5 Remember the scheme[h] of Balak, king of Moab,
      And the answer he got from Balaam, son of Beor
   . . . from Shittim to Gilgal,[i]
   That you may know[j] the saving acts of Yahweh."[k]

6 "With what shall I come before Yahweh,
      Bow[l] to the God who is on high?[m]
   Shall I come before him with whole burnt offerings,[n]
      With calves a year old?

7 Will Yahweh[o] accept thousands of rams,
      Streams of oil[p] by the ten thousands?"
   Shall I give my firstborn for my sin,[q]
      The fruit of my body for the wrong I have done?

8 He told you,[r] O man, what is good
   Yahweh wants nothing of you, except that you
   Do justice,
      Love kindness,[s]
      And walk wisely[t] with your God.

a The form of the heading in the MT is unique, but not ungrammatical. The LXX ἀκούσατε δὴ λόγον κυρίου · κύριος εἶπεν has suggested to commentators, as a minimum, insertion of הַדָּבָר after אֵת, or additional change to דְּבַר אֲדֹנָי and of אֹמֵר to אָמַר. But the LXX λόγον κυρίου could represent a change to a more familiar form of words, and יהוה אָמַר would be odd.

b The MT אֵת, common for "striving/contending *with*" an opponent, is without good parallel in the sense required here, "plead *before* someone." Wellhausen and many others have preferred אֶל, which is elsewhere attested for "(plead) *to*" e.g., Hos 12:5. The LXX πρὸς may attest such a reading.

c The LXX freely translates λαοί ("peoples"), perhaps under influence of 1:2 (Rudolph).

d The MT literally means "streams (from) the foundations of the earth." Wellhausen, followed by many, reads וְהַאֲזִינוּ ("and give ear"). Where this is done, "foundations of the earth" is taken as parallel to הָרִים, and in such a context אֵיתָן, in the sense "perpetual" is out of place. But "give ear" is suspiciously easy. Rudolph on that ground rejects the conjecture and retains the MT in the sense "you primeval ones, you foundations of the earth," cf. Jer 5:15; Ps 24:2; Isa 24:18; Ps 82:5; and Isa 40:21.

Though this is preferable to emendation, it involves what is perhaps an unwarranted extension of אֵתָן to mountains. Here אֵתָנִים is taken as "perpetual streams" from its well-known use with נַחַל (Deut 21:4 and Amos 5:24) and נָהָר (Ps 78:15), and יָם (Exod 14:27). Cf. the S *'umqê* ("deeps"). The Arabic cognates, which have to do with flowing water, may have some force in this case. In the ancient world important rivers were thought of as primeval elements, and are often associated with mountains in cosmogonic accounts, specifically those occurring in treaties. Thus a common pattern in Hittite and Akkadian treaty texts is: ". . . the mountains, the rivers, the springs, the great deep, heaven and earth . . .". מֹסְדֵי אָרֶץ is then a chronological indicator, equivalent to אָרֶץ as in Isa 40:21; cf. Jer 5:15 גּוֹי אֵיתָן and its parallel גּוֹי מֵעוֹלָם ("primeval people"). Hence מֹסְדֵי אָרֶץ is "primeval," or it may be "(at) the base of the world," cf. Ps. 24:2 כִּי־הוּא עַל־יַמִּים יְסָדָהּ.

e The LXX ἤ τί ἐλύπησά σε ἤ τί παρηνώχλησά σοι apparently incorporates two renderings.

f Mur 88 has הֶעֱלִיתִיךָ. G. W. Anderson, "A Study of Micah 6:1–8," *Scottish Journal of Theology* 4 (1951): 192, supposes there is a play on words between הֶעֱלִיתִיךָ and הֶלְאֵתִיךָ but the resemblance in sound is really not close.

g Read עַמּוֹ for עַמִּי ("my people"). The idiom שָׁלַח . . . עִם is confirmed by Exod 33:12, a not dissimilar context. Aaron and Miriam are objects coordinate with "Moses," cf. Ps. 105:26 שָׁלַח מֹשֶׁה עַבְדּוֹ אַהֲרֹן אֲשֶׁר בָּחַר־בּוֹ. עַמִּי ("my people") is not ungrammatical or out of place, but could easily have arisen by scribal error.

h The LXX adds κατὰ σοῦ ("against you"); this is an interpretation.

i This does not fit with the context; that is, "answered" does not go well with the expression of distance traversed "from Shittim to Gilgal." Probably something, of unknown extent, has been lost from the text, and we have no obvious way of conjecturing what it was. The attempt to find the missing element in בֶּן בְּעוֹר gives the conjectures: וַתַּעֲבֹר ("and how you crossed" [?] [Sellin]); בְּעָבְרֶךָ ("your c*r*ossing" [Robinson]); עָבְרֶךָ ("when you were passing" [Weiser]). But this destroys a very appropriate traditional epithet, nicely parallel to "king of Moab." (To delete also "king of Moab" [Robinson, Lindblom, *Micha*, and Weiser] is a foolish consistency). Simple deletion of "from Shittim to Gilgal" (Wellhausen, Marti, et al.) is open to the objection that the phrase is neither meaningless in this context, nor a gloss on anything else.

j "You" is understood from the context; the LXX, T, and V probably imply no reading different from the MT (contra George). The infinitive of purpose does not require an express subject if the subject is the same as that of the main verb, as may be the case here (contra George, who would read תֵּדַע).

k Emendation to צִדְקוֹתַי is overly logical. Hebrew style permits this kind of use of the name of God in speech by the deity, cf. Lam 3:35–36; 2:20, 22; 3:66; and Amos 4:11 (contra BHS). The S "because he knew the righteousness of God" is interpretive.

l The LXX καταλάβω . . . ἀντιλήμψομαι (approximately "lay hold on") is a singular translation, but probably not derived from a different Hebrew text.

m The LXX θεοῦ μου ὑψίστου is a misreading of the Hebrew. The MT displays the not uncommon use of a noun in construct before an abstract noun ("God of height") as equivalent of noun plus adjective ("high God").

n Mur 88 has בעלות.

o BHS etc. delete *metri causa*, but this is not sufficient grounds within a book such as Micah.

p The V *hircorum pinguium*, "fat goats," and similar readings in witnesses to the LXX text are by inner-Greek confusion of χειμάρρων ("torrents") with χιμάρων ("he-goats").

q The LXX ἀσεβείας may translate פֶּשַׁע. On the construction: נתן followed by two nouns, meaning "give something in exchange for," Smith compares Ezek 27:14 סוּסִים וּפָרָשִׁים וּפְרָדִים נָתְנוּ עִזְבוֹנָיִךְ . . . ("[Beth-Togarmah] exchanged for your wares, horses, war horses, and mules").

r I.e., Yahweh has told you; Yahweh in the preceding context supplies an antecedent for the pronominal subject of the verb. The MT is thus not impossible, but the usage is unusual and may have given rise to variations in person in the versions. The LXX ἀνηγγέλη ("it was told") may imply הֻגַּד ("it was told") a reading favored by Wellhausen and many others. The difference in sense is slight. The LXX reading preferred by Ziegler is εἰ ἀνηγγέλη σοι; this apparently arises under the influence of the following question. The V has *indicabo* and the S has *ḥawwîtāk*, "I showed you"; the T gives "it was shown."

s J. Philip Hyatt, "On the Meaning and Origin of Micah 6:8," *ATR* 34 (1952): 232–39, uses Qumran evidence to argue for a sense "faithful love," with *ḥsd* modifying *'hbt*, but this presses the syntax of the Qumran texts too much.

t The sense of הַצְנֵעַ is somewhat uncertain because the verb occurs only very seldom in early Hebrew, and because the ancient versions vary in their renderings. The T has צניע "chaste, discreet, decorous"; at Mic 6:8 Greek versions give "ready" (ἕτοιμον so the LXX and also the S) and "be secure" (ἀσφαλίζου); the V has *sollicitum* "anxious, careful." J. Philip Hyatt, "On the Meaning and Origin of Micah 6:8," *ATR* 34 (1952): 232–39; H. J. Stoebe, "Und demütig sein vor deinem Gott. Micha 6,8," *Wort und Dienst*, N. F. 6 (1959): 180–94; H. L. Ginsberg, "Dqdwqym bšnym 'śr," *Eretz Israel* 3 (1954): 83–84, concur in recognizing a more intellectual quality than the traditional (since Luther) "humble." Hence the present translation "wisely."

u The LXX, κυρίου θεοῦ σου, is a typical expansion.

Commentary

This oracle does not continue the mostly hopeful and consolatory passages that precede, but returns to the note of chiding characteristic of chaps. 1–3. The occurrence of "Hear" recalls 1:2. This tone of reproach continues through the following oracles of chaps. 6 and 7 up to the concluding liturgy 7:8–20.

Recognition that this is a prophetic covenant lawsuit (*rîb*) is important for understanding of the imagery and the sequence of ideas, and also for determining the limits of the oracle.[1] Because vv 6–8 introduce new speakers (the people and the prophet), and are intelligible in themselves, they have been taken by some to be a separate oracle. Gunkel-Begrich's analysis of the rîb-pattern, as refined by Huffmon[2] and Harvey,[3] for all its fluidity, at some point calls for a specific charge, indictment, or sentence comparable to Ps 50:14–15; Isa 1:2–3; Jer 2:10, 11, 13; and Deut 32:15–18, stating what the defendant ought to do or what he has failed to do, or both. Mic 6:1–5 is incomplete and truncated without the concluding question and answer.

"Hear now what Yahweh is saying" are the words of the prophet addressed to the audience, to prepare them for the drama that follows.

Yahweh speaks to the prophet first. He is to appear as Yahweh's representative, almost one might say attorney, in a suit against the people. The mountains and primeval streams are invoked "either as witness or as judges in the controversy between Yahweh and Israel when Israel is indicted for breach of covenant".[4] The specific connection of this invocation to ancient treaty and covenant practice was more fully discussed by Huffmon, who identified this sort of divine lawsuit specifically as a *covenant* lawsuit.[5] In the ancient world these primordial elements are not quite on an equal footing with other gods, but do form part of the fundamental cosmic framework. The rather standard list occurring in the Hittite treaties derives from cosmogonic tradition. Reconstructed from variants, it is: "All the former gods: Nara, Napshara, Minki, Ammunki, Tuhushi, Ammizzadu, Alalu, Anu, Antum, Apantum, Enlil, Ninlil, the mountains, the rivers, the springs, the great deep, heaven and earth, the winds, the clouds." Huffmon argues that these were not members of the divine council, even outside Israel. This may be so, if Huffmon's distinction is not somewhat overlogical. In any case it remains difficult to decide whether invocation of heaven and earth, mountains and streams, was much more than a rhetorical device within Israel's religion. Involved as they were fundamentally as witnesses to the covenant, their naming called forth associations of permanence and numinous age. There is no clear evidence that they were thought of as executing sentence on the condemned.

After the prophet's announcement that Yahweh has a suit against his people Israel, the voice of the deity himself speaks. The speech begins ironically by entertaining the notion that Yahweh somehow may have given the people cause for complaint.[6] Implied is that they are acting as if that were the case; eventually the behavior of the people must be investigated, but first will come vindication of God's ways to them. This stress on how the partners to the covenant have lived up to it leads up to v 6, where the people betray their misconception of the importance of their ritual performance.

The saving acts of God which constituted the people as a community are recited, in briefest fashion, with four emphases: redemption from Egypt, inspired leadership, deliverance from the schemes of Balak and Balaam, and entrance into the land. Mention of Moses, the great leader through whom the fundamental Torah was given, requires no comment. "Aaron," cited with Moses also in Ps 77:21 (EV 20); Josh 24:5; 1 Sam 12:8; and Ps 105:26, evokes associations of priesthood, perhaps in subtle preparation for the priestly language of vv 6–8. It is likely that Miriam is thought of here especially as the

---

1 Hans Jochen Boecker, *Redeformen des Rechtslebens im Alten Testament*, WMANT 14 (Neukirchen: Neukirchener, 1964), pp 101–05, treats 6:1–8 from a legal point of view.

2 H.B. Huffmon, "The Covenant Lawsuit in the Prophets," *JBL* 78 (1959): 285–95.

3 Julien Harvey, "'Le Rîb-Pattern,' Réquisitoire prophétique sur la rupture de l'alliance," *Biblica* 43 (1963): 172–96.

4 George E. Mendenhall, *Law and Covenant in Israel and the Ancient Near East* (Pittsburgh: Biblical Colloquium, 1955), p 40.

5 See note 2 above.

6 Cf. Isa 5:4, "What more could have been done for my vineyard that I did not do?" (מַה־לַּעֲשׂוֹת עוֹד לְכַרְמִי וְלֹא עָשִׂיתִי בּוֹ . . .).

"prophetess" of Exod 15:20.[7] The principal story of Balak and Balaam is told in Numbers 22–24. Recent discovery of a long (but very obscure) Aramaic (?) text, concerning Balaam, son of Beor, from about 700 B.C. combines with other biblical evidence (Num 25:1–3 and 31:16) to make it plain that the figure of Balaam loomed even larger in legend of Micah's time than the Numbers story suggests.[8] Here, in the context of favorable divine acts, the reference is to the involuntary reversal in the story. Balak hires Balaam to curse, but he can only bless Israel, predicting her future triumphant greatness. ". . .from Shittim to Gilgal" is probably a fragmentary line, but not much has been lost, for Shittim is the place in Moab, northeast of the Dead Sea, where Israel was encamped when the Balak-Balaam incident took place (Num 25:1), along with other final events of the wilderness period (Number 26 and Joshua 2). From this final camp the Israelites crossed the Jordan to their first foothold in the promised land, Gilgal. Thus the summary of sacred history leads from Exodus to conquest, from promise to fulfillment.

The purpose clause (v 5d) contains ambiguities, or levels of meaning, impossible to convey in a single translation. One may begin with the more profound level. "To know" can describe a very fundamental religious attitude. In some occurrences, and it may be plausible here, it is covenant language. This is not intellectual or mystical knowledge; it means to recognize one's proper lord or fellow, and to act accordingly, as shown by Huffmon.[9] This knowledge (sometimes, succinctly, "knowledge of God," as in Hos 4:1) is presented here in expanded form, i.e. knowledge of his צִדְקוֹת, itself an untranslatable term that conveys the view that God is known in his gracious acts of power and rescue. Thus Judg 5:11, "There they recite the righteous acts of Yahweh" (. . . שָׁם יְתַנּוּ צִדְקוֹת יהוה . . .). In our passage the acts of God spoken of, beginning with the Exodus, are his צִדְקוֹת. Yet the sense is not only "triumphs," (RSV at Judg 5:11), for the word also bears an ethical or forensic connotation. A צְדָקָה is a *righteous* act. This carries us to the lawcourt scene, where the judge would pronounce one party "right," (צַדִּיק) or where the party in the wrong might even admit that his adversary was right. Thus Exod 9:27 "Yahweh is in the right and I and my people are in the wrong."

If Yahweh is vindicated, then the people are by implication accused, and there ensues a brief dialogue resembling a priestly instruction (torah), in this case, a request for cultic guidance by a layman, answered by the specialist.[10] But though the form is priestly the language is not totally priestly; Rudolph notes that רָצָה ("to be pleased") is part of priestly vocabulary, but not קָדַם ("to come before") or כָּפַף ("to bow down"). In fact the whole intent is to reject the cultic. The speaker is an individual, a representative of the whole benighted people who imagine that ritual is a solution when it is part of the problem.

The acts envisioned follow in climactic order. "Whole burnt offerings" (holocausts) were those totally dedicated to the deity, with no share for the worshipper. Calves a year old are prescribed for certain sin-offerings in Lev 9:3. Rams and oil figure in other sacrificial acts, but the figures in Micah are of course deliberately fanciful. Finally, as a pinnacle of human delusion, the spokesman proposes to offer his son, his firstborn. Such sacrifices were more than mere possibilites, both in other nations of the time and in Israel, at least in certain periods, but the linguistic and archaeological evidence is such that it is difficult to estimate the degree to which such an abomination was practiced.[11] This does not, of course, place

---

7   Rudolph.

8   P. Kyle McCarter, "The Balaam Texts from Deir 'Allā: The First Combination," *BASOR*, No. 239 (Summer, 1980): 49–60, and Baruch A. Levine, "The Deir 'Alla Plaster Inscriptions," *JAOS* 101 (1981): 195–205.

9   H.B. Huffmon, "The Treaty Background of Hebrew Yada'," *BASOR* 181 (Feb., 1966): 31–7.

10   Joachim Begrich, "Die priesterliche Tora," *BZAW* 66 (1936): 63–88 (especially 77–78), lists many examples, e.g., Psalm 15 and 24:3–6, most of them from prophetic imitations of the form such as Amos 4:4–5. See also Klaus Koch, "Tempeleinlassliturgien und Dekaloge," *Studien zur Theologie der alttestamentlichen Überlieferungen,* edd. Rolf Rendtorff und Klaus Koch (Neukirchen: Neukirchener Verlag, 1961), pp 45–60. On pp 54–56 Koch makes the point that the priestly torah itself would have had ethical content and has influenced the prophetic saying here.

11   Moshe Weinfeld, "Burning Babies in Ancient Israel," *UF* 10 (1978) 411–13. Also a recently published text from Ras Shamra may contain a rather striking parallel to Micah 6, but the presence of the key word *bkr* "firtborn" depends on the restoration of the first

this oracle precisely in a time of active practice of such a cruel sacrifice, which must be stated against those who would place this oracle specifically in the time of Manasseh (2 Kgs 21:6). The reply rejects even the thought of such a sacrifice, and the attitude it reflects.

Before passing on to the positive statement of mankind's duty, which refutes and rebukes the hysterical offer made here, one may observe that the prophetic objection to sacrifice is religious in the narrower sense, that is, sacrifice is portrayed as useless to God or offensive to him, whatever its place in the society. If God were hungry, he would not tell the people (Ps 50:12), and the limit of performance is a manifest abomination to God. But as in Psalm 50, rejection of sacrifice as an act of worship implies that it interferes with social obligations as well.

In the reply, reproachful in its restraint, the petitioner is called "man" (אָדָם). Such an address is too unusual to permit us to state the exact connotation. Commentators have thought of the universal applicability of the charge that follows, as though all mankind is intended, but is "kindness" (חֶסֶד) expected outside Israel? Perhaps human creatureliness over against God is stressed.

"Justice" and "kindness" are broad terms for what is expected of those to whom one is joined by a social bond such as a covenant; even "love" fits in the covenant vocabulary.[12]

The third term is obscure because of the rare verb involved. "Walk with" means "live in communion with" cf. Genesis 5. If correctly translated and explained here, the modifier would refer to employment of discretion, prudence, and wisdom in the religious life.

A Note on Vocabulary and Date. Mays points to certain linguistic elements in this passage as late. The cogency of some of these evidences is very slight, e.g., that the names of Moses, Aaron, and Miriam otherwise occur together only in P (Num 26:59). Such an isolated resemblance may be due to chance. But several uses of "Deuteronomic" phraseology are more arresting. פָּדָה ("ransom") for the deliverance from Egypt and בֵּית עֲבָדִים ("house of bondage") are Deuteronomic[13] as is, less strikingly, זָכַר ("remember"). Even so, the force of these observations is difficult to assess. פָּדָה occurs in Josh 24:17 and Ps 78:42; the former may be E and the date of the latter is disputed, with the possibility open that it may be quite early.[14] Note also that it occurs here in poetry as the B-word (cf. Jer 15:21 and Job 6:28) to the A-word העלה ("brought up"). בֵּית עֲבָדִים, cf. Exod 13:3, 14; and 20:2, may be Elohistic, in Weinfeld's judgment. In sum, these expressions may be indications of a late date for this passage, or may indicate the influence of an early form of Deuteronomy or a source of Deuteronomy, which is not impossible in Hezekiah's reign.

---

letter; the restoration is very plausible but not certain.
RS 24.266 Verso 11. 12–15
A bull, O Baal, we will consecrate.
Our vow, O Baal, we will pay.
A [fi]rstborn son, O Baal, we will consecrate.
Our due sacrifice, O Baal, we will pay.
  The (apparent) position of "firstborn" as third in a sequence of proposed offerings renders the resemblance to Micah 6 closer. For the whole text see Andrée Herdner, "Nouveaux textes alphabétiques de Ras Shamra—XXIVᵉ campagne, 1961," in *Ugaritica VII* (Paris: Geuthner and Leiden: Brill, 1978) 1–74.

12   William Moran, "The Ancient Near Eastern Background of the Love of God in Deuteronomy," *CBQ* 25 (1963): 77–87.

13   Moshe Weinfeld, *Deuteronomy and the Deuteronomic School* (Oxford: Clarendon, 1972), pp 320–65.

14   H. Junker, "Die Entstehungszeit des Ps. 78 und des Deuteronomiums," *Biblica* 34 (1953): 487–500, and Hans Joachim Kraus, *Psalmen* 1, BK (Neukirchen-Vluyn: Neukirchener, 1961).

■ **A Curse on the Cheating City**

**Because the rich of the city
cheat the poor, Yahweh will bring
his curse on them.**

6

9	. . . and wisdom, to fear thy name . . .[a]

The voice of Yahweh calls out to the city:
"Hear,[b] O tribe[c] and assembly of the city,

12	Whose[d] rich men are full of violence,

    Whose inhabitants speak falsehoods,
        Whose tongues pronounce deceit.[e]

10	Are there,[f] in the house[g] of the wicked, the treasures of wickedness[h]

    And the cursed scant ephah-measure?[i]

11	Can I tolerate[j] the untrue scale[k]

    And the bag with crooked stones?

13	I for my part am striking you a grievous blow,[l]

Making you desolate because of your sins.[m]

14	You shall eat, but not be satisfied

    And what you do eat will cramp your insides.[n]
You shall overtake[o] something, but not carry it off,[p]
    And if you do carry it off, I will give it up[q] to the sword.

15	You will sow, but not reap.

You will tread olives, but not anoint yourselves with the oil.
You will tread out must, but not drink the wine.[r]

16	But she observes[s] the precepts of Omri,[t]

    And all the practices[u] of the house of Ahab.
        She walks[v] in their counsels.[w]
So I must make her[x] a desolation,
    And all her inhabitants a thing to hiss at.
She shall bear the scorn of my people."

---

a   The MT reads "wisdom he fears your name." This is neither intelligible in itself, nor does it fit the context even if emended. Very commonly it is repointed to יִרְאָה (infinitive Qal) "to fear" your name, cf. Ps 86:11 לְיִרְאָה שְׁמֶךָ. Even so, it is doubtful whether this unusual form of words is a gloss, as is sometimes stated; it does not relate in any obvious way to anything in the context, though it resembles the latter part of v 8 more than anything else. The LXX καὶ σώσει φοβουμένους τὸ ὄνομα αὐτοῦ ("and he will save those who fear his name") is probably just interpretive of the MT, not for וּתְשׁוּעָה לְיִרְאֵי שְׁמוֹ, note σωτηρία for תּוּשִׁיָּה at Prov 2:7. The V and S are similarly interpretive.

b   The LXX and S have the singular, according to context, to agree with "tribe."

c   The MT perhaps can be construed as "Hear! A rod. And who has assigned it?" "Rod" would be the familiar figure

for chastisement, and "assign" is used of divine appointment of an instrument for this use, thus Jer 47:6–7 . . . . חֶרֶב לַיהוָה . . . וַיהוָה צִוָּה־לָהּ . . . שָׁם יְעָדָהּ . . . But this is very forced. Read with Wellhausen מַטֶּה וּמוֹעֵד הָעִיר (from עוּד at the beginning of v 10). For עִיר note the LXX πόλιν (The T does not seem to be relevant). This is superior to other proposals. Cf. perhaps Isa 33:20 קִרְיַת מוֹעֲדֵנוּ. The resulting expression is, however, unusual.

d   The antecedent of the relative is most naturally taken to be "tribe" or "city," v 9, and with many commentators I have transposed the text to bring this out.

e   Some delete this as a gloss borrowed from Ps 120:2–3. but more likely this is an example of conventional phraseology. The LXX ὑψώθη ("is exalted") is for רְמִיָּה as if from רוּם.

f   The MT הַאִשׁ equals הֲיֵשׁ, cf. 2 Sam 14:19. Given the first person form in the parallel line (הַאֶזְכֶּה) many have emended to first person הַאֶשֶּׁה ("Can I forget?" [Well-hausen et al.]) or הַאֶשָּׂא ("Can I forgive?" [Duhm, "Anmerkungen," et al.]). The LXX μὴ πῦρ seems to be a translation of אֵשׁ.

g   This translation of the MT presupposes the form בְּבֵית. Influenced by other references to measures in this context, Duhm ("Anmerkungen") proposed בַּת "bath" for בֵּית, but it is difficult to make this fit with the following אֹצְרוֹת רֶשַׁע.

h   The line has seemed overloaded to commentators, and indeed the repetition of consonants may arouse suspicion of a dittography. No emendation has won really wide acceptance. On the basis of the LXX θησχυρίζων θησαυροὺς some would insert אֹצֵר or אֹצֶרֶת ("which heaps up"), but the LXX is probably an interpretive expansion.

i   All witnesses to the LXX have μετὰ ("with"), but Ziegler (*Duodecim Prophetae*) is no doubt right in conjecturing an original μέτρον ("measure") which would equal the MT.

j   The MT Qal, which means "be right," seems unacceptable. Most have been satisfied with הַאֲזַכֶּה ("shall I justify?") comparing the V *numquid justificabo* (Sellin et al.), i.e., with "scales" as object, or add הוּ- ("him") (Wellhausen et al.).

k   Willi-Plein ingeniously proposes הַאֹזְנָה ("you who weigh") as if from * אזן, "weigh," but the existence of such a verb in Hebrew must be regarded as merely hypothetical.

l   Literally, the MT translates, "I have made grievous smiting of you." For the MT cf. Jer 30:12; 10:9; and Nah 3:19. With the LXX καὶ ἐγὼ ἄρξομαι, the V *coepi* and the S *'eśrê*, almost all moderns read הַחִלּוֹתִי ("I have begun"), but the MT seems defensible.

m   α' has πάσαις ταῖς ἁμαρτίαις, and seems to reflect an addition of כל, but Ziegler, "Beiträge," p 349 (*Sylloge*, p 75), explains the addition as an inner-Greek corruption, from similar passages.

n   It is impossible to say what is intended by the MT, and already the ancient versions seem at a loss. The LXX has καὶ σκοτάσει ("and it will be dark") as if from וְיֶחְשַׁךְ, but only Marti seems to have accepted this. For a concise review of opinion see Marvin H. Pope, "The Word שַׁחַת in Job 9:31," *JBL* 83 (1964): 270–271. One conjecture that has won some favor is . . . יֶשׁ־כֹּחַ, "and (if) there still is strength in you . . . ," (Sellin et al., BH3), this sticks close to the transmitted consonants, but has little other merit. BH3 suggests "it will deceive you." Pope favors:

"Filth (i.e., semen) into the womb you shall take, but you will not deliver," following a suggestion by Ehrlich, *Randglossen*, p 288, but it seems odd to find a contemptuous term for intercourse here, and the syntax is not smooth (Pope ignores the w on *wtsg*. I propose יִשְׁיחֶךָ בְּקִרְבֶּךָ, deriving a sense "cramp" from the S *'abartā* ("diarrhea") cf. the T. "there will be sickness." Similar in result is Albert Ehrman, "A note on יָשַׁח in Mic. 6:14," *JNES* 18 (1959): 156 and "A Note on Micah VI 14," *VT* 23 (1973): 103–5; cf. also O. Garcia de la Fuente, "Notas al texto de Miqueas," *Aug.* 7 (1967): 145–54.

o   The MT וְתַסֵּג could be read as וְתַשִּׂיג ("you will catch"), i.e., in hunting. The MT may be construed as if "you will not carry" from the Hiphil, but the sense is not well established.

p   The sense is as at Isa 5:29, where פלט is used of a lion's "carrying off" his prey. The inconcinnity of the Hiphil and the following Piel has suggested to some that one or the other is incorrect.

q   The LXX has passive for active.

r   1QpMi(14) has ול[א תשת ה[י]ן, but the reading is not materially certain. The LXX omits "wine" because of the preceding use of οἶνον for תִּירוֹשׁ.

s   The MT has a passive, "are observed." This is out of harmony with the active וַתֵּלְכוּ; in general there is a pervasive disharmony in person and number and voice in this passage, which must be resolved somehow. I have corrected to third feminine singular throughout (with Ehrlich, *Randglossen*). Others prefer second masculine singular וַתִּשְׁמוֹר etc. comparing θ', σ', and the T (not the LXX). Is the LXX ἃ φανισθήσεται from a form of שמד or שמם?

t   The LXX has λαοῦ μου which would presuppose עַמִּי; this is a sheer error.

u   The MT has singular, but the LXX and α' have plural, but this is probably a free translation. In either case the sense is collective. On α' see Ziegler, "Beiträge."

v   Read ותלך third feminine singular.

w   1QpMi (14) reads במועצותם (plene).

x   Read אוֹתָה.

Commentary

The fragment ". . .and wisdom, etc." is too obscure to permit comment.

The oracle, in theme of a piece with 2:1–11 and 3:1–4, has perhaps been placed here because its "Hear!" caused it to be associated, by the catchword principle, with "Hear!" (שִׁמְעוּ) of 6:2. At a less superficial level, there is a connection between the extravagance in ritual rejected in 6:7–8 and the accumulation of unjust wealth which is the theme of vv 9–11.

Internally, some disorder seems evident; with many commentators I have placed the relative clause of v 12 right after its antecedent, "city" (recovered by emendation), but I have left other apparent roughness or illogicality in sequence stand.

"Tribe" and "city" are addressed. The indefiniteness of even the emended text makes it inadvisable to identify the city as Jerusalem, or Samaria, specifically. To the villager, the nearest city would have been identified as cooperating in oppressing him, by allowing the dishonest rich to cheat him.

The speech of the rich may be fair and pious, but it is belied by their behavior, which is "violence" or "outrage" (חָמָס), much like Greek *hybris*, a wanton, insolent attack on the person and rights of another. In more specific terms, Micah accuses them of falsifying measures and weights. This was forbidden by Israelite law, Lev 19:35–36 and Deut 25:13–15, cf. Ezek 45:10, and would be recognized as an offense in any society of a certain complexity in commercial dealings. We can perhaps best appreciate Micah's indignation if we think of this cheating as going on, not only in a market situation, for Israelite villagers would have limited dealings in a market, but more frequently in the buying of grain in emergencies, or the repayment of loans to creditors or payments of rents and tithes to landlords.

A pungent contemporary commentary on the situation presupposed in Micah 6, with its mention of a "cursed ephah-measure," is found in Scott's *The Moral Economy of the Peasant*: "The most transparent and despised method of circumventing local traditions was to devise a landlord's basket that held more. The ingenuity of landowners and their agents in the design of such baskets was seemingly inexhaustible. Some baskets were constructed so as to ballon out as they received rice, others were shaped to prevent leveling and ensure a heaping basket, certain methods of pouring increased the basket's capacity, and if it were shaken vigorously several times as it was filled, it would hold more. . . . The capacity of absentee landlords to adapt a special 'rent-basket' that was always larger than the 'village basket' came to be a galling symbol of their power to impose thier will."[1] Mutatis mutandis—Scott describes modern Viet Nam—this illuminates the bitterness of the complaint against the city in Micah.

The next section, describing the punishment to be inflicted by God, is cast in the form of what I have elsewhere called "futility curses,"[2] that is, the guilty will undertake a course of action and inevitably be frustrated in it. The nearest biblical parallels are Deut 28:30–31 and 38–40, with briefer examples in Lev 26:26 and, in the prophets, Hos 4:10, "They shall eat but not be satisfied; they shall play the harlot but not increase," cf. 5:6; 8:7; 9:12; 9:16; and Amos 5:11: "You have planted pleasant vineyards, but you shall not drink their wine." Biblical curses of this pattern, and other prophetic threats, have parallels in the curses attached to Near Eastern treaties. It is clear that Micah, like other prophets, drew on a traditional stock of maledictions, and it is plausible to suppose that he meant to imply that just these evils were coming because the Israelites had broken their covenant with God.

The precise sense of the phrases "precepts of Omri" and "all the practices of the house of Ahab" escapes us, but most likely this is an allusion to abuse of legal forms and institutions; the judicial murder of Naboth has been aptly compared, cf. 1 Kings 21. It is not surprising that people of Judah should be accused of following an Israelite example, cf. 2 Kgs 17:19, "(They followed) the customs that Israel had practised," (בְּחֻקּוֹת יִשְׂרָאֵל אֲשֶׁר . . . עָשׂוּ). For חֻקָּה ("custom" or "practice") followed by a king's name see 1 Kgs 3:3: Solomon followed "the practices of his father David" (בְּחֻקּוֹת דָּוִד אָבִיו).

The final doom separates the accused from the group called "my people"; the evil city will eventually experience the contempt of the oppressed.

---

1   James C. Scott, *The Moral Economy of the Peasant* (New Haven and London: Yale, 1976), p 71.

2   Hillers, *Treaty-Curses*, pp 28–29.

■ **Injustice: Its Own Punishment**

The prophet bewails a society where injustice has become its own punishment; pervasive disregard of right has made it impossible for people to be secure even in the most intimate relations of life, with friends and family.

7

1 How I[a] regret
That I have become like a harvester[b] of summer fruit,
  Like a gleaner at the vintage.
There is no cluster to eat,
  Or fig such as I longed for.[c]

2 The pious man is gone[d] from the land;
  There is no one upright among its people.
All of them lie in ambush[e] to shed blood;
  One hunts another with a net.[f]

3 [g]Their hands are good at evil.[h]
The prince asks for a bribe;[i]
  The judge[j] judges for profit;
    The great man[k] pronounces whatever he pleases.[l]
So they twist it. . . .[m]

4 The best of them is like a brier,[n]
  The most upright like a hedge.
The expected time of punishment has come,[o]
  Just now confusion[p] comes on them.

5 Do not rely on a friend;
  Do not[q] trust a lover.[r]
Guard the doors of your mouth[s]
  From the woman you sleep with.

6 For son treats father like a fool,
  Daughter rebels against her mother,
    Daughter-in-law against mother-in-law.
A man's own slaves[t] are his enemies.

7 But I will wait expectantly for Yahweh,
  I will hope in God who saves me.
    My God will hear me.

a   Ehrlich (*Randglossen*) suggests that both here and in Job 10:15 (the only other occurrence of לִי אַלְלַי) לִי has arisen by dittography. But the similar construction אוֹי לִי vouches for the MT.

b   The MT אֹסְפֵּי, as if from abstract אֹסֶף, and עֹלְלֹת ("gleanings") abstract and feminine, suggest a comparison of the speaker to the pitiful gleanings left after the harvest. Such a simile is acceptable in itself, but out of harmony with the second line, where the speaker desires to eat the fruits of the harvest. Read אֹסֵפִי, participle with *ḥireq compaginis,* a relatively common form which has been mistaken for a construct plural by the MT. Cf. the LXX συνάγων and the V *qui colligit.* (So Robinson, Weiser, and George.) Misreading of the first agent-noun may have led to change of the second, which should be emended to עֹלֵל (a Qal participle?—the precise original form is doubtful because this rare verb is attested only in Polel; Robinson construes it as Polel participle without *m*). A

similar end is achieved by Sellin, who takes אֹסְפִי as a participle, but reads בְּעֹלְלֹת ("in the time of gleaning"). This has the disadvantage of combining in one action (which is not the same as one picture or one simile) the vintage and fruit harvest, which are kept separate in line 2, as in nature. An alternate understanding retains nouns denoting harvest activity, and takes the phrases as temporal: "I have become as at the time of the gathering of fruit, as in the gleaning after the vintage" (Franz Delitzsch, *Biblischer Commentar über den Propheten Jesaia* [Leipzig: Dörffling und Franke, ³1897] et al.). But, if grammatically possible, it is a less likely form of simile.

c   Literally this means "my appetite desired." The LXX οἴμμοι has connected אותה with אוי.

d   The LXX ὅτι (which might be from כִּי) at the beginning of this phrase.

e   The LXX δικάζονται would come from יָרִיבוּ, but this destroys the image, and must have arisen out of the legal terminology that follows.

f Many delete, as producing a metrically over-long line, or prefer a different sense; already α' and σ' (cf. the V) have ἀναθέματι (connect with חֵרֶם ["cursed thing"]); Marti, following Felix Perles, *Analekten zur Textkritik des Alten Testaments* (Leipzig: Engel, 1905), reads צוּד חֵנָם, cf. Lam 3:52; similarly Nowack reads חֵנָם, but these do not make much of an improvement on the MT. Lindblom, *Micha*, et al. add the word to v 3 (see below).

g The MT is corrupt beyond convincing restoration, and where the versions are more intelligible they seem to have wrested a meaning from the same Hebrew text, rather than to have had a better one. Even apparently clear bits may not be entirely in order. The present translation aims to offer a consensus, commonplace rendering. Only a small selection of conjectures is given; most of those which rely on deletion of words present in the text or on substantial rearrangement have not been reported.

h "Their (supplied, cf. the LXX, S and V) hands are upon the evil to do it well," i.e., "diligently, thoroughly," literally "make (it) good" with play on הרע (so Brown-Driver-Briggs, *Lexicon*); this achieves approximately the sense of the present translation without emendation, but the explanation is somewhat forced. Read לְהָרַע כַּפֵּיהֶם הֵיטִיבוּ and cf. the LXX ἑτοιμάζουσιν; thus approximately BHS BH³, and many others, following Wellhausen, literally "They have made their hands good at doing evil."

i An accusation of venality is suggested by the following intelligible words: "the judge . . . for recompense," and e.g., Isa 1:23, hence "a bribe" has been added to the translation. Perhaps שֹׁחַד "bribe" or a similar term has fallen out; note the S has "gold."

j Supply שֹׁפֵט ("judges"), which was lost by haplography.

k Not represented in the LXX, but a satisfactory, though uncommon, parallel to שָׂר and שֹׁפֵט; note 2 Sam 3:38 . . . . . . כִּי־שַׂר וְגָדוֹל נָפַל הַיּוֹם חַזֶּה ("For a prince and great man has fallen today"). In Prov 25:6 גָדוֹל is parallel to מֶלֶךְ ("king"). The proposal to transfer this term to after שָׁאַל, and reading plural גְּדֹלוֹת destroys the parallelism and produces a sense of "the prince asks for great things" which as a vague accusation of haughtiness is not especially appropriate to this context.

l הַוַּת is cognate with Ugaritic *hwt* and Akkadian *awātu* "word"; in the OT it seems to occur sometimes in some such sense, for it is used as the object of דִּבֶּר, "speak," in Ps 38:13 (cf. Ps 91:3) and is associated with "tongue" in Ps 52:4 and Prov 17:4 and with "mouth" in Ps 5:10 (EV 9); mostly it carries a pejorative sense.

נַפְשׁוֹ seems to make the point that it is his own word, not a real דְּבַר מִשְׁפָּט (Deut 17:9), and might be taken to emphasize the possessive suffix. But this combination of words is unparalleled and probably unidiomatic, pointing to a corruption. Nowack and Marti read הַוָּתוֹ ("according to his greed"), cf. Prov 10:3. Since in that passage הַוַּת is parallel to נֶפֶשׁ in the sense of "appetite," perhaps נפשׁ in Micah 7 is a double reading, equal to הות.

m The verb is otherwise unknown, the sense being derived from a supposed connection with עֲבֹת ("cord, rope") by a

process plausible at best (rope is twisted, hence the verb means "twist"). The third feminine singular suffix lacks an antecedent. Wellhausen's conjecture yielded a similar sense: עִוְּתוּהָ from עות (Piel ["bend, pervert"]). Others insert an object, מִשְׁפָּט, or even מְצַפֶּיךָ from v 4, which is very arbitrary. Still others assume a metathesis from יְתָעֵבוּ ("they abominate"), also understanding "justice" as the object (Lindblom, *Micha*, and Sellin). The LXX ἐξελοῦμαι ("I will take away" [joined to the following clause]), is unexplained; it may be guesswork, like the S *w'aslīw ṭābathōn* ("and they have rejected their own good").

n Prov 15:19 דֶּרֶךְ עָצֵל כִּמְשֻׂכַת חָדֶק ("The way of the sluggard is like a thorny hedge") confirms the parallelism of חָדֶק and מְסוּכָה (variation of *ś* and *s* in the same word) and suggests the general sense of the simile: the unjust magistrates are an obstacle in the way of justice. The LXX ὡς σὴς ἐκτρώγων ["like a devouring moth" [cf. the S]) involves some sort of misreading. Wellhausen achieves harmony between the parallel members by reading מחדק in the phrase "the best of them is *from the thorn-hedge;* the most upright, etc." Most have preferred a redivision to כִּמְסוּכָה or יִשְׁרָם מְסוּכָה (so BH³ BHS, with many). Rudolph aptly points out that the insertion of *k*, though minor, is unnecessary; cf. e.g., Isa 40:6 for parallel cola with and without the *k* of comparison. The LXX καὶ βαδίζων ἐπὶ κανόνος ("and walking on a rule" [?]) involves some kind of confusion.

o Read בָּא וּפְקוּדָה () יוֹם מִצְפֶּה. The following colon "Just now confusion comes on them" seems unproblematic, and gives guidance as to the sense of the first. יוֹם is acceptable in such a context, which in the light of Isa 22:5 and 37:3 (equals 2 Kgs 19:3) I take to be a reference to a terrible "day" whose qualities are described by abstract nouns. פְּקוּדָה is "visitation" in the sense "punishment," cf. Hos 9:7 בָּאוּ יְמֵי הַפְּקֻדָּה ("the days of punishment have come") and Jer 8:12; 10:15; and Isa 10:1–4. מְצַפֶּיךָ ("your spies, lookouts") is out of place in such a context. I have assumed an abstract noun, "looking for, expectation, dread." Usage of צפה and derivatives does not confirm such a negative sense, so perhaps some greater corruption is present. The second person suffixes are out of place, and perhaps arose under the influence of v 5. Feminine בָּאָה is apparently influenced by פְּקוּדָה; read masculine, with יוֹם as subject.

p Mur 88 has מב'כתם (*waw* above the line). The LXX has κλαυθμοὶ αὐτῶν as if from בכה ("weep").

q Mur 88 has ואל, cf. the LXX καὶ μή.

r "Lover, beloved, intimate," cf. Ps 55:14 (EV 13); Prov 2:17; 16:28; and Jer 3:4. The LXX confuses this word with the homonym meaning "chief, chiliarch."

s The LXX τοῦ ἀναθέσθαι τι αὐτῇ ("to offer anything to her") is probably just a free translation.

t Literally this means "men of his house," but Sellin citing Gen 17:23; 17:27; 39:14; and Job 19:15 shows that this means specifically "slaves" rather than "family members."

On the text of 7:6 in Matthew, see Robert H. Gundry, *The Use of the Old Testament in St. Matthew's Gospel*, Supplements to Novum Testamentum, Vol XVIII (Leiden: Brill, 1967), pp 78–79.

Commentary

The general theme of this section resembles that of other oracles in Micah, but there is no especially close tie to anything in the immediate context to explain why the oracle is placed just where it is.

It seems most likely that the "I" of v 1 is the prophet himself, though some have thought of Zion as the lamenter. The picture of a society where a lone man cannot find anyone to trust is most consistently maintained by assuming that from the beginning an individual speaks.

The unity, authorship, and date of 7:1–7 have occasioned much discussion. The position taken here: that the passage is a unity which may well be by Micah, can claim no more than plausibility. Since v 4 ends with a threat, if we understand the general sense of the corrupt text, some have believed that this is the end of the poem, and that a new poem begins at v 5, especially since in v 5 there is a shift to the imperative.[1] Others secure a tighter unity in these verses by reordering to the sequence 3, 5, 6, 4,[2] or delete v 4b as a late gloss, thus eliminating a main difficulty.[3] In my view, the theme of vv 5–6 is "There is none that doeth good," and thus closely related to vv 1–4.

Verse 7 is a separate problem, with commentators about equally divided as to whether it belongs with the preceding or succeeding verses. Here it has been treated with the preceding poem, because of the conjunction, "But I" (וַאֲנִי); cf. Hab 3:18 "Yet I will rejoice in the Lord." The resulting first person ending of the poem then turns out to correspond to the first person opening. Of course, even if v 7 belongs with the foregoing, it may still serve as a bridge to vv 8–20.

Evidence for authorship and date of the passage is slender. Of the vocabulary, "the pious man" (חָסִיד, v 2) is cited by some as proof of a date after the time of Micah, since its usage cannot be proved to be earlier than Deuteronomy (33:8) and Jeremiah (3:12), according to Renaud.[4] This is not especially weighty, since the term is so rare outside the Psalms that we may doubt the adequacy of our evidence, and since in Deuteronomy it occurs only in what is probably an ancient poem, and since certain Psalms which use it may well be quite old (Psalm 18 [equals 2 Sam 22]; 50; and 89). Our poem has been thought to be dependant on Isa 57:1, or Mal 3:24, or especially on Jer 8:23–9:5 (EV 9:1–6). But though these passages are related in theme or vocabulary, this observation does not demonstrate the direction of influence, especially since the topos "Do not trust a friend" is probably age-old.

The opening lines present a figure. Like a gleaner after the late gathering of grapes or figs, the prophet is looking—in vain—for some last remaining good man in the land. Jeremiah (5:1–5) was later to picture himself in a similar fruitless search. The ensuing description of a greedy, unjust people provides the literal counterpart to the initial figure. Yet there is a deep congruity between figure and reality, rooted in the prophet's concern for the poor. Leaving bits of the crop to be gleaned was an important traditional way of securing the very poorest from starvation (Lev 19:9–10, 23:22; and Deut 24:19–21) and the uprightness of Boaz showed itself in his generous observance of this practise (Ruth 2–3). Implicit in the picture of a frustrated, hungry gleaner is an accusation of injustice and lack of pity.

The "good man" is, in this context, one who practices the expected pieties toward fellowman and God. All such are gone, and greed and injustice have gone so far that one would fear to practise traditional virtues. It is the courts that are the worst, to judge from the very difficult text (cf. Mic 3:1–4, 9–12).

The punishment has come in the form of the conditions they themselves have created. The appropriate behavior under the circumstances is a universal suspicion, for none is to be trusted. A similar description of social disintegration occurs in various literatures. In the Old Testament itself, we have Jer 9:3–4. Alfred Jeremias gathered Babylonian parallels;[5] Egyptian parallels were

---

1 So Marti and many others.
2 Sellin and others.
3 Renaud, *La formation.*
4 Ibid.
5 Alfred Jeremias, *Babylonisches im Neuen Testament* (Leipzig: Hinrichs, 1905), pp 97–99; see also B. Reicke, "Liturgical Traditions in Mic. 7," *HTR* 60 (1967): p 358, and Rykle Borger, "Gott Marduk und Gott-König Šulgi als Propheten," *BO* 28 (1971): pp 3–24.

given already in Erman,[6] and the classical occurrences are cited by Smith.[7] The topos is not likely to be an invention of Micah's, but there is no reason to doubt that it accurately portrays conditions in his time. If modern assistance is needed in imagining the kind of society depicted here, one may turn to *The Mountain People* by Colin M. Turnbull, which describes the Ik, reduced by starvation to an individualism and lovelessness hard to recognize as human.[8]

The prophet closes with a conventional, but not thereby inauthentic, expression of personal trust in God.

Hab 3:18 contains a similar looking-away from present distress.

Mic 7:6 is quoted, and applied to Jesus' effect on human relations, in Matt 1:35–36 and Luke 12:53.

---

6   Adolf Erman, *Die Literatur der Aegypter* (Leipzig, Hinrichs, 1923) pp 132, 138, and 155.

7   Smith.

8   Colin M. Turnbull, *The Mountain People* (New York: Simon and Schuster, 1972).

■ **A Closing Liturgy of Hope**

In a closing liturgy the chastened people expresses hope in Yahweh; they are answered by a prediction of expansion and triumph; they pray for restoration of divine rule; and praise the mystery of divine forgiveness.

7

8 Do not rejoice over me, my enemies;
 Though I fall, I will get up again.[a]
Though I sit in the dark,
 Yahweh will be my light.[b]

9 I will bear the anger of Yahweh
 Because I have sinned against him,
Until he pleads my cause
 And accomplishes justice for me.
He will bring me out to the light;
 I will see his salvation.

10 Then my enemies will see it
 And shame will cover them;
For they said to me:
 Where[c] is Yahweh your God?
My eyes will look on them;
Then they will be trodden down,
 Like the mud in the streets.[d]

11 That day will be a day for building your walls,[e]
 Your boundaries will be enlarged[f] on that day,

12 Then[g] they will come to you[h]
From Ashur and from as far as[i] Egypt,[j]
 From Egypt and as far as the Euphrates;
From sea to sea and from mountain to mountain.[k]

13 Then the earth shall be a desolate waste
 To its inhabitants, because of their evil deeds.

14 Shepherd your people with your staff,
 The flock that belongs to you,
Which dwells[l] alone in the scrub, in the midst of fertile land.
 May they feed in Bashan and Gilead[m]
  As in days of old.

15 As when you went out of the land of Egypt,[n]
 Show us[o] your wonders.

16 Foreign nations shall see and despair of all their power.
 They will put their hands over their mouths,
 Their ears will be deaf.

17 They will lick the dust like snakes,
 Like those that creep over the ground.[p]
They will come quaking out of their dens[q] to Yahweh, our God,[r]
 They will be terrified and afraid[s] of you.

18 What other god is like you,
 One who forgives iniquity
  And pardons rebellion
   For the survivors of his people?
Who will not hold on to his anger forever,
 For he delights in clemency.

19 Who will have pity on us again,
 Who will tread down[t] our iniquities.
You will throw[u] all our sins[v] into the depths of the sea.

20 May you show loyalty to Jacob,
 Love for Abraham,
That which you promised to our fathers from of old.

a   It is rare to have the perfect where future time is intended. The LXX καὶ ἀναστήσομαι may have read the common converted perfect וְקַמְתִּי.

b   The LXX future, φωτιεῖ, seems to construe this as a verbal form; is אוֹר perfect like קַמְתִּי?

c   Brown–Driver–Briggs, *Lexicon*, 32a: "Idiomatically, with the sf. anticipating the noun to which it refers. . . . 2 Kgs 19:13 אַיוֹ אֵפוֹא חֲכָמֶיךָ. The conjecture of Wellhausen (followed by BH³ and BHS), אַיֵּה, seems to prosaicize the text.

d   Marti et al. would delete because the same expression occurs also in Ps 18:43 (EV 42) and Isa 10:6, but this has little force in view of the fondness for conventional expressions in Hebrew literature.

e   Contrary to the Masoretic accent (athnach), the first clause ends at הַהוּא, yielding a sentence pattern like Zeph 1:15 יוֹם עֶבְרָה הַיּוֹם הַהוּא ("a day of wrath is that day"). For "day" modified by an infinitive phrase, cf. Isa 58:5, יוֹם עַנּוֹת אָדָם נַפְשׁוֹ . . . and Jer 46:10, יוֹם נְקָמָה לְהִנָּקֵם . . . יוֹם הַהוּא מִצָּרָיו . . . must at least be understood as equivalent to הַיּוֹם הַהוּא, and perhaps the article should be inserted, or read יוֹם הוּא as in v 12. The LXX has (joined to the preceding clause) ἡμέρας ἀλοιφῆς πλίνθου. ἐξαλειψίς σου ἡ ἡμέρα ἐκείνη . . . ("on the day of plastering of brick. Your plastering/destruction is that day"). לבנות has been taken to mean "bricks" and this is the starting-point of the misunderstanding, though some details escape us.

f   Read חָקֵקְךָ or חֻקֶּךָ. Isa 26:15 רִחַקְתָּ כֹּל־קַצְוֵי־אָרֶץ . . . ("you extended all the boundaries of the land") may be cited in defense of the essential correctness of the MT; cf. Isa 33:17 אֶרֶץ מֶרְחַקִּים . . . ("a land that stretches far"). The LXX ἀποτρίψεται ("will rub away") could represent מחק, cf. Hos 8:5; the S "will be taken up" is obscure. The sequence ירחק חק is suggestive of dittography.

g   In sense, this must be the equivalent of בַּיּוֹם הַהוּא. Note Mur 88 ביום.

The general idea of this verse is clear: people will stream to the rebuilt Zion from the far corners of her empire; beginning with "from" the description of the boundaries proceeds by giving the outer limits. The sense is "from a territory stretching from Ashur to Egypt, etc." Cf. Isa 27:12. The text has suffered in detail.

h   Read וְעָדֶיךָ יָבוֹאוּ with Sellin et al.; cf. the LXX ἥξουσιν.

i   For the MT וְעָדֵי read וַעֲדֵי (Hitzig, Wellhausen and many others). Cf. Ps 72:8 וְיֵרְדְּ מִיָּם עַד־יָם וּמִנָּהָר עַד־אַפְסֵי־אָרֶץ.

j   A variant name for Egypt here and in the following verse; also in 2 Kgs 19:24 (equals Isa 37:25) and Isa 19:6. Like the S, some have wanted to find Tyre (צֹר) in these occurrences, but this is out of place in a listing of ideal boundaries such as this. The LXX goes badly astray from here on. See now, Hayim Tawil, "The Historicity of 2 Kings 19:24 (= Isaiah 37:25). The Problem of Ye'ōrê māṣôr," *JNES* 41 (1982): 195–206, who connects ye'ōrê māṣôr to a very precise set of historical and geographical circumstances in the time of Sennacherib, which seems to neglect the poetic and conventional nature of the language here.

k   Read מִיָּם עַד יָם as in BHS, which must be approximately correct, though commentators differ over details. Cf. Amos 8:12; Zech 9:10; Ps 72:8; Zech 14:8; and Joel 2:20. Also read וּמֵהַר עַד הַר (with Marti et al.); cf. the V *et ad montem de monte*, similarly some LXX mss, and θ'. The first phrase, involving the sea, is a staple of boundary descriptions. Magne Saebø, "Grenzbeschreibung und Landideal im Alten Testament, mit besonderer Berücksichtigung der min-'ad-Formel," *ZDPV* 90 (1974): p 19, makes the point that where the sea is a border, the West is always the Mediterranean, and the East is also a sea in some sense, as in Exod 23:31 and Josh 12:7. Mountains figure less often in such descriptions; "from mountain to mountain" raises the question: which? But see Num 13:29 and Deut 1:7; also Josh 11:2; 12:8; 9:1; 10:40; and Judg 1:9. Saebø points out that Lebanon is the northern border in several boundary passages (Deut 11:24 and Josh 1:4, both somewhat problematic).

l   The participle refers to the people (see Commentary), but though a plural involves little change in the text and has been preferred by Marti and others, the MT singular with *ḥireq compaginis* agreeing with the grammatical singular collective noun is acceptable and yields the same sense.

The S '*ānā* arises from inner-Syriac change out of '*ābā* ("thicket").

m   Cf. Jer 22:6 for use of Gilead in an evaluative, metaphorical sense (of the house of the king of Judah).

n   The LXX has ἐξ Ἀιγύπτου; this shorter reading is preferred by Marti and others (BHS).

o   The MT has "I will show him." A simple solution is הַרְאֵנוּ ("show us" [Wellhausen and many others]); Ehrlich, *Randglossen*, has הַרְאֵהוּ ("show him"); and Robinson reads הַרְאֵה ("show"). The LXX has ὄψεσθε ("you will see"); this is a free translation.

p   IQpMi(14) in commentary *probably* on this verse, spells plene וזוחלי.

q   The Hebrew word perhaps has this meaning, continuing the comparison to animals, or it could mean "fastnesses," of human strongholds; the evidence is insufficient to decide the question.

r   The MT is perhaps possible, though reference to Yahweh in third person is out of harmony with the direct address at the end of the line. The V omits אֶל; Ehrlich (*Randglossen*) also would delete אֶל, and read the divine name as vocative. (Similarly Rudolph אֵלֶיךָ "to you, Yahweh.") BHS following Marti et al. deletes the whole phrase.

s   The MT has וייראו; Mur 88 has ויראו.

t   The picture of "treading down" sins is unparalleled in the Bible, but not so bizarre as to be indefensible. R. P. Gordon, "Micah vii 19 and Akkadian kabāsu," *VT* 28 (1978): p 355 points to Akkadian *kabāsu* ("tread") in the

sense "forgive" with "sin" as the object. Slight emendation yields שׁ/יכבס ("wash away"), a metaphor familiar
from Jer 2:22 and Ps 51:4, 9. Rudolph cites Greek
κατακλύσει in support of this emendation (from
κατακλύζω which sometimes means "wash") but this
reading is found only in some witnesses to Cyril's
commentary (Ziegler's Cyr^F) and is an inner-Greek
development from καταλύσει ("he will destroy") attested
in a subgroup of the Lucianic recension.

u   The LXX has third person ἀπορρίψει; this is like the S,
T, and V, followed by some commentators (and BHS),
but the versions probably just smooth out the change in

person. Second person is in place, for the direct address
to God is implied constantly after the opening question
(v 18) and is explicitly resumed here.

v   The MT "their sins" is probably a mistake for חַטֹּאותֵנוּ.
Cf. the LXX ἀμαρτίας ἡμῶν and also the S and V; a
reading preferred by Wellhausen and many since. (2 mss
Kenn., 2 de Rossi חטאתינו). Horace D. Hummel,
"Enclitic *Mem* in Early Northwest Semitic, Especially
Hebrew," *JBL* 76 (1957) p 95, following Dahood,
proposes that the *m* is enclitic.

Commentary

Since Gunkel[1] this passage has been recognized as a
prophetic liturgy; earlier Stade[2] had described it as a
psalm and made an exhaustive listing of parallels.
Speakers change, and the mood and tone shift from
section to section. First (8–10) the suffering people
speak. They are defiant of their enemies, humbly confi-
dent in God. Then (11–13) a prophetic voice announces
a glorious time coming when the city and land will be
enlarged and all peoples will stream in with tribute. The
congregation utters a prayer (14–17) for the return of
the divine shepherd, to rule them in peace and terrify
their enemies. The liturgy ends (18–20) with a hymnic
confession of the greatness of divine compassion, spoken
by the congregation.

Though there is no specific link to the immediately
preceding context, this closing liturgy does resume and
bring to resolution a number of the book's themes: the
wretched state of the people of God, Israel's suffering at
the hand of enemies, a promise of glorious restoration,
and the advent of the divine shepherd-king. The emphasis on divine forgiveness, however, is much more prominent here than elsewhere in the book.

Because of the lack of reference to very specific
historical conditions, the liturgy is difficult to date. The
"enemy" or "enemies" are unidentified, and that the
people are in desperate condition could be true of many
periods. It is not certain that the "walls" (v 11; גְּדֵרָיִךְ) are
the walls of Jerusalem (or Samaria) for the term is
unusual, and the sense could be metaphorical or general
("the nation's walls"). If v 12 does refer to gathering of

scattered Israelites, which is uncertain, such a prophecy
would fit beginning with the fall of Samaria. Many
commentators have assigned this liturgy to a late date; I
prefer to hold that it fits conditions in Micah's time, but
to leave open the possibility of later origin.

Recently it has become popular for commentators to
hold that 7:7/8–20 is of North Israelite origin, sometimes considering it part of a longer Deutero-Micah
beginning at ch. 6. Willis has an extensive review of
opinion on the structure and provenance of Micah 7:7–
20, with copious bibliography.[3] Willis gathers the arguments in favor of a North Israelite provenance, which he
finds convincing, though he modifies this view by proposing that the passage was reapplied to the Judacan
situation. His organization of the arguments is followed
here. Setting aside the somewhat curious view defended
by Eissfeldt and Dus, that "the One who dwells alone in a
forest in the midst of Carmel" is a title of Yahweh,[4] four
arguments for a Northern origin remain: 1) that the
places named are all in North Israel; 2) the traditions
mentioned are almost exclusively North Israelite; 3) Mic
6:1–7:6 is probably from North Israel, and this piece has
been placed after it as having the same provenance; 4)
(given little weight by Willis) this passage is similar
linguistically to North Israelite texts such as Hosea and
Deuteronomy. These arguments, in various forms and
combinations, have seemed convincing to an impressive
number of scholars.[5] The author of 7:8–20 is held to
have been a North Israelite contemporary of Micah.

To the first point, the place names are Carmel (?),
Bashan, and Gilead. But it seems ruled out that כַּרְמֶל

1   H. Gunkel, "Der Micha-Schluss," *ZS* 2 (1924): 145–
      78.

2   Bernhard Stade, "Streiflichter auf die Entstehung
      der jetzigen Gestalt der alttestamentlichen Prophet-
      enschriften," *ZAW* 23 (1903): 153–71.

3   J.T. Willis, "A Reapplied Prophetic Hope Oracle,"
      VTS 26 (1974): 64–76.

4   Otto Eissfeldt, *Der Gott Karmel*, Sitzungsberichte der

deutschen (Preussischen) Akademie der Wissenschaften zu Berlin. Klasse für Sprachen, Literatur
und Kunst (Berlin: Akademie Verlag, 1953), pp 7–8
und Jan Dus "Weiteres zum nordisraelitischen Psalm
Micha 7, 7–20," *ZDMG* 115 (1965): 14–22.

5   For Eissfeldt and Dus see previous note (4). Also see
      A. van Hoonacker, *Les douze petits prophètes*, Études
      Bibliques (Paris: Gabalda, 1908); F.C. Burkitt,

even is a place name here; it is a common noun. Bashan and Gilead are specific places, of course, but while this establishes the writer's *interest* in reoccupation of those territories in Northern Transjordan, it says nothing of his origin. Because we can locate the places, we must not imagine we have located the author! Jeremiah could write a Book of Consolation for Ephraim (chaps. 30–31), and an earlier Judaean could have done the same. But the Micah passage is not even that; it could well be a reflection of ideals inherited from the times of the Davidic empire by a prophet with deep interest in the fall of Samaria (chap. 1). The two places have a kind of symbolic meaning; Bashan is traditionally luxuriant, and for "Gilead" see Jer 22:6 "You are a Gilead to me. . .yet surely I will make you a desert."

The force of the second argument rests on one's confidence in the ability of scholars to identify such traditions as the exodus, the oath to the fathers, and the incomparability of Yahweh, as Northern. In my view the first two are all-Israelite, and the last is all Near Eastern, an onomastic and theological commonplace.

The third argument, from proximity to 6:1–7:6 would have little force even if 6:1ff. were clearly Northern, being only a kind of guilt by association, but in fact the Northern origin of the earlier passage rests on very weak evidence (discussed above: mention of Omri and Ahab; "Deuteronomic" vocabulary in 6:1–8). Finally, an argument from linguistic similarities to Northern texts would have some force if made with any methodological rigor, but this is lacking.

To sum up, a theory of Northern provenance for Micah 7:8–20 remains of some potential interest, but is still unproven, and—this puts the matter in perspective—is not especially illuminating for reading the passage. We encounter a familiar case in Old Testament studies, that the experience (defeat, exile, misery, etc.) is so typical for ancient Israel, and the portrayal no less so, that the student strives in vain to recover the specific occasion.

The first speaker is the devastated people, personified; perhaps we are meant to think of the personified city. The metaphorical oppositions falling/rising and darkness/light are extremely common in Old Testament poetry, and doubtless in world literature, but just for that reason suited for liturgy.

The people collectively acknowledges its sins; the divisions and tensions within the society disappear here. This tone is prepared for by the acknowlegment of universal guilt in the previous poem "the good man is gone from the land." The expectation that Yahweh will "plead one's cause" and "accomplish justice" for a person is metaphor derived from the judicial scene where the poor man needed a protector against a powerful enemy; now Yahweh is no longer conceived of as a menacing, angry figure.

The rather unattractive note struck in v 10 is nevertheless typical of Old Testament thought: as the enemy has done to Israel, so Israel will do to them (cf. Lam 1:22; 3:65–66; and 4:21–22). An exact parallel to v 10 is Obad 10; to "my eye will see" cf. Mal 1:5 "and your eyes will see." To the final metaphor cf. Isa 10:6 "like the mud in the street."

Rather abruptly a different speaker appears, and with a different message. Zion (and Judah) will be rebuilt, the land enlarged, and "they" will stream to it from far and wide.

This will happen in the "that day" of prophetic expectation; cf. Mic 2:4 and 4:6. "Your walls" (גְּדֵרַיִךְ) is not the common term for "city walls" (חוֹמוֹת), but may be a rarer alternate; cf. Ps 89:41 and Ezra 9:9, against Janssen.[6] Cf. also Ps 80:13 (EV 12) "Why did you break down her walls?" (לָמָּה פָּרַצְתָּ גְדֵרֶיהָ). But the term may be less specific than "city wall," and this could be a reference to destruction of walled towns in Judah in 701 (by Sennacherib).

Enlarging of the nation's size, if that is the sense of the difficult line that follows, is similar to the hope expressed in Isa 49:19–21: "The children born in your time of

"Micah 6 and 7 a Northern Prophecy," *JBL* 45 (1926): 159–61; B. Reicke, "Liturgical Traditions in Mic. 7," *HTR* 60 (1967): 349–367; A.S. van der Woude, "Deutero-Micha: Ein Prophet aus Nord-Israel?" *Nederlands Theologisch Tijdschrift* (1971): 365–78; and H.L. Ginsberg "Dqdwqym bšnyn 'śr," *Eretz Israel,* 3 (1954): 83–84.

6   Enno Janssen, *Juda in der Exilszeit, FRLANT,* Heft 51

(Göttingen: Vandenhoeck and Ruprecht, 1965), p 90.

bereavement will yet say in your ears: 'The place is too narrow for me; make room for me to dwell in'". Cf. Isa 54:2–3 "Enlarge the place of your tent."

Those who will "come" to the new land and city are left unidentified, so that one may think of the scattered people, or of foreign peoples. Both ideas occur elsewhere in Micah (4:1–2 and 2:12), and many times elsewhere; there seems no clear reason for preferring one or the other. There would be a kind of illogicality in having foreigners come on pilgrimage to Zion, and at the same time have their own lands laid waste (v 13) or themselves be trodden down like mire, but these are separate parts of the eschatological vision, not to be pressed, or relieved by textual rearrangement or other change.

The third portion of the liturgy is spoken by the people, the "flock," who pray for secure and abundant life under the rule of the shepherd-king. This is to be brought about by repetition of the wonders displayed at the Exodus, with foreign countries reduced to creeping impotence. But if so much is clear, the line "which dwells alone in the scrub in the midst of fertile land" is not. כַּרְמֶל has been taken to be the proper name Carmel here, but there is no historical circumstance known to us which confined the people of God, or a remnant thereof, to the Carmel. This must refer somehow to the present unfavorable conditions of the people. Some[7] have thought of returned exiles living in undesirable parts of the country while the occupying people has the good land. It seems to me more likely that this pictures the conditions resulting from destruction of the towns by slaughter, and deportation of the population. The empty land rapidly reverts to scrub,[8] and the people, many of them impoverished even before the invasion, revert to more primitive ways of life, hunting and husbandry.[9] Such a state of affairs is depicted in Isa 6:11 and 7:21–25. There is a comparable description of a desolate Babylon in 710–709 B.C., in an inscription of Sargon II.[10] The state of the text suggests caution, but with that limit one may suppose that Judah or parts of it must have experienced conditions such as these late in Micah's day.

The "you" in "when you went out of the land of Egypt" refers to God, not the people as is more common; cf. Exod 13:21; 33:14; and 2 Sam 5:24. The brief section dealing with the amazed reaction of the nations recurs to a theme found elsewhere in Micah (4:1–2; 4:13; 5:5 [EV 6], and 14 [EV 15]) and in the rest of the Bible. Michael Barré has noted parallels in an Amarna letter and elsewhere.[11]

The final section of the liturgy is not sharply set off from the foregoing, since the speaker remains the same, but there is a shift to a more hymnic style. The term "survivors of the people" recalls 2:12; 4:7; 5:6, and 7. The terms in parallel in v 20 ("loyalty" [אֱמֶת] and "love" [חֶסֶד]), with the following reference to God's oath, must be understood specifically as the loyalty and fidelity to be displayed to a covenant partner. "Abraham" is unparalleled as a title for the people, but in this context such an understanding seems forced on us. The phrase by itself could mean "love like your love to Abraham" cf. Isa 55:3, "faithful love (as) for David" (חַסְדֵי דָוִד הַנֶּאֱמָנִים), but the parallel colon, "loyalty to Jacob" (אֱמֶת לְיַעֲקֹב), is against it.

7   Smith and Weiser.

8   Denis Baly, "Forest," *IDBS*.

9   Emmanuel LeRoy Ladurie, *The Territory of the Historian*, trans by Ben and Siân Reynolds (Chicago: Un. of Chicago Press, 1979), p 92.

10   C.J. Gadd, "Inscribed Prisms of Sargon II from Nimrud," *Iraq* 16 (1954): 173–201 (especially p 92–94).

11   Michael L. Barré, "Cuneiform Parallel to Ps 86: 16–17 and Mic 7:16–17," *JBL* 101 (1982): 271–75.

Bibliography
Indices

Bibliography

1. Commentaries (listed in order of their publication)

Keil, Carl Friedrich
Biblischer Commentar über die Zwölf kleinen Propheten, BC III/4 (Leipzig: Dörffling und Franke, 1866, ²1873, ³1888).

Hitzig, Ferdinand
Die zwölf kleinen Propheten, 4th ed. by Heinrich Steiner, Kurzgefasstes exegetisches Handbuch (Leipzig: S. Hirzel, 1881).

Wellhausen, J.
Skizzen und Vorarbeiten, Fünftes Heft: *Die kleinen Propheten übersetzt, mit Noten* (Berlin: Reimer, 1892).

Smith, George Adam
The Book of the Twelve Prophets I, Expositor's Bible (New York: A. C. Armstrong, 1896).

Marti, Karl
Das Dodekapropheton, KHC 13 (Tübingen: J. C. B. Mohr, 1904).

Margolis, Max L.
Micah (Philadelphia: Jewish Publication Society, 1908).

von Orelli, Conrad
Die zwölf kleinen Propheten, Kurgefasster Kommentar zu den Heilgen Schriften Alten und Neuen Testamentes A, 5 Abteilung, 2 Hälfte (Munich: Becksche, ³1908).

Smith, John Merlin Powis, William Hayes Ward, and Julius A. Bewer
A Critical and Exegetical Commentary on Micah, Zephaniah, Nahum, Habakkuk, Obadiah and Joel, ICC (Edinburgh: T. & T. Clark, 1911).

Nowack, W.
Die kleinen Propheten, HK III Abteilung, 4 Band (Göttingen: Vandenhoeck and Ruprecht, ³1922).

Schmidt, Hans
Micha in SAT, Abteilung 2, Band 2. *Die grossen Propheten* (Göttingen: Vandenhoeck und Ruprecht, ²1923).

Sellin, Ernst
Das Zwölfprophetenbuch, KAT Bd. 12, Erste Hälfte: *Hosea-Micha* (Liepzig: Diechertsche, ² & ³ 1929).

Robinson, Theodore H.
Die zwölf kleinen Propheten, HAT 14 (Tübingen: Mohr, 1938).

Bewer, Julius A.
The Book of the Twelve prophets: Vol. I: *Amos, Hosea and Micah*, Harper's Annotated Bible (New York: Harper, 1949).

Weiser, Artur
Das Buch der zwölf Kleinen Propheten I: Die Propheten Josea, Joel, Amos, Obadja, Jona, Micha, ATD Teilbd. 24 (Göttingen: Vandenhoeck & Ruprecht, ²1956).

George, Augustin
Michée Sophonie Nahum, La Sainte Bible, Vol. 27 (Paris: Cerf, 1952).

McKeating, Henry
The Books of Amos, Hosea and Micah, Cambridge Bible Commentary (Cambridge: University Press, 1971).

Rudolph, Wilhelm
Micha—Nahum—Habckuk—Zephanja, KAT Bd. 13/3 (Gütersloh: Gütersloher Verlagshaus Gerd Mohn, 1975).

Allen, Leslie C.
The Books of Joel, Obadiah, Jonah and Micah, The New International Commentary on the Old Testament (Grand Rapids, Mich.: Eerdmans, 1976).

Mays, James Luther
Micah: A Commentary (Philadelphia: Westminster, 1976).

van der Woude, A. S.
Micah (Nijkerk: Callenbach, 1976).

2. Select Books, Monographs, and Articles (alphabetically)

Abel, F.-M.
Géographie de la Palestine II (Paris: Gabalda, 1938).

Adas, Michael
Prophets of Rebellion (Chapel Hill, North Carolina: Univ. of North Carolina, 1979).

Aharoni, Yohanan
"Trial Excavation in the 'Solar Shrine' at Lachish. Preliminary Report," *IEJ* 18 (1968): 157–69.

Ahlström, G. W.
"'eder," *VT* 17 (1967): 1–7.

Idem
"Is Tell ed-Duweir Ancient Lachish?" *PEQ* 112 (1980): 7–9.

Albright, W. F.
"Contributions to the Historical Geography of Palestine," *AASOR* 2 (1921): 1–46.

Idem
"Egypt and the Early History of the Negeb," *JPOS* 4 (1924): 131–61.

Allegro, John M.
Qumrân Cave 4. Discoveries in the Judaean Desert of Jordan, V (Oxford: Clarendon, 1968), 36 and Pl. XII ("168. Commentary on Micah").

Idem
"Uses of the Semitic Demonstrative Element z in Hebrew," *VT* 5 (1955): 309–12.

Allen, Leslie C.
The Books of Joel, Obadiah, Jonah and Micah, The New International Commentary on the Old Testament (Grand Rapids, Mich.: Eerdmans, 1976).

Alt, Albrecht
"Micha 2, 1–5 Γης αναδασμος in Juda," *NTT* 56 (1955): 13–23; reprinted in *Kleine Schriften zur Geschichte des Volkes Israel*, III (Munich: Beck'sche, 1959), 373–81.

Andersen, Francis I. and David Noel Freedman
Hosea, The Anchor Bible (Garden City, N. Y.: Doubleday, 1980).

Anderson, G. W.
"A Study of Micah 6:1-8," *Scottish Journal of Theology* 4 (1951): 191–97.

Avi-Yonah, Michael
"Mārēshāh, Māre'šāh (Hebrew)," *EM*.

Idem
The Madaba Mosaic Map (Jerusalem: Israel Exploration Society, 1954).

Avi-Yonah, Michael and Amos Kloner
"Maresha (Marisa)," *EAEHL* III (1977): 792–91.

Baly, Denis
"Forest," *IDBS*.

Bardtke, Hans
"Die Latifundien in Juda während der zweiten Hälfte des achten Jahrhunderts v. Chr.," *Hommages a André Dupont-Sommer* (Paris: Adrien-Maisonneuve, 1971), 235–54.

Barré, Michael L.
"A Cuneiform Parallel to Ps 86:16–17 and Mic 7:16–17," *JBL* 101 (1982): 271–75.

Barthélemy, Dominique
Les devanciers d'Aquila, VTS X (1963)

Idem
"Redécouverte d'un chaînon manquant de l'histoire de la Septante," *RB* 60 (1953): 18–29.

Barthélemy, Dominique and J. T. Milik
Qumran Cave I. Discoveries in the Judaean Desert I (Oxford: Clarendon, 1955), 77–80 and Pl. XV ("Commentaire de Michée").

Bartlett, J. R.
"The Use of the Word ראש as a Title in the Old Testament," *VT* 19 (1969): 1–10.

Begrich, Joachim
"Die priesterliche Tora," BZAW 66 (1936): 63–88. Reprinted in *Gesammelte Studien zum Alten Testament*, ed. Walther Zimmerli (Munich: Chr. Kaiser, 1964), 232–60.

Benoit, F., J. T. Milik, and R. de Vaux
Les Grottes de Murabba'ât. Discoveries in the Judaean Desert, II (Oxford: Clarendon, 1961).

Bentzen, Aage
King and Messiah (London: Lutterworth, 1955).

Bewer, Julius A.
The Book of the Twelve Prophets: Vol. I: Amos, Hosea and Micah, Harper's Annotated Bible (New York: Harper, 1949).

Idem
"Textkritische Bemerkungen zum Alten Testament," in *Festschrift Alfred Bertholet*, ed. W. Baumgartner, O. Eissfeldt, K. Elliger, L. Rost (Tübingen: Mohr, 1950), 65–76.

Beyer, Gustav
"Beiträge zur Territorialgeschichte von Südwestpalästina im Altertum," *ZDPV* 54 (1931): 113–70.

Beyerlin, W.
Die Kulttraditionen Israels in der Verkündigung des Propheten Micah, FRLANT 54 (Göttingen: Vandenhoeck and Ruprecht, 1959).

n.a.
La Bible de Jerusalem (Paris: Cerf, ²1974).

Bliss, F. J.
"First Report on the Excavations at Tell ej-Judeideh," *PEFQSt* (1900): 87–101.

Idem
"Second Report on the Excavations at Tell ej-Judeideh," *PEFQSt* (1900): 199–222.

Bliss, F. J. and R. A. Stewart Macalister
Excavations in Palestine during the Years 1898–1900 (London: Palestine Exploration Fund, 1902).

Bloch, Marc
French Rural History, Tr. Janet Sondheimer (Berkeley and Los Angeles: Univ. of California, 1966).

Boecker, Hans Jochen
Redeformen des Rechtslebens im Alten Testament, WMANT 14 (Neukirchen-Vluyn: Neukirchener, 1964).

Bordreuil, Pierre
"Michée 4:10–13 et ses paralleles ougaritiques," *Semitica* 21 (1971): 21–28.

Borée, W.
Die alten Ortsnamen Palästinas ([Leipzig, ²1930] reprinted Hildesheim: Olms, 1968).

Borger, Rykle
"Gott Marduk und Gott-König Šulgi als Propheten," *BO* 28 (1971): 3–24.

Boyd, B.
"Lachish" *IDBS*.

Brinkman, J. A.
A Political History of Post-Kassite Babylonia 1158–722 B. C. Analecta Orientalia 43 (Rome: Pontifical Biblical Institute, 1968).

Brockelmann, C.
Grundriss der vergleichenden Grammatik der semitischen Sprachen, Vol. II, Syntax (Hildesheim: Olms, 1961 [reprint of Berlin, 1913 ed]).

Idem
Hebräische Syntax (Neukirchen Kreis Moers: Buchhandlung des Erziehungsvereins, 1956).

Broshi, Magen
"The Expansion of Jerusalem in the Reigns of Hezekiah and Manasseh," *IEJ* 24 (1974): 21–26.

Idem
"Judeideh, Tell," *EAEHL* III 694–96.

Brown, Francis
"The Measurements of Hebrew Poetry as an Aid to Literary Analysis," *JBL* 9 (1890): 71–106.

Brown, Francis, S. R. Driver, and Charles A. Briggs
A Hebrew and English Lexicon of the Old Testament (Oxford: Clarendon, 1907).

Brueggemann, Walter
"Vine and Fig Tree: A Case Study in Imagination and Criticism," *CBQ* 43 (1981): 188–204.

Bruno, Arvid
Das Buch der Zwölf. Eine rhythmische und textkritische Untersuchung (Stockholm: almqvist and Wiksell, 1957).

Bryant, David J.
"Micah 4:14–5:14: an Exegesis," *ResQ* 21 (1978): 210–30.

Buccellati, Giorgio
Review of Vernant et al., Divination et Rationalité, *OrAnt* 16 (1977): 239–40.

Büchler, A.
"אדר = Fell in LXX zu Micha 2, 8," *ZAW* 30 (1910): 64–65.

Budde, Karl
"Das Rätsel von Micha I," *ZAW* 37 (1917/18): 77–108.

Idem
"Eine folgenschwere Redaktion des Zwölfprophetenbuchs," *ZAW* 39 (1921): 318–29.

Idem
"Micha 2 und 3," *ZAW* 38 (1919/20): 2–22.

Idem
"Verfasser und Stelle von Mi 4, 1–4 (Jes 2, 2–4)," *ZDMG* 81 (N. F. 6) (1927): 152–58.

Burkitt, F. C.
"Micah 6 and 7 a Northern Prophecy," *JBL* 45 (1926): 159–61.

Byington, Steven T.
"Plow and Pick," *JBL* 68 (1949): 49–54.

Calderone, P. J.
"The Rivers of 'Maṣor'," *Biblica* 42 (1961): 423–32.

Calvin, John
Commentaries on the Twelve Minor Prophets, Vol. Third: Jonah, Micah, Nahum. Tr. John Owen (Grand Rapids, Mich.: Eerdmans, 1950).

Cannawurf, E.
"The Authenticity of Micah IV 1–4," *VT* 13 (1963): 26–33.

Carmignac, J.
"Notes sur les Peshârîm," *RQ* 3 (1962): 505–38.

Idem
"Precisions apportées au vocàbulaire de l'hébreu biblique par la Guerre des fils de Lumière contre les fils de ténèbres," *VT* 5 (1955): 345–65.

Caspari, C. P.
Über Micah den Morasthiten und seine prophetische Schrift (Christiana: Malling, 1852).

Cathcart, Kevin J.
"Micah 5, 4–5 and Semitic Incantations," *Biblica* 59 (1978): 38–48.

Idem
"Notes on Micah 5, 4–5," *Biblica* 49 (1968): 511–14.

Cazelles, H.
"Histoire et géographie en Michée IV 6–13," *4th World Congress of Jewish Studies. Papers I* (Jerusalem: 1967) 87–89.

Idem
"Micah." *Encyclopaedia Judaica* (New York: Macmillan, 1971), XI, coll. 1480–83.

Cheyne, T. K.
Micah, with Notes and Introduction, The Cambridge Bible for Schools and Colleges (Cambridge: Cambridge Univ. Press, 1889).

Childs, Brevard S.
Introduction to the Old Testament as Scripture (Philadelphia: Fortress, 1979).

Christensen, Duane L.
Transformations of the War Oracle in Old Testament Prophecy (Missoula: Scholars Press, 1975).

Clauss, H.
"Die Städte der El-Amarnabriefe und die Bibel," *ZDPV* 30 (1907): 1–79.

Cohen, A., ed.
The Twelve Prophets (Bornemouth: Soncino, 1948).

Cohn, Norman
"Medieval Millenarism: Its Bearing on the Comparative Study of Millenarian Movements," in *Millenian Dreams in Action,* Comparative Studies in Society and History, Sup. II, ed. Sylvia L. Thrupp (The Hague: Mouton, 1962), 31–43.

Idem
The Pursuit of the Millennium, revised and expanded edition (New York: Oxford Univ., 1970).

Collin, Matthieu
"Recherches sur l'histoire textuelle du prophète Michée," *VT* 21 (1971): 281–97.

Condamin, Albert
"Interpolations ou transpositions accidentelles?" *RB* 7 (1902): 379–97.

Copass, B. A. and E. L. Carlson
A Study of the Prophet Micah (Grand Rapids, Baker Book House, 1950).

Coppens, J.
"Le cadre littéraire de Michée V:1–5," in *Near Eastern Studies in Honor of William Foxwell Albright,* ed. Hans Goedicke (Baltimore and London: Johns Hopkins, 1971) 57–62.

Crook, Margaret B.
"The Promise in Micah 5," *JBL* 70 (1951): 313–20.

Cross, Frank Moore
Canaanite Myth and Hebrew Epic (Cambridge, Mass.: Harvard, 1973).

Deissler, Alfons
"Micha 6, 1–8: Der Rechtsstreit Jahwes mit Israel um der rechte Bundesverhältnis," *TrTZ* 68 (1959): 229–34.

Delitzsch, Franz
Biblischer Commentar über den Propheten Jesaia (Leipzig: Dörffling und Franke, ³1897).

Idem
Micha und der Herrscher aus der Vorzeit (Leipzig &

Erlangen: Deichertsche; Uppsala & Stockholm: Almqvist & Wiksells, 1923).

Demsky, A.
"The House of Achzib. A Critical Note on Micah 1:14b," *IEJ* 16 (1966): 211–15.

Dever, William
"Iron Age Epigraphic Material from the Area of Khirbet el-Kôm," *HUCA* 40–41 (1969–70): 139–204.

Donner, H.
"Die soziale Botschaft der Propheten im Lichte der Gesellschaftsordnung in Israel," *OrAnt* 2 (1963): 229–45.

Donner, H. and W. Röllig
Kanaanäische und aramäische Inschriften, 3 vols (Wiesbaden: Harrassowitz, 1962–64).

Driver, G. R.
"Birds in the Old Testament," *PEQ* 87 (1955): 5–20.

Idem
"Hebrew Notes on Prophets and Proverbs," *JTS* 41 (1940): 162–75.

Idem
"Linguistic and Textual Problems: Minor Prophets II," *JTS* 39 (1938): 260–73.

Duhm, B.
"Anmerkungen zu den Zwölf Propheten," *ZAW* 31 (1911): 81–110.

Dus, Jan
"Weiteres zum nordisraelitischen Psalm Micha 7, 7–20," *ZDMG* 115 (1965): 14–22.

Ebach, Jürgen
"Sozialethische Erwägungen zum alttestamentlichen Bodenrecht," *Biblische Notizen* 1 (1976): 31–46.

Ebeling, Erich
"Das Verbum der el-Amarna Briefe," *Beiträge zur Assyriologie*, edd. F. Delitzsch and P. Haupt, Vol. 8 (Leipzig: Hinrichsche and Baltimore: Johns Hopkins, 1912) 39–79.

Ehrlich, Arnold B.
Randglossen zur hebräischen Bibel, Vol. V (Leipzig: Hinrichs, 1912).

Ehrman, Albert
"A Note on Micah VI 14," *VT* 23 (1973): 103–05.
Idem
"A Note on שׁי in Mic. 6:14," *JNES* 18 (1959): 156.
Idem
"A Note on Micah II 7," *VT* 20 (1970): 86–87.

Eissfeldt, Otto
Der Gott Karmel, Sitzungsberichte der deutschen (Preussischen) Akademie der Wissenschaften zu Berlin. Klasse für Sprachen, Literatur und Kunst (Berlin: Akademie Verlag, 1953).
Idem
"Ein Psalm aus Nord-Israel," *ZDMG* 112 (1962): 259–68.

Elliger, Karl

"Die Heimat des Propheten Micha," *ZDPV* 57 (1934): 81–152.

Erman, Adolf
Die Literatur der Aegypter (Leipzig: Hinrichs, 1923).

Ewald, Heinrich
Die Propheten des Alten Bundes, vol. 1 (Göttingen: Vandenhoeck & Ruprecht, ²1867).

Fichtner, Johannes
Obadja, Jona, Micha, Stuttgarter Biblehefte (Stuttgart: Quell, 1957).

Fisher, L. R.
"The Temple Quarter," *JSS* 8 (1963): 34–41.

Fitzmyer, Joseph
"l^c as a Preposition and a Particle in Micah 5, 1 (5, 2)," *CBQ* 18 (1956): 10–13.

Fohrer, Georg
"Micha 1," *Das Ferne und nahe Wort*, Festschrift Rost, BZAW 105 (1967): 65–80.
Idem
"Neuere Literatur zur alttestamentlichen Prophetie," *TRu* 19 (1951): 277–346.
Idem
"Neuere Literatur zur Alttestamentlichen Prophetie (Fortsetzung)," *TRu* N. F. 20 (1952): 192–271; 295–361.
Idem
"Neue Literatur zur alttestamentlichen Prophetie (1961–1970)," *TRu* 40 (1975): 193–209; 337–377; 41 (1976): 1–12.
Idem
"Zehn Jahre Literatur zur alttestamentliche Prophetie (1951–1960)," *TRu* 1962: 1–75; 235–97; 301–74.

Frezza, F.
Il libro di Michaea, Ascendenze filogico-letterarie semiticonordoccidentali (Diss. Pont. Inst. Biblico 1977).

Fritz, Volkmar
"Das Wort gegen Samaria Mi 1, 2–7," *ZAW* 86 (1974): 316–31.

Fuhs, Hans F.
Sehen und Schauen, Die Wurzel ḥzh im alten Orient und im Alten Testament, Forschung zur Bibel, 32 (Würzburg: Echter Verlag, 1978).

Gadd, C. J.
"Inscribed Prisms of Sargon II from Nimrud," *Iraq* 16 (1954): 173–201.

Gailey, James H.
Micah to Malachi, Layman's Bible Commentaries Vol. 15 (Richmond: John Knox, 1962).

García de la Fuente, O.
"Notas al texto de Miqueas," *Aug* 7 (1967): 145–54.

Gaster, Theodor H.
"Notes on the Minor Prophets," *JTS* 38 (1937): 163–65.
Idem
"The Combat of 'Aleyân-Ba'al and Môt: Two Missing Portions," *JRAS* (1936): 225–35.

Idem

Thespis, new and revised edition (Garden City, N.Y.: Doubleday, 1961).

Gemser, B.

"The rîb—or controversy-pattern in Hebrew mentality," in *Wisdom in Israel and in the Ancient Near East, VTS* 3 (1955): 120–37.

George, Augustin

"Michée (Le livre de)," *DBS,* Vol. 5 (Paris: Letouzey et ané, 1955) Cols. 1252–63.

Idem

Michée Sophonie Nahum, La Sainte Bible, Vol. 27 (Paris: Cerf, 1952).

Gese, Hartmut

"Die hebräischen Bibelhandschriften zum Dodekapropheton nach der Variantensammlung des *Kennicott,*" *ZAW* 69 (1957): 55–69.

Gesenius

Gesenius' Hebrew Grammar, ed. and rev. E. Kautzsch, tr. and rev. A. E. Cowley (Oxford: At the Clarendon Press, ²1910).

Giesebrecht, F.

Review of Zeitschrift für die alttestamentliche Wissenschaft, 1. Jahrg., *TLZ* 6 (1881): cols. 441–44.

Ginsberg, H. L.

"Dqdwqym bšnym 'śr," *Eretz Israel* 3 (1954): 83–84.

Gold, V. R.

"Mareshah," *IDB.*

Idem

"Moresheth," *IDB.*

Gonzáles Núñez, Angel

"El Rocío del Cielo," *Estudios Biblicos* 22 (1963): 109–39.

Gordis, Robert

"A Note on טוב," *JTS* 35 (1934): 186–88.

Gordon, R. P.

"Micah vii 19 and Akkadian kabāsu," *VT* 28 (1978): 355.

Gottlieb, Hans

"Den taerskende kvie Mi IV 11–13," *Dansk teologisk tijkssdrift* 26 (1963): 167–71.

Graesser, Carl F.

"Standing Stones in Ancient Palestine," *BA* 35 (1972): 34–63.

Graetz, H.

Emendationes in plerosque Sacrae Scripturae Veteris Testamenti libros, ed. W. Bacher (Breslau: Schlesische Buchdruckerei, ²1895).

Gray, George Buchanan

The Book of Isaiah I–XXXIX, I.C.C. (Edinburgh: T. & T. Clark, 1912).

Gressman, Hugo

Der Messias, FRLANT, Heft 43 (N.F. 26) (Göttingen: Vandenhoeck and Ruprecht, 1929).

Grether, Oskar

Name und Wort Gottes im Alten Testament, BZAW 64 (1934).

Grimm, Karl J.

"The Meaning and Etymology of the Word תּוּשִׁיָּה in the Old Testament," *JAOS* 22 (1901): 35–44.

Guariglia, Guglielmo

Prophetismus und Heilerwartungs—Bewegungen als völkerkundliches und religionsgeschichtliches Problem, Wiener Beiträge zur Kulturgeschichte und Linguistik XIII (Vienna: Berger, 1959).

Gundry, Robert H.

The Use of the Old Testament in St. Matthew's Gospel, Supplements to Novum Testamentum Vol XVIII (Leiden: Brill, 1967).

Gunkel, H

"Der Micha-Schluss," *ZS* 2 (1924): 145–78. (Eng. trans. "The Close of Micah, a Prophetical Liturgy" *What Remains of the Old Testament* 1928, 115–49).

Guthe, Hermann

"Der Prophet Micha," in *HSAT,* 4th ed. by D. Bertholet, Vol. II (Tübingen: Mohr, 1923) 53–66.

Halévy, J.

"Le livre de Michée," *Revue Sémitique* 12 (1904): 97–117, 193–216, 289–312; 13 (1905): 1–22.

Hammershaimb, Erling

"Einige Hauptgedanken in der Schrift des Propheten Micha," *Studia Theologica* 15 (1961): 11–34.

Idem

"Some Leading Ideas in the Book of Micah," in *Some Aspects of OT Prophecy from Isaiah to Malachi,* Teologiske Skrifter, 4 (Copenhagen: Rosenkelde og Bagger, 1966) 29–50.

Hanson, P. D.

"Apocalypticism," *IDBS.*

Hardmeier, Christof

Texttheorie und biblische Exegese, Beiträge zur evangelischen Theologie, Band 79 (Munich: Kaiser, 1978).

Harrelson, Walter

"Nonroyal Motifs in the Royal Eschatology," *Israel's Prophetic Hertiage,* edd. Bernhard W. Anderson and Walter Harrelson (New York: Harper, 1962) 147–65.

Harvey, Julien

"Le 'Rîb-Pattern,' Réquisitoire prophétique sur la rupture de l'alliance," *Biblica* 43 (1963): 172–96.

Hasel, G. F.

"Remnant," *IDBS.*

Haupt, Paul

The Book of Micah (Chicago: University of Chicago Press, 1910). Reprinted from *AJSL* 27 (1910) and 26 (1910).

Idem

"The Book of Micah," *American Journal of Semitic Languages and Literatures* 27 (1910): 1–63.

Idem

"Critical Notes on Micah," *AJSL* 26 (1910): 201–52.

Idem

"Micah's Capucinade," *JBL* 29 (1910): 85–112.

Hentschke, R.
Die Stellung der vorexilischen Schriftpropheten zum Kultus, BZAW 75 (1957): 104–7.

Herdner, Andrée
Corpus des tablettes en cunéiformes alphabétiques, Mission de Ras Shamra, Tome X (Paris: Geuthner, 1963).

Herntrich, V.
"The 'Remnant' in the Old Testament," *TDNT* Vol. IV, ed. Gerhard Kittel, tr. and ed. Geoffrey W. Bromley (Grand Rapids: Eerdmans, 1967).

Hertz, J. H.
"Micah vi. 8," *Expository Times* 46 (1935): 188.

Hesse, Franz
"Wurzelt die prophetische Gerichtsrede im israelitischen Kult?" *ZAW* 65 (1953): 45–53.

Hillers, Delbert R.
"Amos 7, 4 and Ancient Parallels," *CBQ* 26 (1964): 221–25.

Idem
"A Convention in Hebrew Literature: the Reaction to Bad News," *ZAW* 77 (1965) 86–90.

Idem
"*Hôy* and *Hōy*-Oracles: A Neglected Syntactic Aspect" (Freedman Volume, forthcoming)

Idem
Lamentations, Anchor Bible, Vol. 7A (Garden City, N. Y.: Doubleday, 1972).

Idem
Treaty-Curses and the Old Testament Prophets, Biblica et Orientalia 16 (Rome: Pontifical Biblical Institute, 1964).

Hitzig, Ferdinand
Die zwölf kleinen Propheten, 4th ed. by Heinrich Steiner, Kurzgefasstes exegetisches Handbuch (Leipzig: S. Hirzel, 1881).

Hoffmann, Georg
"Versuche zu Amos," *ZAW* 3 (1883): 87–126.

Hoftijzer, J. and G. van der Kooij
Aramaic Texts from Deir 'Alla (Leiden: Brill, 1976).

van Hoonacker, A.
Les douze petits prophètes, Études Bibliques (Paris: Gabalda, 1908).

Horgan, Maurya P.
Pesharim: Qumran Interpretations of Biblical Books, Catholic Biblical Quarterly Monograph Series, 8 (Washington, D. C.: Catholic Biblical Association, 1979).

Houbigant, Carolus Franciscus
Notae criticae in universos Veteris Testamenti libros (Frankfurt am M.: Varrentrapp and Wenner, 1777).

Huffmon, H. B.
"The Covenant Lawsuit in the Prophets," *JBL* 78 (1959): 285–95.

Idem
"The Treaty Background of Hebrew Yada'," *BASOR* 181 (Feb., 1966): 31–7.

Hummel, Horace D.

"Enclitic *Mem* in Early Northwest Semitic, Especially Hebrew," *JBL* 76 (1957): 85–107.

Hyatt, J. Philip
"On the Meaning and Origin of Micah 6:8," *Anglican Theological Review* 34 (1952): 232–39.

Ilan, Z.
"גדוד ולחי בספר מיכה," *Beth M 20* (1975): 209–18.

Van Imschoot, P.
"Le prophète Michée et son Temps," *Collationes Gandavenses* 17 (1930): 176–81.

Janssen, Enno
Juda in der Exilszeit, FRLANT, Heft 51 (Göttingen: Vandenhoeck and Ruprecht, 1956).

Jeppesen, Knud
"New Aspects of Micah Research," *Journal for the Study of the Old Testament*, Issue 8 (1978): 3–32.

Jepsen, Alfred
"חזה ḥāzāh," *TWAT*.

Idem
"Kleine Beiträge zum Zwölfprophetenbuch. 2. Micha," *ZAW* 56 (1938): 85–100.

Jeremias, Alfred
Babylonisches im Neuen Testament (Leipzig: Hinrichs, 1905).

Jeremias, Joachim
"Moreseth-Gath, die Heimat des Propheten Micha," *PJB* 29 (1933): 42–53.

Jeremias, Jörg
"Die Deutung der Gerichtsworte Michas in der Exilszeit," *ZAW* 83 (1971): 330–54.

Idem
Theophanie: Die Geschichte einer alttestamentlichen Gattung, WMANT Vol. 10 (Neukirchen-Vluyn: Neukirchener, 1965).

Jerome, St.
S. Hieronymi Presbyteri Opera, Pars I: Opera Exegetica, Vol. 6, *Commentarii in Prophetes Minores*, Corpus Christianorum, Series Latina, Vol 76 (Turnhout: Brepols, 1969).

Junker, H.
"Die Entstehungszeit des Ps. 78 und des Deuteronomiums," *Biblica* 34 (1953): 487–500.

Kahle, Paul
The Cairo Geniza (Oxford: Blackwell, ²1959) 226–28.

Idem
"Die im August 1952 entdeckte Lederrolle mit dem griechischen Text der Kleinen Propheten und das Problem der Septuaginta," *ThLZ* 79 (1954): cols 81–94.

Kallai, Zechariah
"Judah and Israel—A Study in Israelite Historiography," *IEJ* 28 (1978): 251–61.

Kallai-Kleinmann, Zechariah
"Libnah," *EM*. (Heb.)

Idem
"Moresheth-Gath," *EM*. (Heb.)

Kaminka, Armand
Studien zur Septuaginta an der Hand der zwölf

Kleinen Prophetenbücher (Frankfurt am M.: Kauffmann, 1928).

Kapelrud, Arvid S.
"Eschatology in the Book of Micah," *VT* 11 (1961): 392–405.

Katz, Peter
Justin's Old Testament Quotations and the Greek Dodekapropheton Scroll, Studia Patristica Vol. I 1957 343–53 = Texte und Untersuchungen zur Geschichte der altchristlichen Literatur 63. V. Reihe, Band 8 (Berlin: Akademie Verlag, 1957).

Kaufman, Yehezkel
The Religion of Israel, abidged and tr. Moshe Greenberg (Chicago: University of Chicago Press, 1960).

Keil, Carl Friedrich
Biblischer Commentar über die Zwölf Kleinen Propheten, BC III/4 (Leipzig: Dörffling und Franke, 1866, ²1873, ³1888).

Kellermann, Diether
"Überlieferungsprobleme alttestamentlicher Ortsname," *VT* 28 (1978): 423–32.

Kennicott, Benjamin
Vetus Testamentum Hebraicum cum Variis Lectionibus Tomus secundus (Oxford: Clarendon, 1780).

King, Philip J.
"Micah." *The Jerome Biblical Commentary,* edd. Raymond E. Brown, Jospeh A. Fitzmyer, and Roland E. Murphy (Englewood Cliffs, New Jersey: Prentice-Hall, 1968) 283–89.

Kleinert, Paul
Obadja, Jona, Micha, Nahum, Habakkuk, Zephanja, Theologisches-homiletisches Bibelwerk, ed. J. P. Lange (Bielefeld & Leipzig: Velhagen and Klasing, ²1893).

Knabenbauer, Joseph
Commentarius in prophetas minores, 2nd ed. by M. Hagen, Cursus Scripture Sacrae 2nd section, 24 (Paris: Lethielleux, 1924).

Knierim, Rolf
"Exodus 18 und die Neuordmung der mosaischen Gerichtsbarkeit," *ZAW* 73 (1961): 146–71.

Knudtzon, J. A.
Die El-Amarna Tafeln, 2 vols. (Leipzig: Hinrichs, 1915).

Koch, Klaus
"Tempeleinlassliturgien und Dekaloge," *Studien zur Theologie der alttestamentlichen Überlieferungen,* edd. Rolf Rendtorff and Klaus Koch (Neukirchen: Neukirchener Verlag, 1961) 45–60.

Köbert, G.
"môrād (Mi 1,4) Tränke," *Biblica* 39 (1958): 82–83.

Kraus, Hans-Joachim
Psalmen 1, BK (Neukirchen-Vluyn: Neukirchener, 1961).

Kselman, John
"A Note on Isaiah II 2," *VT* 25 (1975): 225–27.

Ladame, F.
"Les chapitres IV et V du livre de Michée," *RTP* 35 (1902): 446–61.

Ladurie, Emmanuel LeRoy
The Territory of the Historian, tr. Ben and Siân Reynolds (Chicago: University of Chicago Press, 1979).

Laetsch, Theo
Bible Commentary: The Minor Prophets (St. Louis: Concordia, 1956).

de Lagarde, Paul
Onomastica sacra, Vol. I (Göttingen: Rente, 1870).

Lanternari, Vittorio
The Religions of the Oppressed (New York: Knopf, 1963).

Laufer, Berthold
Ostrich Egg-shell Cups of Mesopotamia and the Ostrich in Ancient and Modern Times, Anthropology Leaflet 23 (Chicago: Field Museum of Natural History, 1926).

Laurentin, André
"Wᵉ 'attāh - kai nun, Formule caractéristique des textes juridiques et liturgiques (à propos de Jean 17,5)," *Biblica* 45 (1964): 168–97 and 413–32.

Lescow, Theodor
"Das Geburtsmotiv in den messianischen Weissagungen bei Jesaja und Micha," *ZAW* 79 (1967): 172–207.

Idem
Micha 6, 6–8: Studien zu Sprache, Form und Auslegung, Arbeiten zur Theologie, I Reihe, Heft 29 (Stuttgart: Calwer, 1966).

Idem
"Redaktionsgeschichtliche Analyse von Micha 1–5," *ZAW* 84 (1972): 46–85.

Idem
"Redaktionsgeschichtliche Analyse von Micha 6–7," *ZAW* 84 (1972): 182–212.

Levine, Baruch A.
"The Deir 'Alla Plaster Inscriptions," *JAOS* 101 (1981): 195–205.

Lewy, Guenter
Religion and Revolution (New York: Oxford, 1974).

Lewy, Julius
"Lexicographical Notes," *HUCA* 12–13 (1937–38):97–101.

Limburg, James
"The Root ריב and the Prophetic Lawsuit Speeches," *JBL* 88 (1969): 291–304.

Lindblom, Johannes
Micha literarisch untersucht, Acta Academiae Aboensis, Humaniora Vl 2 (Helsingfors: Åbo Akademi, 1929).

Idem
Prophecy in Ancient Israel (Philadelphia: Fortress, 1962).

Lipiński, E.
"באחרית הימים dans les textes préexiliques," *VT* 20 (1970): 445–50.

Idem

"Nimrod et Aššur," *RB* 73 (1966): 77–93.

Lippl, Joseph and Johannes Theis

Die Zwölf Kleinen Propheten I, 1 Hälfte (Bonn: Hanstein, 1937).

Löhr, Max

"Zwei Beispiele von Kehrvers in den Prophetenschriften," *ZDMG* 61 (1907): 1–6.

Loewenstamm, S.

"Beth leaphrah (Hebrew)," *EM*.

Loretz, O.

"Hebräische TJRWŠ und JRŠ in Mc 6, 15 und Hi 20, 15," *UF* 9 (1977): 353–54.

Idem

"Fehlanzeige von Ugaritismen in Micah 5, 1–3," *UF* 9 (1977): 358–60.

Luria, B. Z.

"The Political Background for Micha: Ch. 1 (Hebrew)," *Beth Mikra* 71,4 (1977): 403–12, English summary p 532.

Luther, Martin

Luther's Works, Vol. 18: *Lectures on the Minor Prophets* I, ed. Helton C. Oswald (St. Louis: Concordia, 1975), 207–68, lectures on Micah delivered 1524–26.

Lutz, Hanns Martin

Jahwe, Jerusalem und die Völker, WMANT 27 (1968): 171–77.

Lux, R. C.

"An Exegetical Study of Micah 1, 8–16," *Dis Abstracts* 37 (1976/77): 3717-A.

Margolis, Max L.

Micah (Philadelphia: Jewish Publication Society, 1908).

Marsh, John

Amos and Micah, Torch (London: SCM, 1959).

Marti, Karl

Das Dodekapropheton, KHC 13 (Tübingen: J. C. B. Mohr, 1904).

Marty, Jacques

Michée, in *La Sainte Bible*, Bible du Centenaire, Tome II: Les Prophètes (Paris: Société Biblique de Paris, 1947), 768–783 and xxxiii–xxxiv.

Mauchline, John

"Implicit Signs of a Persistent Belief in the Davidic Empire," *VT* 20 (1970): 287–303.

Mays, James Luther

Micah: A Commentary (Philadelphia: Westminster, 1976).

Idem

"The Theological Purpose of the Book of Micah," in *Beiträge zur Alttestamentlichen Theologie*, edd. H. Donner, R. Hanhart, R. Smend (Göttingen: Vandenhoeck and Ruprecht, 1977), 276–87.

McCarter, P. Kyle

"The Balaam Texts from Deir 'Allā: The First Combination," *BASOR* No. 239 (Summer, 1980): 49–60.

McKeating, Henry

The Books of Amos, Hosea and Micah, Cambridge Bible Commentary (Cambridge: University Press, 1971).

Meek, Theophile J.

"Some Emendations in the Old Testament," *JBL* 48 (1929): 162–68.

Mendenhall, George E.

Law and Covenant in Israel and the Ancient Near East (Pittsburgh: Biblical Colloquium, 1955).

Idem

The Tenth Generation (Baltimore: Johns Hopkins, 1973).

Milik, J. T.

"Fragments d'un Midrash de Michée dans les manuscrits de Qumran," *RB* 59 (1952): 412–18.

Miller, Patrick D.

"Synonymous-Sequential Parallelism in the Psalms," *Biblica* 61 (1980): 256–60.

Moran, William

"The Ancient Near Eastern Background of the Love of God in Deuteronomy," *CBQ* 25 (1963): 77–87.

Moreshet, Menaham

"Whr hbyt lbmwt yʻr," *Beth Miqra* 12 (1966/67): 123–26.

Moriarty, F. L.

"The Chronicler's Account of Hezekiah's Reform," *CBQ* 27 (1965): 399–406.

Mowinckel, Sigmund

"Mikaboken," *Norsk Teologisk Tidsskrift* 29 (1928): 3–42.

Mühlmann, Wilhelm E.

Chiliasmus und Nativismus (Berlin: Dietrich Reimer, 1961).

Müller, Werner E.

Die Vorstellung vom Rest im Alten Testament, ed Horst Dietrich Preuss (Neukirchen: Neukirchener, 1973).

Na'aman, N.

"Sennacherib's Campaign to Judah and the Date of the LMLK Stamps," *VT* 29 (1979): 61–86.

Neiderhiser, Edward A.

"Micah 2:6–11: Considerations on the Nature of the Discourse," *BTB* 11 (1981): 104–07.

Nielsen, Eduard

Oral Tradition, Studies in Biblical Theology, no. 11 (Chicago: Allenson, 1954).

Nielsen, Kirsten

Yahweh as Prosecutor and Judge: An Investigation of the Prophetic Lawsuit (Rib- Pattern), Journal for the Study of the Old Testament, Supplement Series, 9 (Sheffield: Univ. of Sheffield, 1978).

Nöldeke, Th.

"Mene tekel upharsin," *ZA* (1886): 414–18.

Noth, Martin

"Das Amt des 'Richter Israels'," *Festschrift A. Bertholet* (Tübingen: J. C. B. Mohr, 1950), 404–17.

Nowack, W.
"Bemerkungen über des Buch Micha," *ZAW* 4
(1884): 277–91.

Idem
Die kleinen Propheten, HK III Abteilung, 4 Band
(Göttingen: Vandenhoeck and Ruprecht, ³1922).

Oded, Bustenay
"Mass Deportations in the Neo-Assyrian Empire—
Facts and Figures," *Eretz-Israel* Vol. 14, H. L.
Ginsberg Vol (Jerusalem: Israel Exploration
Society, 1978), 62–68, Hebrew, English summary
124*–125*.

Idem
*Mass Deportations and Deportees in the Neo-Assyrian
Empire* (Wiesbaden: Reichert, 1979).

von Orelli, Conrad
Die zwölf kleinen Propheten, Kurzgefasster Kom-
mentar zu den Heiligen Schriften Alten und
Neuen Testamentes A, 5 Abteilung, 2 Hälfte
(Munich: Becksche, ³1908).

Perles, Felix
Analekten zur Textkritik des Alten Testaments
(Leipzig: Engel, 1905).

Pope, Marvin H.
"The Word שַׁחַת in Job 9:31," *JBL* 83 (1964):
269–78.

Posner, A.
Das Buch des Propheten Micah (Frankfurt am Main:
Kauffmann, 1924).

Praetorius, Fr.
"Zum Micha-Schluss," *ZS* 3 (1924): 72–73.

Proksch, Otto
"Gat," *ZDPV* 66 (1943): 174–91.

Idem
Die kleinen prophetischen Schriften vor dem Exil,
Erläuterungen zum Alten Testament, 3 Teil
(Calw & Stuttgart: Vereinsbuchhandlung, 1910).

Rainey, A. F.
"Gath," *IDBS*.

Idem
"The Identification of Philistine Gath," *Eretz Israel*
12, Nelson Glueck Memorial Volume (Jerusalem:
Israel Exploration Society, 1975), 63*–76*.

Idem
"The Toponymics of Eretz-Israel," *BASOR* 231 (Oct.,
1978): 1–17.

Idem
"Wine From the Royal Vineyards," *BASOR* No.
245 (1982): 57–62.

Ramsay, George W.
"Speech-Forms in Hebrew Law and Prophetic
Oracles," *JBL* 96 (1977): 45–58.

Reckendorf, H.
Arabische Syntax (Heidelberg: Carl Winter, 1921).

Reicke, B.
"Liturgical Traditions in Mic. 7," *HTR* 60 (1967):
349–367.

Reider, Joseph
"Etymological Studies in Biblical Hebrew," *VT* 4
(1954): 276–95.

Reinke, Laur
Der Prophet Micha (Giessen: Emil Roth, 1874).

Renaud, B.
La formation du livre de Michée, Études Bibliques
(Paris: Gabalda, 1977).

Idem
Structure et attaches littéraires de Michée IV–V,
Cahiers de la Revue Biblique, 2 (Paris: Gabalda,
1964).

Richter, Georg
"Erläuterungen zu dunkeln Stellen in den kleinen
Propheten," *Beiträge zur Förderung Christlicher
Theologie*, 18, 3/4 Heft (1914) 275–473. "Micha,"
374–394.

Rieszler, Paul
Die kleinen Propheten oder das Zwölfprophetenbuch
(Rottenburg a. N.: Bader, 1911).

Rinaldi, Giovanni
*I Profeti Minori, Fascicolo III: Michea-Nahum-Abacuc-
Sofonia-Aggeo-Zaccaria-Malachia* (Turin: Marietti,
1969).

Roberts, J. J. M
"The Davidic Origin of the Zion Tradiion," *JBL*
92 (1973): 329–44.

Idem
"Zion Tradition," *IDBS*.

Robinson, Theodore H.
Die zwölf kleinen Propheten, HAT 14 (Tubingen:
Mohr, 1938).

Rohland, Edzard
*Die Bedeutung der Erwählungstraditionen Israels für
die Eschatologie der alttestamentlichen Propheten*, Diss.
Heidelberg, 1956.

Roorda, Taco
Commentarius in Vaticinium Michae (Leipzig:
Weigel, 1869).

Rosenbaum, Jonathan
"Hezekiah's Reform and the Deuteronomistic
Tradition," *HTR* 72 (1979): 23–43.

Rosenmüller, Ernst
Scholia in Vetus Testamentum, Part 7, Vol. 3
(Leipzig: Barth, 1814).

de Rossi, Giovanni
Variae lectiones Veteris Testamenti, Vol. III (Parma:
Ex regio typographeo, 1786).

Rottenberg, Meir
"שמעו עמים כלם," *Beth Miqra* 78 (1979): 266–68.

Rowley, H. H.
"Hezekiah's Reform and Rebellion," in *Men of God*
(London: Nelson, 1963), 98–132.

Rudolph, Wilhelm
Micha—Nahum—Habakuk—Zephanja, KAT Bd.
13/3 (Gütersloh: Gütersloher Verlagshaus Gerd
Mohn, 1975).

Idem
"Zu Micha 1, 10–16," *Wort, Lied und Gottesspruch
. . . Festschrift für J. Ziegler*, Forschung zur Bibel
(1972): 233–38.

Ryssel, Viktor
"Die arabische Uebersetzung des Micah in der Pariser und Londoner Polyglotte," *ZAW* 5 (1885): 102–38.

Idem
Untersuchungen über die Textgestalt und die Echtheit des Buches Micha (Leipzig: S. Hirzel, 1887).

Saarisalo, Aapeli A.
"Topographical Researches in the Shephelah," *JPOS* 11 No. 2 (1931): 14–20.

Saebø, Magne
"Grenzbeschreibung und Landideal im Alten Testament, Mit besonderer Berücksichtigung der min- 'ad -Formel," *ZDPV* 90 (1974): 14–37.

Schmidt, Hans
Micha, in SAT, Abteilung 2, Band 2. *Die grossen Propheten* (Göttingen: Vandenhoeck and Ruprecht, ²1923).

Idem
Der Mythos vom wiederkehrenden König im Alten Testament, Schriften der Hessischen Hochschulen, Universität Giessen, Jahrgang 25, Heft 1 (Giessen: Töpelmann, 1925).

Schumpp, Meinrad, O. P.
Die Heilige Schrift für das Leben erklärt Vol. X/2, Herders Bibelkommentar (Freiburg: Herder, 1950).

Schwantes, S. J.
"Critical Notes on Micah 1:10–16," *VT* 14 (1964): 454–61.

Idem
A Critical Study of the Text of Micah, Unpublished Ph.D. dissertation, Johns Hopkins, 1962.

Idem
"A Note on Micah 5:1 (Hebrew 4:14)," *AUSS* 1 (1963): 105–07.

Scott, James C.
The Moral Economy of the Peasant (New Haven and London: Yale, 1976).

Sebök, Mark
Die syrische Uebersetzung der zwölf kleinen Propheten (Breslau: Preuss und Jünger, 1887).

Seebass, Horst
"'aḥªrît," *TWAT*.

Sellin, Ernst
Das Zwölfprophetenbuch, KAT Bd. 12, Erste Hälfte: Hosea-Micha (Leipzig: Deichertsche, ²&³1929).

Sievers, Eduard
"Alttestamentliche Miszellen," *Berichte über die Verhandlungen des königl. Sächsischen Gesellschaft der Wissenschaften zu Leipzig*, Phil.-hist. Klasse LIX (Leipzig: Teubner, 1907): 3–109.

Smith, George Adam
The Book of the Twelve Prophets I, Expositor's Bible (New York: A. C. Armstrong, 1896).

Idem
The Historical Geography of the Holy Land (New York and Evanston: Harper and Row, ²⁵1931, reprint 1966).

Smith, John Merlin Powis, William Hayes Ward, and Julius A. Bewer
A Critical and Exegetical Commentary on Micah, Zephaniah, Nahum, Habakkuk, Obadiah and Joel, ICC (Edinburgh: T. & T. Clark, 1911).

Ibid
"Some Textual Suggestions," *AJSL* 37 (1920–21): 238–40.

Ibid
"The Strophic Structure of the Book of Micah," in *Old Testament and Semitic Studies in Memory of W. R. Harper*, edd. R. F. Harper et al (Chicago: Univ. of Chicago, 1908), Vol. II, 415–38.

Smith, Louise Pettibone
"The Book of Micah," *Interpretation* 6 (1952): 210–227.

Smith, W. Robertson
The Prophets of Israel and Their Place in History, new ed. by T. K. Cheyne (London: Adam and Charles Black, 1895).

Sperber, Alexander
The Bible in Aramaic, Vol. 3 (Leiden: Brill, 1962).

Stade, Bernhard
"Bemerkungen über das Buch Micha," *ZAW* 1 (1881): 161–72.

Ibid
"Bemerkungen zu vorstehendem Aufsatze," *ZAW* 4 (1884): 291–97.

Idem
"Streiflichter auf die Entstehung der jetzigen Gestalt der alttestamentlichen Propheten-schriften," *ZAW* 23 (1903): 153–71.

Idem
"Weitere Bemerkungen zu Micha 4.5," *ZAW* 3 (1883): 1–16.

Staerk, W.
"Der Gebrauch der Wendung בְּאַחֲרִית הַיָּמִים im alttestamentlichen Kanon," *ZAW* 11 (1891): 247–53.

Stamm, J. J. and M. E. Andrew
The Ten Commandments in Recent Research, Studies in Biblical Theology, Second Series, No. 2 (Naperville, Ill.: Allenson, 1967).

Stendahl, Krister
The School of St. Matthew (Uppsala: Almqvist and Wiksells, 1954).

Stoebe, H. J.
"Und demütig sein vor deinem Gott. Micha 6,8," *Wort und Dienst* N. F. 6 (1959): 180–94.

Strugnell, J.
"Notes en marge du volume V des 'Discoveries in the Judaean Desert of Jordan'," *RQ* 26 (1970): 163–276. P 204 concerns 4QpMi = 4Q168.

Tawil, Hayim
"The Historicity of 2 Kings 19:24 (= Isaiah 37:25). The Problem of Ye'ōrê māṣôr," *JNES* 41 (1982): 195–206.

Theodore of Mopsuestia
Commentarius in XII prophetas minoras, Patrologiae

Graecae Tomus LXVI, ed. J. P. Migne (Paris: 1864).

Thiele, Edwin R.
The Mysterious Numbers of the Hebrew Kings, Revised ed. (Grand Rapids: Eerdmans, 1965).

Thiersch, H.
"Die neueren Ausgrabungen in Palästina,"
Jahrbuch des Kaiserlichen Deutschen Archäologischen Instituts, Archäologischer Anzeiger, Vol. XXIII (1908), cols. 344–413.

Thomas, D. Winton
"The Root צנע in Hebrew and the Meaning of קדרנית in Malachi III, 14," *JJS* 1 (1948–49): 182–88.

Thrupp, Sylvia L., ed.
Millennial Dreams in Action, Comparative Studies in Society and History, Supplement II (The Hague: Mouton, 1962).

Tournay, R.
"Quelques relectures bibliques antisamaritaines," *RB* 71 (1964): 504–36.

Treitel
"Wert und Bedeutung der LXX zu den Zwölf kleinen Propheten," *MGWJ* 73 (1929): 232–34.

Turnbull, Colin M.
The Mountain People (New York: Simon and Schuster, 1972).

Ungern-Sternberg, Rolf Freiherr von
Der Rechtsstreit Gottes mit seiner Gemeinde. Die Botschaft des Alten Testaments, Vol. 23/III (Stuttgart: Calwer, 1958).

Ussishkin, David, Yohanan Aharoni, Olga Tufnell
"Lachish," *EAEHL*, III (1977): 735–53.

Vaughan, Patrick H.
The Meaning of "bāmâ" in the Old Testament, Society for Old Testament Study, Monograph Series 3 (New York: Cambridge Univ., 1974).

de Vaux, R.
"Le 'reste d'Israel' d'après les prophètes," *RB* 42 (1933): 526–39.

Vermes, G.
The Dead Sea Scrolls in English (Baltimore: Penguin, 1965).

Vernant, J. P., et al.
Divination et rationalité (Paris: Seuil, 1974).

Vetter, D.
"חזה ḥzh schauen," *THAT*.

Vilnay, Zeev
"The Topography of Israel in the Book of the Prophet Micah (Hebrew)," *BJPES* (1939): 1–19.

Vogt, Ernst
"Fragmenta Prophetarum Minorum Deserti Juda," *Biblica* 34 (1953): 219–72.

Vollers, Karl
"Das Dodekapropheton der Alexandriner," *ZAW* 3 (1883): 219–72.

Idem
"Das Dodekapropheton der Alexandriner (Schluss)," *ZAW* 4 (1884): 1–20.

Vuilleumier, René and Carl A. Keller
Michée Nahoum Habacuc Sophonie, Commentaire de l'Ancien Testament Xlb (Neuchâtel: Delachaux et Niestlé, 1971).

Wade, G. W.
The Books of the prophets Micah, Obadiah, Joel and Jonah, Westminster Commentaries (London: Methuen, 1925).

Wagner, Max
Die lexikalischen und grammatikalischen Aramaismen im alttestamentlichen Hebräisch, BZAW 96 (1966).

Wakeman, M. K.
"The Biblical Earth Monster in the Cosmogonic Combat Myth," *JBL* 88 (1969): 313–20.

Weil, Hermann M.
"Le chapitre 2 de Michée expliqué par le Premier Livre des Rois, chapitre 20–22," *RHR* 121 (1940): 146–61.

Weinfeld, Moshe
"Burning Babies in Ancient Israel," *UF* 10 (1978): 411–13.

Idem
Deuteronomy and the Deuteronomic School (Oxford: Clarendon, 1972).

Weingreen, J.
"The Title Moreh Sedek," *JSS* 6 (1961): 162–74.

Weiser, Artur
Das Buch der zwölf Kleinen Propheten I: Die Propheten Josea, Joel, Amos, Obadja, Jona, Micha, ATD Teilbd. 24 (Göttingen: Vandenhoeck & Ruprecht, ²1956).

Welch, Adam C.
"Micah V. 1–3 (Eng. 2–4)," *The Expository Times* 13 (1902): 234–36.

Wellhausen, J. in Friedrich Bleek
Einleitung in das Alte Testament, ed. J. Wellhausen (Berlin: Reimer, ⁴1878).

Idem
Skizzen und Vorarbeiten, Fünftes Heft: *Die kleinen Propheten übersetzt, mit Noten* (Berlin: Reimer, 1892).

Welten, Peter
Die Königs-Stempel, Abhandlungen des Deutschen Palästinavereins (Wiesbaden: Harrassowitz, 1969).

Werbeck, W.
"Michabuch," *RGG*, Vol. 4 (Tübingen: J. C. B. Mohr, ³1960), cols. 929–31 (Bibliography).

Idem
"Zwölfprophetenbuch," *RGG*, Vol. 6 (Tübingen: J. C. B. Mohr, ³1962), cols 1969–70.

Westermann, Claus
"Micha 5, 1–3," in *Herr, tue meine Lippen auf*, ed. Georg Eichholz, Vol. 4 (Wupptertal-Barmen: Emil Müller, 1961), 54–59.

Wildberger, H.
"Die Völkerwallfahrt zum Zion Jes. II 1–5," *VT* 7 (1957): 62–81.

Idem
"שאר übrig sein," *THAT*.

Idem

    Jesaja, BK 10/1 (Neukirchen-Vluyn: Neu-kirchener Verlag, 1972).

Willi-Plein, Ina

    Vorformen der Schriftexegese innerhalb des Alten Testaments, BZAW 123 (1971).

Willis, J. T.

    "The Authenticity and Meaning of Micah 5:9–14," *ZAW* 81 (1969): 353–68.

Idem

    "Fundamental Issues in Contemporary Micah Studies," *Restoration Quarterly* 13 (1970): 77–90.

Idem

    "Micah 2:6–8 and the 'People of God' in Micah," *BZ* N. F. 14 (1970): 72–87.

Idem

    "Micah IV:14–V5–A Unit," *VT* 18 (1968): 529–47.

Idem

    "ממך לי יצא in Micah 5:1," *JQR* 58 (1967–68): 317–22.

Idem

    "A Note on ואמר in Micah 3:1," *ZAW* 80 (1968): 50–54.

Idem

    "On the text of Micah 2,1aα–B," *Biblica* 48 (1967): 534–41.

Idem

    "A Reapplied Prophetic Hope Oracle," *VTS* 20 (1974): 64–76.

Idem

    Review of Theodor Lescow, Micah 6, 6–8. Studien zu Sprache, Form und Auslegung, *VT* 18 (1968): 273–78.

Idem

    "Some Suggestions on the Interpretation of Micah I 2," *VT* 18 (1968): 372–79.

Idem

    "The Structure of Micah 3–5 and the Function of Micah 5:9–14 in the Book," *ZAW* 81 (1969): 191–214.

Idem

    "The Structure of the Book of Micah," *Svensk Exegetisk Årsbok* 34 (1969): 5–42.

Wolf, Abraham

    "l' z't hmnwḥh," *Beth Miqra* 25–26 (1965): 14–41.

Wolf, Eric R.

    Peasant Wars of the Twentieth Century (New York, Evanston, and London: Harper and Row, 1969).

Wolfe, Rolland E.

    "The Book of Micah," *IB*, VI (New York and Nashville: Abingdon, 1956), 897–949.

Wolff, Hans Walter

    Dodekapropheton 1: Hosea, BK 14/1 (Neukirchen-Vluyn: Neukirchener, ²1965).

Idem

    Hosea: A Commentary on the Book of the Prophet Hosea, tr. Gary Stansell; Hermeneia (Philadelphia: Fortress, 1974).

Idem

    Micah the Prophet, tr. Ralph D. Gehrke (Philadelphia: Fortress, 1981).

Idem

    Micha, Biblischer Kommentar XIV/12 (Neukirchen-Vluyn: Neukirchener, 1980).

Idem

    "Micah the Moreshite—the Prophet and his Background," in *Israelite Wisdom,* ed. John G. Gammie et al. (Missoula, Montana: Scholar's Press, 1978), 77–84.

van der Woude, A. S.

    "Deutero-Micha: Ein Prophet aus Nord-Israel?" *Nederlands Theologisch Tijdschrift* (1971): 365–78.

Idem

    Micah (Nijkerk: Callenbach, 1976).

Idem

    "Micah IV 1–5: An Instance of the Pseudo-Prophets Quoting Isaiah," *Symbolae biblicae et mesopotamicae F. M. Th. de Liagre—Böhl Dedicatae,* edd. M. A. Beek et al. (Leiden: Brill, 1973), 396–402.

Idem

    "Micah in Dispute with the Pseudo-Prophets," *VT* 19 (1969): 244–60.

Idem

    "Micah I 10–16," in *Hommages a André Dupont-Sommer* (Paris: Adrien-Maisonneuve, 1971), 347–53.

Idem

    "Micha II 7a und der Bund Jahwes mit Israel," *VT* 18 (1968): 388–91.

Yadin, Yigael

    The Scroll of the War of the Sons of Light against the Sons of Darkness, tr. B. and C. Rabin (London: Oxford Univ., 1962).

Zeidel, Moshe

    "Micha chap. VI (Its Parallels and a Commentary) (Hebrew)," *Tarbiz* 17 (1945): 12–20.

Ziegler, Joseph

    "Beiträge zum griechischen Dodekapropheton," *Nachrichten von der Akademie der Wissenschaften in Göttingen,* Philolog.-Hist. Klasse (Göttingen: Vandenhoeck and Ruprecht, 1943), 345–412 = *Sylloge,* 71–138.

Idem

    "Die Einheit der Septuaginta zum Zwölfprophetenbuch," *Beilage zum Vorlesungsverzeichnis der Staatl. (Akademie zu Braunsberg/Ostpr.* 1934/35) 1–16 = *Sylloge,* 29–42.

Idem

    "Der griechische Dodekapropheton-Text der Complutenser Polyglotte," *Biblica,* 25 (1944): 297–310 = *Sylloge,* 229–242.

Idem

    "Studien zur Verwertung der Septuaginta im Zwölfprophetenbuch," *ZAW* 60 (1944): 107–31 = *Sylloge,* 243–67.

Idem

    Sylloge: Gesammelte Aufsätze zur Septuaginta.
    Mitteilungen des Septuaginta-Unternehmens der
    Akademie der Wissenschaften in Göttingen X
    (Göttingen: Vandenhoeck and Ruprecht, 1971).

Idem

    "Der Text der Aldina im Dodekapropheton,"
    Biblica, 26 (1945): 37–51 = *Sylloge*, 306–20.

Zimmerli, Walther

    Ezechiel, I Teilband, *BK*, XIII/1 (Neukirchen-
    Vluyn: Neukirchener, 1969).

2. Foreign Words

a / Hebrew

אָדָם	68(e), 79
אָדָר	35(k)
אָהֵב	41(e)
אָחִיו	67
אָמַר	32(k), 35(e), 41(a), 42
אֹסֶף	83(b)
אֶרֶץ	69
בְּכוֹר	78(11)
בָּמוֹת	18(n), 20
בְּצִירָה	38(e)
בָּצַר	38(e)
גָּדֵל	25(a)
גָּדֵר	90
גָּלוּ	30
דָּבָר	13(a,e), 75(a), 84(l)
הָגָּר	76(r)
הָדָר	35(n), 36(p)
הַגֹּנֵעַ	76(t)
הַר	49(d)
חָדָר	36(p)
חָזָה	13(e)
חַטָּאת	17(n), 20, 89(v)
חָמָר	33
חָמָס	82
חָסֵר	79, 85, 91
חָרָם	61
חֲשֵׁכָה	44(f)
טוֹב	26(i), 43
טָמְאָה	36(r)
יֹלֶדֶת	66
יָם	88(k)
יָצָא	20
יִרְאָה	80(a)
יָרַד	20, 30
יָרַשׁ	27(n)
יִשְׂרְפוּ	18(s)
כֹּחַ	45(k)
כָּפַךְ	78
מוֹצָאָה	65(e)
מִי	17(m)
מִפְתָּה	22(f)
מַצֵּבוֹת	73
נִגְעָה	22(h)
נָהָר	49(f)
נָמַסּוּ	17(h)
נָשַׂג	34(d)
עָבַת	84(m)
עָמַד	65(i), 67
עָנָה	22(e)
עֹפֶל	56(b,c)
פָּעַל	31(b)
פָּרַס	42(i)
פָּרַץ	39
פֶּשַׁע	17(n), 20
פְּתִיחָה	68(h)
צֶדֶק	78
קֶדֶם	65(e), 78
קֶסֶם	46, 48
קָצִין	41(d), 42
רֹאשׁ	49(d)
רִיב	77
רֵעַ	26(j), 43
רָעָה	67, 69, 78
שְׁאֵרִית	39, 42, 70
שָׁלֹם	26
שָׁמַע	81
שַׁעַר	23
שַׂר שָׁלוֹם	65(n)
תָּחֲנוּךְ	60(b)
תָּרִיעִי	58(b)

b / Greek

ἀγαπᾶν	41(e)
ἁμαρτὶα	17(n), 89(v)
ἀνατολή	65(e)
ἀνηγγέλη	76(r)
ἀπωσάμην	54(b)
βασιλέων	13(c)
Γεθ	25(a)
ἐμπήσουσιν	18(s)
ἐπεγερθήσονται	68(c)
ἐπιχαρούμεθα	60(b)
ζητοῦντες	41(e)
ἤγειραν	44(d)
ἡμέρα	31(c)
κατακόψουσι	18(s)
κατακριθήσεται	60(b)
καταλήφη	34(d)
κατάλοιποι	41(d), 42, 47(b)
καταλύσει	89(t)
κληρονόμους	28(r)
λόγος	13(a), 16(a), 75(a)
μεγαλύνεσθε	25(a)
ὀχυρώματι	38(e)
πληγή	22(f)
ποίμνιον	65(j)
πορνείας	18(v)
σαλευθήσεται	17(h)
σειρήνων	22(e)
σκοτία	44(f), 81(n)
τακήσονται	17(h)
ὕβρις	82
φάραγγα	18(r)
χάος	18(r)
χηρείαν	28(y)

c / Akkadian

karmu	18(q)
ṭābu	26(i)
nasiku	68(e)
awatu	84(l)
kabāsu	88(t)

d / Aramaic

tab	26(i)

e / Ugaritic

'al	25(b)
'pr pltt	26(d)
ṭb	26(i)
tk.ḥqpt.il.klh	38(b)
hwt	84(l)

3. Subjects

Aramaean
69
Assembly of Yahweh
32
Assyria
59, 69
Assyrians
5, 18, 63

Babylon
2, 56(g), 59, 91
Balaam
66, 77f.
Bethlehem
6, 62(a), 64(a), 65
Birth
66

Cannibalism
5, 43
Covenant
77, 79, 91
Covenant language
78
Covenant lawsuit
77
Curse
78, 82

David
7, 23, 57, 65f., 69
Davidic Dynasty
66
Davidic empire
56, 69, 90
Deprivation
5
Deutero-Micah
89
Deuteronomic phraseology
79
Deuteronomic vocabulary
90
Deuteronomistic writings
14
Dew simile
71
Divination
72
Divine council
77

Divine lawsuit
77
Divine power
65
Doom
7, 9, 15, 22f., 33, 38f., 45,
82

Exile
6, 54f., 59
Exilic community
67

Flock
55f., 67
Foreign elements
6, 72
Forgiveness
89
Formulas of Introduction
10

Gath
25(a), 27(n)
Grace
7f., 39

Harvest
83
Heavenly council
19
Hezekiah
1f., 5f., 8f., 14, 42, 57, 59,
74
Hezekiah, Reform of
9, 19, 74
High places
20
Holocaust
78
Holy war
61
Hope
7, 33, 72, 77

Idolatry
20, 73
Idols
72f.
Images
73
Injustice
19
Instruction
50

Jerusalem
5, 7, 15, 18, 19f., 23, 28,
48, 50, 52, 55f., 60, 81, 89
Judgment
7, 8, 17(d), 19, 33, 42f.,
45f., 74
Justice
33, 42, 48, 51, 85, 90

Kenosis
50
Kindness
99
Kingdom of God
69
Kingship
54, 59
Knowledge
78

Lament
3, 23, 30, 32, 85
Land
7, 32, 36(r), 37, 61, 91
Land, division of
33
Land, redistribution of
7
Love
91

Messenger formula
44(a), 45
Messiah
6, 66
Messiah-figure
46
Messianic king
66, 68, 72
Messianic prophecy
66
Messianic woes
6
Messianism
57
Micah
As prophet of new age
4, 7
Authentic material
2
Authorship
51f.
Date of
2, 15

History of
4
Identity of
14
Life and times of
1
Present form of
2, 8
Redaction of
3
Texts and versions
9, 10
Title
15
Millennial hope
57
Millennial movements
66
Moresheth
13(b), 14, 27(n)
Mourning
23, 28, 46
Myth
7, 66

Nativism
4(20), 6
New age
4f., 21
Northern Kingdom
5, 27(q)

Oracles
Hopeful
3
Hôy
3
Judgment
3
Salvation
42
Social criticism
3

Parallelism
10
Peace
6f., 51, 67
Pilgrimage
50, 52, 91
Poetic form
10
Poor
5f., 35

4. Modern Authors